GIRLS IN AMERICA

GIRLS IN AMERICA

Their Stories, Their Words—

Beauty Queens, Synchronized Swimmers,
Double Dutchers, Rugby Players, Cheerleaders, and Teenage Moms

CAROL CASSIDY

Foreword by
KATHA POLITT

Photographs by
ARLENE SANDLER AND JOYCE GEORGE

New York

Library of Congress Cataloging-in-Publication Data

Girls in America / [edited by] Carol Cassidy.

   p. cm.

  ISBN 1-57500-084-9 (Hardcover)

  1. Teenage girls — United States Interviews. I. Cassidy, Carol, 1962-

  HQ798 .A733 1999

  305.235 — dc21   99-40418

                    CIP

Photographs of teenage mothers by Joyce George and photographs of pageant contestants and athletes by Arlene Sandler.

The publisher has made every effort to secure permission to reproduce copyrighted material and would like to apologize should there have been any errors or omissions.

Book Design by Tania Garcia

TV Books, L.L.C.

Publishers serving the television industry.

1619 Broadway, Ninth Floor

New York, NY 10019

www.tvbooks.com

GIRLS IN AMERICA

CONTENTS

❧

ACKNOWLEDGMENTS

❧

This is a stone soup project, where you knock on doors with an empty cauldron — an idea — and hope people will throw in the odd potato or onion. The joy is that so many contribute lobster and saffron and wine.

People participate because they believe the resulting feast will be worth it, and theirs to share.

I celebrate this work and the joyful, generous gifts of all the women who took part, and I open my heart to all of them and offer this invitation: Please come one summer night for supper and I'll feed you from my garden.

I thank each girl who took part in this project. Whether or not your words appeared in the films and the book, your story shaped this work. I thank everyone at the Independent Television Service (ITVS) and at TV Books, especially Emily Stevens, Nondas Voll, Lois Vossen, Peter Kaufman, Keith Hollaman, and Rachel Reiss. I thank Susi Walsh from the Center for Independent Documentary.

I thank Rachel May.

I thank my mother and father, Judy and Bill Weaks; my sisters, Karen, Kelly, Chris, and Casey; and my brother, Bill.

Most of all I thank my beloved, my soul, my Stephen.

This book is for Kelsey and Kaytea, for Julia, for Emily, Kate, Lane, Dale, and Chloe, and all the girls I love.

FOREWORD

Katha Pollitt

What happens to those little girls we all know — clever, funny, curious, wild? The ones whose mothers can't get them into a dress — or who love dresses so passionately they put on their favorite one to take a bath? The ones who want not just to ride horses, but to be a horse? The ones who see exactly what the grownups are up to — and secretly promise themselves never, ever to become one?

"You all die at fifteen," wrote the great eighteenth-century French writer Denis Diderot to his mistress Sophie Volland. Hardly! As Carol Cassidy reveals in the interviews gathered here, nothing could be further from the truth than the stereotype that young girls are lacking in assertiveness, drive, or desire. The beauty contestants interviewed here are no Barbie® dolls — they are ardent competitors, many of them, curiously, former tomboys. The teenage mothers — in current political discourse the very symbol of "dependency" — seem to expect of themselves an impossible degree of autonomy, in which a boyfriend's promise of a baby crib is the most one can expect from others, and probably more than will be delivered. The lucky girls are the athletes, who have found a way to take their drives toward self-expression, mastery, and adventure into a female arena that isn't also a trap. Only the athletes talk about their new womanly bodies as if they truly belong to themselves. By contrast, the beauty contestants have the detachment toward their bodies of drag queens, self-consciously turning themselves into something halfway between an industrial product and a mirage. For the young mothers, sexuality seems to have little to do with their own desires or pleasures, and everything to do with pleasing others — their worried, hectoring mothers by staying virgins, their boyfriends by "giving it up."

Girls in America is a deeply troubling book. After all, these young people are making their lives out of the materials we give them, the materials of our culture. What does it say about us, the adults, that girls compete for scholarship money not by reading a thousand books or painting a thousand paintings, but by painfully wrapping their breasts in duct tape and, should they be black or biracial, by minimizing their ethnic features with blue contact lenses and maybe a nose job, too? Why is it only in girls' sports — cheerleading, synchronized swimming, double Dutch — that smiling matters? Why is teen motherhood much more common among American girls than it is in many other wealthy Western countries? American girls aren't so different from French girls or Danish girls in their level of sexual activity, after all. The difference is that American grownups have decided to not to make sexual information and contraception — not to mention abortion — easily available and uncontroversial, while simultaneously leaving millions of poor and working class kids without much to postpone parenthood for.

What about parents? Mothers are problematic in these pages. They love their girls — few daughters seemed to doubt that — and the less privileged ones work their fingers to the bone to give their kids a better life. But few of them listen to their girls, talk with them about sex and boys, except to lecture them on the potential of both for disaster, and too often their expectations are so high and so rigid, their own burdens so great, as to frighten their daughters from confiding in them at the very moment when they most could use real guidance. Fathers are another story. For many of the girls in these pages, Dad has decamped and plays no real role in his daughter's life beyond an occasional phone call, and maybe not even that.

Given these often harsh realities, one comes away from *Girls in America* amazed at our daughters' strength, resilience, ingenuity, and hope. Michelle, who plays rugby, wants to be housewife — but a housewife who, unlike her fundamentalist parents, supports gay rights and knows more about computers than the guys at the computer store. Adelaide, raised in a group home and penniless and pregnant at eighteen, teaches herself to drive and gets her license with no help from anyone.

A girl who could do that — what *couldn't* she do, with a little help and support? That is the question these interviews pose.

PREFACE

The Documentary Series

I am one of five sisters from a Philadelphia family. I grew up on the stories of girls and women. We talked in a circle at baby showers, in bedrooms, dressing as bridesmaids, in the church basement as Girl Scouts, and in the kitchen, drying dishes.

The girls in my life were always smarter, tougher, funnier, more complex, and more interesting than the girls I saw on TV, in movies, in magazines. As an independent documentary filmmaker, I want to use my tools and training to bring these lives to light.

I designed a project called "Baby Love" in 1995. I wanted to talk with teenage mothers. My basic question to them was, "What the heck...? What happened? What can we do to make sure other girls don't get pregnant? What would you say to other girls?"

Several of my cousins were teenage mothers, and growing up it seemed to me that having a baby was the one irreversible thing a girl could do, the one thing that would set her life on a different course forever.

The documentary was funded by The Independent Television Service. ITVS was created in 1989 to increase the diversity of programming on public television. It was established by an act of Congress to "encourage the development of programs that involve creative risks and address the needs of underserved audiences." ITVS is funded through the Corporation for Public Broadcasting.

With an all-woman film crew, I worked through high schools to meet with groups of girls who were mothers and mothers-to-be. At that time there were five high schools in New York City that were just for pregnant girls and girls who had babies. We worked there and also at ten schools in Georgia—urban, rural, suburban, in between. We talked with girls from different ethnic and socioeconomic backgrounds.

We explained the project and asked girls if they'd like to take part. We told them we'd like to do personal interviews, on camera, that would last from twenty to sixty minutes. We said we were interested in their stories and they could say or not say whatever they chose. We told them participation required written parental consent in advance. We thought we might work with ten or twelve girls. The response was overwhelming. We had to stop at just over a hundred.

The girls were wonderful and frank, compelling and engaging, hilarious and heart-breaking. All of the women who worked on the film crew were moved and amazed at the girls' great eagerness to talk. Many girls told us no one ever asked their opinion before. Girls' talk is belittled as yakking, babbling, chatter. But in girls' talk lies the code to their souls.

I wanted to talk with other girls, girls who don't have babies, to find out more about their experience of adolescence. The project expanded and continued over the course of three years with renewed support from ITVS. For "Run Like a Girl," we interviewed athletes: synchronized swimmers, double dutch jumpers, rugby players, and cheerleaders. For "Smile Pretty," we talked with girls who compete in beauty pageants.

In choosing these areas of focus, I just followed my heart. Pageants as we know them are a purely American variation on a theme that comes to us from ancient mythology. The drama creates a forum in which to explore the boundaries of beauty, the power of prettiness, and the quest for perfection for which all American girls are encouraged to crusade. I was interested in athletes because many people see team sports as girls' salvation, and I wanted to see how physical prowess can shape a girl's life.

The larger idea was to encourage girls to tell their own stories and speak their own truth about their experience of growing up female today.

We traveled all over the country and conducted three hundred interviews. We talked with city girls, country girls, girls in the suburbs, recent immigrants, and thoroughly American descendants of the people of Africa, Asia, Europe, and South America. We worked in California, South Carolina, New York, Tennessee, Massachusetts, and Georgia. The girls came from all kinds of families: blended, extended, Leave-It-to-Beaver, single mom, no mom, ward of the state.

The girls talked mostly about family, school, sex, boys, work, power, ambition, competition, struggle, violence, lon friendship, and growing up. They talked about how they see the ies, how others react to them, how they cope with growth and (They talked about gender and identity.

We invited each girl to direct her own interview, to talk abou that mattered to her. We also told each girl to reject questions sh(want to answer. In this way we tried to offer girls as much control sible over the interview. My feeling is that girls are pushed : enough without a film crew adding to the pressure. Also, I was to cultivate and nurture a garden of stories told from girls' true I approached the girls as experts on their own lives. We heard th ries as they chose to tell them. We took them at their word.

There is something generous and magical about the act of telli ries from our own lives. We thank every girl who took part, w or not her words are included in the book and the films. Each ; formed this work, infused this work with breath and heart ar What we humbly offered each girl in return was a chance to tell h of the story, to explain her take on things, to talk about how an she felt or thought or acted as she did.

Mothers told us over and over again, "I talk to my daughter time, I tell her everything she needs to know, I tell her all the tim grown women, we call out our wisdom from further down the hollering back a warning, shouting out encouragement, whisj support. That's great, but what about *listening* to our daughter: their flowered stories, their barbed insults, their prickly questions swollen sobs? This is a book about listening to our girls, paying tion, attending them.

We heard over and over from girls of all backgrounds, but espe from those who had babies: "I will listen to my daughter, she ca me anything, she can come to me, and she won't have to be ashar

Stories gave birth to stories. When the crew piled into the van : end of each day of shooting, we told our own tales of bewildermen conspiracy, subterfuge and triumph. Listening to girls helps us reca own ocean-drowned youth, for mourning and celebration, for r tion and the earning of wisdom.

In this way we connect to the girls of our lives, the girls long l(

our older bodies, the girls that emerge from our wombs and the girls born to our sisters and friends.

One of the most remarkable lessons of doing this work is the discovery that girls from widely divergent paths tell overlapping stories. A girl from a group home on the devastated edge of town and a girl from a rosy middle-class Mormon home could finish each others' sentences. Listening, we can trace the points at which two girls diverged, where one took the rougher road, and the other dodged a bullet and eased along.

These stories resonate with themes that connect girls despite the details of their lives. The simple fact of being a girl can override ethnicity, race, economics, region, luck, and even love in shaping adolescence.

I organized the interviews around themes that rose repeatedly like ocean waves and echoed through various stories. I linked girls from different backgrounds in the book to recreate for the reader the sense of continuity we had on the road. I wanted to highlight the universality of girls' experience, because this is what we felt while doing this work.

The stories take a spiral rather than linear form. Girls contradict themselves, repeat some things, double back and take another look. This is true for the way the book is put together as well. You'll hear the distant toll of one girl's song in another's story, many pages away. This again reflects our field experience, listening to the stories as they were told.

I have tried to respect the sound of each voice, word choice, cadence, and rhythm of speech.

I asked each girl, out of my own curiosity, "Why did you want to take part in this project?" A lot of girls said they wanted to warn other girls about mistakes they'd made, tell them what kind of boys to watch out for, encourage them to develop their own interests, tell them things get better after the casual brutality of eighth grade. Many said they were tired of the cheesy portrayals of girls on TV and hoped to contribute their own story to help create an image that is more realistic and complex.

Ultimately, this work is not about babies or pageants or sports. It's about the ways in which American girls become women, and how girls do the work of their young lives: forging women's hearts from the fire and ore of American adolescence.

INTRODUCTION

It's like waking up as a cockroach.

At nine or ten you're a skipping, grinning, boney-maroney little girl — rough and ready, half-way up a tree.

The bell tolls by twelve, a personal midnight. A new, unrecognizable body rules your life. Roofers hoot and holler when you walk down the street. Boys at school taunt you for developing too soon or not soon enough. Old friends become obsessed with diets, clothes, and makeup. Compared to the sleek, sexy girls on TV, you're fat, ugly, loud and mouthy, rude, geeky, dorky, awkward, frigid, and you smell.

You care. You are prickly, exquisitely sensitive, easily piqued by the leer, the frown, the rejection. Other girls are praised and petted for being quiet, docile, pretty, helpless, thin. Your parents may have raised you to be strong and secure. But you pick up on the cultural standard that boy things are better than girl things. The worst insult one boy can hurl at another is "girl, girlie, sissy...you run like a girl, you throw like a girl."

Suddenly shy of your smarts, you may be struck dumb. You may keep your mouth shut, refuse to eat or speak. You try to be pretty, try to be thin, try to be sexy, perfect, cute and nice and sweetie-pie.

You strap on a bra, shave your legs, tweeze your eyebrows, try some makeup, get a hairdo and a monthly visit from your Little Friend, bemoan your nose, your hips, your feet, your face.

What happens to girls? In the freest nation on Earth, at the birth of a new century, what is happening to half of the kids we're raising? How does our culture influence girls? How can parents raise happy, healthy, strong, secure girls when so much of what girls absorb is out of our control? How do ordinary girls accomplish their extraordinary molding and melding at the body slam of adolescent ch-ch-ch-changes?

❧

What happens to girls?

Girls have a secret life. Girls learn to keep quiet about pain, rage, intelligence, desires, ideas, and dreams. They learn to protect their parents from the details of their experience. They keep their wisdom, friendship, love, power, and hope among themselves.

But girls will talk if you listen, with respect and without judging. They tell stories of bull-headed rebellion, quiet courage, lonely surrender. If you listen, their stories are brutal and bruising, heart-swelling, hilarious, and true.

This is a book about American girls, how they are muddling and struggling, cringing and singing through their teenage years.

Some get talked into sex at twelve, and become mothers at fourteen. Some work thirty hours a week for ten years to compete as synchronized swimmers, smiling above water and struggling underneath. Other competitive girls wear their swimsuits with high heels. Some girls run away, do drugs, steal cars. Some form life-long, life-saving links to sisters and best friends.

This book is a look at what happens to girls, in their own lives, their own stories, in their own words. I hope adults will share the book with girls they care for and, after reading it, they'll turn to those girls and *listen* more carefully than before.

This is a book designed to spark all night heart-to-heart talks. It's a book for anyone who has ever been, or cared about, a young American girl.

 IDENTITY

Chelsea is a swish of golden hair

flashing in a blurry field of stinking mud. She is the fastest girl on the rugby team. She'll crash into you, knock you flat, and run away laughing. Andrea used to run in the mud but now she stands, poised, posed, on a pageant stage in a slim white gown, silent, smiling like a bride.

Their stories reveal the power of other people to shape a girl's gender identity, inspiring in some girls a gracious embrace of the ideal, and in others a kicking, raging resistance.

These girls fight hard every day to let their true selves live, like Michelangelo freeing saints from stone.

ANDREA, EIGHTEEN
WEST COLUMBIA, SOUTH CAROLINA

I was a big tomboy. I grew up on the trampoline, on the four-wheelers, on the motorcycles, just anything that dealt with wallerin' in the dirt or fightin' with the boys. Go-carts, football—I was an outside little girl. I wanted to get dirty. I loved my Barbies, but I used to rip their heads off. I was a typical tomboy.

I don't think you could have gotten me in one of those frilly ruffled dresses when I was little. I would have died. You would have had to tie me down to get me into one. And then I would have been out in the dirt, wallerin' in it.

I used to hate to even go to church, 'cause I hated dresses. They itched! They bugged me. I didn't like the dress shoes. I hated the hose. Used to hate the little bows my mom put in my hair. I used to fight with her all the time. And she always used to tell me, "You gotta sit proper and you gotta do this and do that." I just cried my little eyes out if my mom made me sit there and act all prim and proper. She always wanted to dress me up and I used to hate it.

All I wanted to do, I wanted to play. I didn't care about my clothes. I just wanted to put on some raggy little shorts and just go and do my own little thing and go on about myself. The dress thing was not me.

That's the difference between me and someone who grew up being a little priss all the time. I'm like, myself. I don't worry about, "Well, I got to be prim and proper here." I'm like, "If you don't like me for who I am, I'm sorry." That's the way I am. I go into things with an open mind and open heart. If they like me, they like me. If they don't, well, I can't help it.

I was quite on the heavy side when I was a little girl. I used to get picked on all the time. If I got looked at the wrong way, I'd bust out crying. I was still kind of on the hefty side in seventh and eighth grade. I reckon right when puberty hit in...I don't even remember losing the weight or anything. All I remember is just, next thing I know...it was almost like waking up one morning and I was totally different.

That's why I'm in beauty pageants today. I've grown up so much that I have a good time being the person that I turned out to be. I've totally changed from what I was when I was younger. I really am totally different from what I was like as a little girl. Totally, but not drastically at all.

I don't even know when I really did change out of that, but I remember I did. I don't even think it was an age I can remember. I reckon you just kinda change. It's something you wanna do. I got into watching my mom do her hair and her makeup and next thing I knew, I started getting more into dolls and stuff. I think I probably decided I wanted to go and do the hair thing. I remember when crimping and styling stuff was in, and your mom used to wet your hair and braid it and you'd wake up in the morning like you had a spiral perm.

I reckon it probably was around sixth grade. Puberty had a lot to do with it. You start getting interested in … boys. You start noticing stuff. I used to go back to my mom's bedroom and sneak some makeup, maybe she won't see it. I think that's when I decided I needed to grow up and be a girl like I was supposed to be when I was born.

I remember when I first started wearing my training bra. I was so excited. I was like, "What am I gonna do? I'm growing up!" I didn't want to. That was the last thing I wanted to do.

The first time I got my period, my mom was at work. I woke up and I was like, "What's going on?" I called my mom and said, "Mom, what do I do?" She laughed at me. She started telling everybody that was standing around her at work, "Andrea's starting her period." Thanks, Mom. Now when I see these people in public, they're gonna be like, "Oh, how're you doing with your period and your cramps?" I was scared to death. I didn't know what to do. I was going, "I don't like this at all." My mom said, "Well, you've got to live with this the rest of your life." I was going, "Please, no! I don't want to."

I was still kind of a tomboy. You really haven't developed a look yet. You're wanting to get into makeup but you aren't at that age where your mom's gonna let you, so you have to deal with what you look like then. But I reckon you could say you felt a little isolated because you weren't sure what you were going to look like, how you were going to be. So it was kind of like you always kept to yourself, kept secluded until you got to that age that you knew, "Well, maybe I'm gonna turn out pretty decent."

I first done a pageant in ninth grade. It was the freshman pageant at my high school. I didn't know how to walk, I didn't know how to wear my hair, my makeup. I was just going in it knowing nothing. I had a really good friend who done pageants so she kinda got me into them. She showed me the fun in it.

It's like anybody going to play football on the weekends, or basketball. It's just something for girls to do, 'cause there's not a whole lot of hobbies that girls like to do. Either you're a tomboy and you play softball and stuff like that, or you're just gonna be a dud and don't do nothing except hang out with your friends. I don't compete for the crowns and for the banners. I do it to get money for college. I'm not gonna say it's an easy thing to get money for, but it's a good challenge for me. If it challenges me, I'm up for it.

When you go up on stage, there is a certain type of walk. Some girls got the model walk, and you've got to overpower them and it's hard. And then you've got the girl who's got the perfect hair, the perfect figure, and you've got to try to have the perfect hair, a better dress than them, and it's hard. Some people have more money and some people just don't care to dress up that much. It all depends on your smile, your poise. Your personality means more than anything. A girl can go up there and not look good at all but have the cutest personality, and that girl is gonna win. Because they got to have a girl who's gonna go out and do parades and be friendly with everybody, carry on a conversation like they've known them for years. Walks, smiles, dresses — you're just competing all together, it's a whole bundle of stuff.

Some of my titles are Miss South Carolina World, Miss Poultry, Miss Peanut, and I recently won — two weeks ago — Miss Southern Belle. I have a good time meeting a lot of people. It brings out a personality in you. It teaches you, when you go out into the world, to be yourself. It helps you when you need to go to a job interview. It gives you self-confidence. It gives you confidence that you're yourself, and you can go out there and present yourself for who you are and everybody — more than likely everybody — is gonna like you or they're not gonna like you.

The first time I ever done swimsuit was Miss Teen, in front of thousands of people. If I'm in a swimsuit, I'm kinda skittish around everybody. You put your bathing suit on and you look around at everybody else and you go, "God, I look fat." I have my robe on and everyone else is just walking around. I'm going, "If I looked like you, I would do that, too." The first time I went up on stage, we were lined up five in a row. You want to run off the stage. Everybody's staring at you. You have to turn around and walk back. You go, "Can't I just walk backwards?"

I tell myself, don't worry about anybody else. Be happy for what you

are and who you are. Whenever I see other girls that might be skinnier or taller or more gorgeous…some girls, you go, "God, you make me sick!" But I just try to overlook it and be happy for what God gave me.

I think doing swimsuit is a good thing because it gives me confidence in myself. If I can get up there in a swimsuit, then I think I'm doing pretty good. I try, anyways.

Girls like me, I don't have any boobs, so I have to add 'em. A lot of times I will get like cloth boobs sewn into my dress. My mom just bought me the jelly type. They're a lot more comfortable than the cotton ones. They feel like the silicone implants that girls get. They're just like…jelly. They're just like part of your skin. It's wild. You can stick them in your bra, and you can wear them every day. I put 'em on and you don't even know it, you don't even feel it. It just clings to you and with your body heat, it shapes to the form of your body. It's weird. You put those in your bra to enhance your boobs, and make the dress fit right and look right. Because this dress is made to have the figure and the boobs, and if you don't have 'em, you've got to add 'em to make it look right. So that's the first thing I grab every time I go. Most everybody seems to have boobs. I'm the only one that seems to have to worry about it. I mean, these little girls are thirteen and bigger than me. I feel like an idiot, but I can't help it.

A lot of girls use duct tape to tape their boobs up. To get them to stay and give them cleavage. I done it one time and I'll tell you, I'll never do it again! It hurts! It really takes two people. You pretty much lean over and push your boobs up, and someone else will tape you underneath. It keeps your boobs up right where you had them. Oh, it's painful! You start right underneath your armpit and do kinda like a smiley face kinda look. Just to get 'em to hold up. If you have a dress that's low cut and you need to have some cleavage, and adding some fake boobs isn't gonna help, a lot of girls will tape. Some girls either use duct tape or that gray tape, and it hurts.

I done it for one dress I had and I'll never do it again 'cause it hurt so bad. It doesn't really hurt when it's on. It's taking it off. 'Cause it's literally just stuck to your skin. You're trying to rip it and it doesn't want to come off. God, it's awful! Ever have a Band-Aid over hair, and you take it off, and it's pulling? That's what it feels like. It just pulls and it's like you're taking an inch off at a time. You finally go, "Just rip it!"

That's what my Mom did. She went, "one, two, three," and she ripped it off. It just feels like I'm gonna be ripped in half! I looked at the tape and saw my skin on it. It had taken the first layer of my cells off. I had a red mark all the way around and I was tender. I'm not doing that again.

But girls do it all the time, even girls who don't need it. I mean, compared to me. Every time I turn around, "I need some tape, Mom!" When I went to the Miss Teen pageant, everybody was hollering, "Give me the tape! Give me the tape!" I was going, "Ugh, stay away from me." And they were like, "Come on, you might need to." And I was like, "I don't think so, you're not taping me." I've got what I've got, and if I ain't got any more, I'm not trying to make it look like I do.

A lot of girls really go through some pain to get the perfect figure, to get the perfect look. A lot of girls will tape around their waist, hips, anything they can tape up to look slimmer. But, oh, I'm not doing it, 'cause I'm not suffering! It's not worth it to me, 'cause I'm up there for myself, for who I am, not for what I'm not.

I hate doing my hair, 'cause it's aggravating. Sometimes you do a pageant and your hair goes up perfect. Sometimes it's the weather. It wants to curl or it's too flat or it's too soft. It's a pain 'cause you've got to make sure everything is right. And when your hair don't do right it puts you in bad mood. I think probably the hair is the worst thing for me 'cause it's so thick and you can't do a whole lot with it. I've got to hire somebody to do my hair.

I wash my hair the night before, because if you wash your hair that day and try to fix it, it's gonna be too soft. You want it to be not perfectly clean, but still clean. You take your shower. I usually will roll my hair and do my makeup while my curls are being set. You have probably ten different things you have to do to your face. From the eyebrows to the eyelashes to the eyeliner to the...I mean, everything, everything, there is a certain way you do everything. And after you do that, you have to get your stuff together. Your hose and, if you have 'em, the fake boobs you put in your dress. Your shoes. It's a lot of preparation to make sure you got everything. So many times I've almost left my earrings, which is a big essential thing that you need. You have to backtrack and you've got to have someone that backtracks over you, to make sure you have this, this, this, and this. If it weren't for my mom, I'd probably forget everything.

I usually get my dresses from a place called Foxy Lady. My mom brought me three thousand dollars worth of dresses on credit, so I could choose and send the rest back. The one I really liked was just too skimpy. The lady at the store called me and said, "I've got another one. It's coming from New York." She sent it to me and I fell in love with it. It had the stand-up collar and the little train and everything. I loved it until I looked at the price. It was two thousand dollars. The other dress was one thousand dollars. But it didn't need a lot of alterations, just the sleeves and the hem. It's not as expensive as if you were to get a dress made. I bought a dress before that that I've only worn twice, but I don't really like it any more. I'll probably get rid of that one—it was a thousand dollars. I think I'm gonna rip it apart and do something else with it.

When you get a dress made or get a dress fitted for you, you can't gain weight. If I gain an *ounce* in any direction, I mean, I can't wear it. I stay away from the junky stuff. I try to eat as many vegetables as possible. I'm actually gonna have to cut back more from what I'm eating now. I still eat all the time. I eat what I want, but I don't eat as much. So you don't gain as much. I'm gonna have to start getting away from that and start doing a little more dieting. I don't think my Mom would like it if I were to gain weight and I couldn't wear that expensive dress any more. She'd probably kill me.

As soon as I'm off the stage, I'm like, "I've got to get this thing off, it's so uncomfortable!" I've got dresses that I can't sit down in, 'cause they'll wrinkle or rip. I'm undressing, walking down the hallway. My mom is like, "Don't just throw it on the ground."

First thing that comes off is the shoes, and the panty hose, which are so annoying. I take those off and I'll just throw on a pair of jeans, a T-shirt, tennis shoes, and I'm ready to go. You don't know how much you adore your tennis shoes 'til you put on a pair of high heels for four hours. Then you put on your tennis shoes, and God, what a relief! I cannot stand being dressed up all the time. I'm totally different. Every time I leave a pageant, everybody's like, "Is that the girl that just won?"

I have my hair pinned up and I'm just throwing bobby pins out. I'll take my hair down and put it in a ponytail. All the hair spray and ughhh...it makes me sick! It's even worse trying to get it all off than it is to put it all on. You got so much makeup on, you could put your hands on your face and just see it, and it's—ughh! I can't stand wearing a lot of makeup. I like getting all that stuff off, it drives me nuts. I hate it. But the hair, the makeup — you've got to do it. You don't have a choice.

I reckon sometimes when you get up in the morning you're like, "God, I gotta do my hair, I gotta do my makeup." You get to the point where you're just like, "I don't want to do any of it." You just want to put your hair in a ponytail and go. You don't care what you look like. You just want to go back to that little girl who didn't care, who just got up and played all the time, and that's all she had to worry about. I would love to go back to being a little girl again. I wish I could go be like the boys, just go play and do what I want to do. But I can't.

CHELSEA, SIXTEEN
EL DORADO HILLS, CALIFORNIA

When I was a little girl, a lot of people thought I was a boy. I swear, everybody thought I was a boy 'cause I had my hair cut short, like in a bowl cut, and it was shaved underneath. I always hung out with all the guys. I didn't really have any girl friends 'cause I didn't really relate to them, you know. I liked playing sports and I liked the things guys did. I didn't like Barbies or anything, and I always dressed like a guy. Lots of people thought I was a guy.

In junior high school I started growing my hair out 'cause I was just tired of everybody thinking I was a boy. I thought, "I might as well just grow my hair out. That'll just be one less thing I have to worry about." A lot of people, they're always like, "Are you gay or something?" Nah. It's just, I don't wanna be prissy. There's just so much of that. Most of the girls I see, they're wearing trendy little stuff. They all gob on the makeup and goop up their hair. All these girls, *(mimicking a prissy voice)* "Oh, my hair, how do I look?" and "Am I trendy enough?" Who cares? It's not gonna matter anyways.

I get it a lot from my sisters. They're like, *(mimicking)* "Oh, let me dress you up! You should wear a skirt to school! Let me curl your hair." Sometimes I'll let them do that, like if I go to a dance or something, but otherwise I'm just kinda like, "naaah." It's too much to maintain. It's so annoying. You have to worry about so much more. I don't need the added stress. But I kinda feel the pressure 'cause people like, they wonder, "Oh, you don't wear makeup?" "No." So, I feel it. But it doesn't our older bodies, the girls that emerge from our wombs and the girls born to our sisters and friends.

One of the most remarkable lessons of doing this work is the discovery that girls from widely divergent paths tell overlapping stories. A girl from a group home on the devastated edge of town and a girl from a rosy middle-class Mormon home could finish each others' sentences. Listening, we can trace the points at which two girls diverged, where one took the rougher road, and the other dodged a bullet and eased along.

These stories resonate with themes that connect girls despite the details of their lives. The simple fact of being a girl can override ethnicity, race, economics, region, luck, and even love in shaping adolescence.

I organized the interviews around themes that rose repeatedly like ocean waves and echoed through various stories. I linked girls from different backgrounds in the book to recreate for the reader the sense of continuity we had on the road. I wanted to highlight the universality of girls' experience, because this is what we felt while doing this work.

The stories take a spiral rather than linear form. Girls contradict themselves, repeat some things, double back and take another look. This is true for the way the book is put together as well. You'll hear the distant toll of one girl's song in another's story, many pages away. This again reflects our field experience, listening to the stories as they were told.

I have tried to respect the sound of each voice, word choice, cadence, and rhythm of speech.

I asked each girl, out of my own curiosity, "Why did you want to take part in this project?" A lot of girls said they wanted to warn other girls about mistakes they'd made, tell them what kind of boys to watch out for, encourage them to develop their own interests, tell them things get better after the casual brutality of eighth grade. Many said they were tired of the cheesy portrayals of girls on TV and hoped to contribute their own story to help create an image that is more realistic and complex.

Ultimately, this work is not about babies or pageants or sports. It's about the ways in which American girls become women, and how girls do the work of their young lives: forging women's hearts from the fire and ore of American adolescence.

The girls talked mostly about family, school, sex, boys, babies, work, power, ambition, competition, struggle, violence, loneliness, friendship, and growing up. They talked about how they see their bodies, how others react to them, how they cope with growth and change. They talked about gender and identity.

We invited each girl to direct her own interview, to talk about things that mattered to her. We also told each girl to reject questions she didn't want to answer. In this way we tried to offer girls as much control as possible over the interview. My feeling is that girls are pushed around enough without a film crew adding to the pressure. Also, I was trying to cultivate and nurture a garden of stories told from girls' true hearts. I approached the girls as experts on their own lives. We heard their stories as they chose to tell them. We took them at their word.

There is something generous and magical about the act of telling stories from our own lives. We thank every girl who took part, whether or not her words are included in the book and the films. Each girl informed this work, infused this work with breath and heart and life. What we humbly offered each girl in return was a chance to tell her side of the story, to explain her take on things, to talk about how and why she felt or thought or acted as she did.

Mothers told us over and over again, "I talk to my daughter all the time, I tell her everything she needs to know, I tell her all the time." As grown women, we call out our wisdom from further down the road, hollering back a warning, shouting out encouragement, whispering support. That's great, but what about *listening* to our daughters — to their flowered stories, their barbed insults, their prickly questions, their swollen sobs? This is a book about listening to our girls, paying attention, attending them.

We heard over and over from girls of all backgrounds, but especially from those who had babies: "I will listen to my daughter, she can tell me anything, she can come to me, and she won't have to be ashamed."

Stories gave birth to stories. When the crew piled into the van at the end of each day of shooting, we told our own tales of bewilderment and conspiracy, subterfuge and triumph. Listening to girls helps us recall our own ocean-drowned youth, for mourning and celebration, for reflection and the earning of wisdom.

In this way we connect to the girls of our lives, the girls long lost in

really matter to me. It's just a lot of added costs. I mean, how much does lipstick cost? Like fifteen bucks? That's crazy. It's just paint. What are guys gonna think anyways? If you have to put all this stuff on your face, what do you look like for real?

You kinda wonder, do guys want all that makeup? I mean, it's only fake. It's just like painting. Don't they want the real thing? You can't know if that's what they want. But, if they only want you because you wear makeup, then why would you want them anyways?

I have a girly side. I mean, it's not like I'm some macho tough chick all around. I mean, I like guys and everything, and I'll sometimes wear a dress to a dance or something, and get dressed up and stuff like that.

I think I kinda always knew I had strength and power. I've always been pretty aggressive. A lot of girls don't always try their hardest 'cause they're kind of afraid of the image they might portray, like they're some sort of sports fanatic. They want to be viewed as a prissy little girl, you know, *(simpering)* "putting on their makeup." I never really cared what other people think 'cause I've always been kind of a tomboy.

I was gonna play Powder Puff — like girls' football. I thought it was gonna be tackle football, but it's just flag. So it's not really football. I wanna play tackle 'cause that's the funner way. Rugby's great 'cause it's a contact sport. It kinda gives you an adrenaline rush. You just get to run and tackle them.

It's a lot funner to tackle in the mud 'cause you don't get so scratched up. In most other sports, you don't really wanna get muddy, 'cause, you know, *(girly-girl voice)* "You're girls and you should stay clean." In rugby, you can get all muddy, and like, mud dripping off your hair. I just think it's a cool sport because of that.

Girls in general, they're not allowed, in society, to be more aggressive and actually use their strength and their power. So I think it's just kinda fun, kinda like showing off. You just use all your strength and take somebody down. It's not really like you're mad or anything. It's just, you actually have a sport where you can use all your strength.

You get a rush and you run and you just slam into them, man, and you can feel it like in slow motion, going down, you're just like "roahhhr" and you splat into the mud and all the mud goes up everywhere. When you tackle somebody it just helps — you're just like *"grrrrrrr."* It just gives you more of a boost.

I'm not really sure which position I'm gonna play. They have me as a wing and as a break, and those're two totally different parts. The wing is really fast. I don't wanna brag, but I'm pretty fast. I think I could do really well with that and just beat them all, you know, 'cause I'm fast. With the wing you get to run a lot and with the break you get to be more strong. You get to push people around, kinda have a little more aggression in there, get down in the mud, tackle some people, get rough.

Chelsea and her older sister, Alexis.
Alexis: When she was littler, she was a tomboy. She's like growing out of that now. I like dressing her up for dances and stuff.
Chelsea: I don't want you to put makeup on me.
Alexis: I usually just put on some eyeshadow and mascara. She doesn't like that. Oh, and foundation.
Chelsea: It stinks! Smells like old people.
Alexis: I like to curl her hair and stuff. I usually just put it in steam curlers. I leave them in for like an hour or two and then I take them out and I put hairspray in it.
Chelsea: One time I had to go buy shoes and I just left the curlers in my hair and went to the mall. People were like, "Gosh, you're really brave. You're going out in curlers!" I'm like, "I don't care." My sister was embarrassed. She didn't want to walk with me. She was like, "I don't know you! Stay away from me."
Alexis: But I still helped you pick out shoes.

Chelsea and her mom.
Mom: Chelsea's been pheasant hunting a couple times. When she was eight, Grandpa got her her own rifle. She was pretty little and he got her this child-sized rifle.
Chelsea: It's not a rifle, it's a shotgun.
Mom: Oh, a shotgun, excuse me. Her uncle took her out shooting with it. And it left a huge bruise on her shoulder. Chelsea's not your wimpy kind of girl anyway. But to leave this big old bruise!
Chelsea: Well, that was when I was little. He's got a ton of really cool guns. He has steel targets and stuff out by his house. It's really fun to go out there and shoot. It's awesome.
Mom: Chelsea's one of these go-for-it kids. She'll try anything. She's very

athletic. She's really good at a lot of things. She's a good water-skier and skate-boarder and snow-boarder. You name it, she'll try it. When I was her age, I liked to ride motorcycles.

Chelsea: Even though you won't let us.

Mom: Well, I have scars I don't want you to have.

Chelsea: Too late.

Mom: She went out for boys' wrestling a couple years ago. I wasn't real thrilled about that. But at least rugby is all girls. That was guys. I wasn't too excited to have her out there wrestling with these burly, sweaty boys.

Chelsea: I can still beat them up.

Mom: They were all afraid of her 'cause she, what was it, sumo wrestling? She was picking up girls that were a lot bigger. She was beating up — well, not beating up, but beating — a lot of the girls in sumo wrestling. Even the teacher wouldn't come up against her. She was always the kind of kid that she'd be carrying in the firewood when she was real little, you know. I used to get to dress her up in white and in little pink dresses, though.

Chelsea: Only when I didn't have any control over it.

Mom: Alexis is a lot more feminine. She's not a wimp or anything.

Chelsea: Yes, she is.

Mom: No, she's not.

Chelsea: Yes, she is.

Mom: She's just different. Chelsea's hair grew, it was short two years ago. She had a boy's style, so she was mistaken for a boy.

Chelsea: Yeah, in sixth grade. It was like a bowl cut, up above my ears and shaved underneath. I started growing it out in seventh grade. I never put my hair up 'cause I never learned how. When I had short hair I never had to worry about it, 'cause it doesn't get in your eyes. When I grew it out, I never learned how to put it up. So it stays down and gets in my face.

Mom: When I was her age, I wanted to wear short dresses and be noticed by boys a lot more than she does. Which I'm kind of glad she's the way she is, because you always worry about your daughters. If she was out there trying to impress the guys, the way I did at that age, I'd be a lot more worried. I think she's got a really good head on her shoulders. She's got her priorities in the right

place. I just hope that going through the teenage years she maintains those attitudes.

Chelsea: Unlike other people (*motions toward Alexis*).

Mom: I was recently married. For the wedding, of course, I wanted them to wear flowery dresses and have their hair fixed and look really pretty for the pictures.

Chelsea: She made me put makeup on. But when you drink, lipstick gets all over the cups.

Mom: Once in a while I'd like to see her dress up and look beautiful. At the eighth grade graduation she wore a beautiful blue velvet dress and had her hair pulled back and Alexis did her makeup and she looked gorgeous. The minute she got out of the car all the other girls, and the boys, too, came up, "Chelsea, you look so pretty. You look gorgeous." Everybody was walking up to her and she was just beaming. She just looked beautiful.

Chelsea: It was kinda weird. Everybody was like, "Is that you? Wow, you look a lot different."

Mom: They said you looked beautiful. They didn't say you looked a lot different.

Chelsea: Same thing. She always tries, when we go school shopping (*mimicking her mother*), "Don't you wanna get this dress? It's so much more pretty. It has pink on it. Look at the flowers." But she can't make me wear frilly stuff. She always, like when I went to get my hair cut when it was short, "Don't you want to grow it out? You know, you could get a girlier haircut." One time she wanted me to get a perm. Curly, like hers.

Mom: I'd take her to get a haircut. They'd fix her hair afterwards so that it looked like a girl haircut. She would put a bag over her head, run in and wet it down as soon as we got home.

Chelsea: You can't stop somebody from being who they are.

Mom: I don't want to stop her from being who she is.

ENDURANCE

 E N D U R A N C E

A delaide comes early to the interview room. I only ask her name and age. She answers for an hour. We stop to change tapes and batteries. Adelaide never stops.

Taneshia laughs at the camera crew. She thinks it's goofy that we're interested in her. She says, "I'm just an average girl."

Taneshia and Adelaide both have lost their mothers. They endure deep soul loneliness, lit with visions of independence. Like other girls, they want to stand on their own two feet without standing alone. Their stories show the courage and persistence of girls determined to create lives and families for themselves.

TANESHIA, SIXTEEN
MALDEN, MASSACHUSETTS

I think I like myself the way I am. I don't care what anybody says. I don't think I'm fine, I don't think I'm sexy. You know, some girls think they're fine and sexy. I just think I'm cute when I want to be. There's times I have my bad days, then I have my good days. That's the way I see it. I don't like when people say, "Oh, you're so pretty." I don't like that. I feel weird. I would like to say, "Mind your business, don't tell me that stuff," 'cause I don't want to hear it. I don't. I feel weird.

Double dutch is like your own mind. It's like what you want to do and when you want to do it. If your coach wants you to try something, you try it. You should never say that you can't do it, because you never know. One day you just come back and you do it. But double dutch is, you do it on your own. Like you just go out there and you do it, no matter if you mess up or not. You just do what you feel, what your body wants to do, what your heart wants to do. I really don't have to listen to what anybody says. I just go out there and I do what I want, when I want to. Whatever my heart tells me to do, I do.

It's in my blood, I've gotta go, I have to jump.

It's like a rush, you need it, like, you keep doing it and doing it. I keep doing it and doing it. It's like a rush to me, it makes me happy. You may hurt yourself every once in a while, but you get up. We still do it, no matter what. It feels good to you and you like it. And other people like it too, they like what you do and how you do it.

I never taught anybody how to jump ropes before. So, I was, like, a teacher. A couple of people asked me to come to their school and teach their team. Because we did it before. We're gonna teach younger girls, so when they go to competition, they know what to expect, and they know what the judges expect.

The younger girls are really talented. They jump as well as we can jump. They can learn from us, because we've been there already. We know what we're doing. We can put it into their heads and they can go on and be champions.

They should be looking up to basketball players and stuff. Me, I'm like an average girl, so it was weird that they were looking up to me. I'm just average. It's not like I'm the best jumper in the world. I don't think anyone should look up to me. I'm there to learn new stuff, too.

They look up to us because we've been there. We've been through life, kind of. We've been through problems, and they want to know what's out there. That's why they look up to us.

My role model is Tyra Banks. She does modeling and that's totally opposite from what I do. I do double dutch. I don't know nobody famous that does double dutch. I've liked Tyra Banks from when I was like eleven, 'cause everyone used to say I look like her.

When I was little I used to do double dutch. Then I was like, "I'll never get nowhere with this," and then I just stopped. Miss Mack, she taught me how to do it all over again last year. It's fun and my friends are on the team, so I like being with them.

Freestyle is like basically all the tricks and the dances. I do a cartwheel in the ropes, I do the high can-can and a round-off in the rope. Then I go down to the mountain climb and I do the cartwheel out of the rope. I do a lot of stuff. I know how to do everything if I put my mind to it. But that's what the coach mapped out for me to do. I took gymnastics a long time ago. I'm just flexible. Whatever Miss Mack asks me to try, I say I'll try. She asked who can do flips and stuff, splits and I was like, "Me!"

When I first started doing the cartwheel, I was like, "I'm not gonna get this. I'm not gonna get it!" I kept saying to Miss Mack, "I can't do it." She's like, "You can do it." And so I was like, "I'm gonna do this," just playing around, you know, "I'm gonna do this!" When I finally did it in the rope, I was like, "Oh my gosh! I did it!" I just surprised myself by that.

Miss Mack is open to changing the routine. I asked her today if I could put some more stuff into it that's not so easy for me. I want to do some hard stuff. We're gonna work on it this week. Start tomorrow. It's too easy to do like little high kicks. I can do more than that. I know I'm experienced, I know how to do that. Even if I don't know how to do it, I'll get it sooner or later. I just want to try some hard stuff.

The mule kick, that's the hard one that I'm trying now. You have to go real low down to the ground, almost like a handstand in the rope. That's a hard one. But I'll keep trying it and trying it 'til I get it. It's worth a lot of points.

We'll have to work on our speed and double compulsory. But our freestyle, we pretty much have that down. Sometimes we get lazy and play around and some people have sore body parts, like I need an ankle brace and a wrist brace 'cause I land too hard. We just gotta stop playing around and get down to business. We got to be serious about this if we want to win. So we just gotta go out there and do our best, if we mess up just get back in, have a good attitude and I don't know, miracles work.

Go in there with a good attitude, you never know, we might win, 'cause we came in there, we did our best, we tried not to mess up. We might take it again. That's what happened last year. We messed up, yeah, but we still won the state championship.

We went to the world championships. Last year there were about two hundred teams. Some from Japan, China, France, all over the place, Canada. We lost there last year. We were mad about it, but we tried, we smiled, and we put all our effort into it. It's supposed to be a good sport. Everybody's sporty about it. You're supposed to be happy, even if you're mad.

Hopefully by the year 2000, like we read in the paper, it'll be in the Olympics. Right now, no one considers it a real sport. It's not like basketball, baseball, hockey. It's something little girls get together and do. That's what people see it as, but it's more than that. Wait until it goes to the Olympics, and they'll see it's really a sport. People take their time and they put their energy and they sweat, they bleed, they hurt, just for this. They'll see it's just like basketball, baseball, and hockey 'cause you sweat, bleed, and hurt in hockey, basketball. We have to work out just like they have to work out in basketball. We do a lot of stuff that is similar to basketball and hockey and baseball. It's a sport. They don't see it as a sport. They just see it as a little game. It's really nothing. Girls get together and just play.

I don't think I'll ever stop permanently because I like to do double dutch. It keeps me on my toes, so I don't think I'll ever stop.

Our coach, she's like us, like a teenager. We're like, "Give me high five, Miss Mack," and she's funny. She jumps with us, too. She goes wild and crazy. Sometimes we play together. I jump with Miss Mack and switch up and stuff. That's why everybody likes Miss Mack. She's like a good friend. She's older, she went through a lot. She tries to coach us, let us know what we have to do in the world and what we shouldn't do in the world. How we present ourselves in the world. You shouldn't go out and be too big and bad. You're not big and bad, you're just shy inside, y'know. Be yourself no matter what.

I have a lot of brothers and sisters. I have eight sisters and four brothers. Including me, I'm the thirteenth one. The fourth oldest. We've always been together. We've never needed nobody to come to birthday parties. We played with our sisters and brothers, we didn't need no friends, really. I depend on my family and they depend on me. Growing up with them, it was hard, 'cause you're not the only child. There's other people that need love and care. In a way it was fun and in a way it was kinda hard. You felt that you need the most attention, but there's other people.

My mother passed away two years ago because she had an aneurysm in her head. My father got remarried and moved to Everett. So I moved in with my cousin. She's forty-five. She has her own kids.

My two little sisters live in Boston. My other two little sisters, they live in Kentucky. I have one brother and four sisters in Cambridge. We're like scattered all over the place. I miss them a lot. I think about them all the time. I got a lot of pictures of my family. I look at the photo albums and stuff when I miss them. I just seen my little sister yesterday. My oldest sister, too. I go visit them. I call them and talk on the phone. They come over my house, spend the night.

Our whole family lived together and then, when my mother got sick, we all just separated. We went our different ways. It's weird 'cause it's just one of me now. I used to be in the habit of calling them when they're not there. Like, "Vanessa, come here!" and she wouldn't be there, because we're all separated, we all live in different places. It's just weird, like it's only me. Like I'm the only child, even though I know I'm not.

I don't hardly see my Dad. I don't know, I don't really want to see him. I feel better not seeing him. He went on with his life and I'm going on with mine. He got remarried, so I feel better not seeing him. I talked to him a couple of times. I feel weird talking to him 'cause I really don't have nothing to say. I'm older now. I really don't talk to him much.

It'll be two years since my mom passed away. I'm doing OK. People say, "Don't you feel sad?" I feel sad, yeah, but I feel she went to a better place. She would want me to go on with my life instead of grieving. So that's what I'm doing. I still think about her. Little things that my sisters do remind me of her. People say that I remind them of my mother. I get sad sometimes, but I just keep going on.

I was bad when I was little. Like, little wise remarks and stuff. Not come in when I was supposed to. "I'm not doing this, I'm not doing that," "can't make me," and stuff like that. Running around, beating up on people. I stopped when I was eleven. After that, I really didn't go outside that much 'cause nothing outside really interested me. I just stayed in and watched TV. Did my homework and slept. That's all I did. In high school, I did the same thing my freshman year, but my sophomore year I was like, "I need to do something better with my time." So Miss Mack thought of the double dutch team. I've been on the team ever since. To, you know, waste some time. But it isn't wasting time, it's like work. I started liking it, so I don't consider it wasting time any more.

I'll probably take a year off, after high school, to work and stuff. So I can have some money for college. But most definitely I want to go to college. Major in pre-med, be a doctor. I want to cut open stuff, you know. I want to be a surgeon, see what's inside the human body, stitch it back up. The only thing I've cut up was chicken. That's to cook the chicken. But I've never cut any frogs up. I've wanted to, but I haven't had the chance. Our biology teacher, she didn't want to go to the pond and catch them, so she said we wasn't going to cut open anything. Hopefully in college I'll get to cut open some little baby pigs and stuff. You know, see what's inside them. See if we have the same things.

Right now, I'm just sending out stuff to colleges, and having them send me stuff back so I can read about it. In my senior year, I'll start doing college tours. My cousin, she doesn't want me to go far out. She says I need to be close to home 'cause I'm still little. I want to go out of state. I want to go far away from home. I want to go down South. I've been to Tuskegee, Alabama. That college is nice and I've been to Clark. Those are the only colleges I've been to so far. I like those colleges, but she wants me to stay close. I don't want to, though.

Hopefully I won't have to pay for college, I'll just get a scholarship. Full scholarship, so I won't have to pay for anything. And I'll just have a nice car, a good paying job, while I'm there. And when I get out, I'll start my own business and I'll be driving around in my beautiful Lexus. I want a Lexus badly so I gotta hit the books and find something to keep me motivated. You know, something I really want to do that pays well, so I can start getting the stuff that I always dreamed of getting. And first that starts with an education 'cause you can't get nowhere without an education.

My cousin tells me I have to manage my money. I opened up a bank account last year and I saved two thousand dollars. So I'm trying. I'll put that money towards college. I had three jobs last year while I was going to school. Babysitting, I did for my family. I got paid for that. I used to work at a food market. And I used to be a tobacco peer leader. One of the counselors I knew asked me, do I smoke? I said no! She was like, "Do you want to be a tobacco peer leader?'" I write to all the tobacco companies, pass out pamphlets, public service announcements for the radio and just write papers to companies. I don't like people who smoke around me or even if I'm just walking by you, I'll be mad. Smoking is not good. It's killing people. My mother used to smoke and I used to hate it. I used to ask her, "Why do you smoke? Why do you smoke?" And she'd be like, "Because I'm stressed." I don't like smoking. Smoking wouldn't work with double dutch. You'd be wheezing, you couldn't jump long — probably pass out from smoking. It's clogging up your lungs. And when you jump you need all the air you can get. All the air you can get.

About getting pregnant... No. I can't see myself. My family would be so mad 'cause they think if you're so young, you shouldn't have kids. And I like my life now, doing double dutch and stuff. So having a kid would just mess it all up. I wouldn't be able to do the stuff I want to do. Go hang out with my friends, do my double dutch. Go to the mall and stuff. A baby would just set you back. I like my life the way it is now.

I would tell younger girls, life is ups and downs and you gotta learn how to deal with the ups and downs. The downs may be real hard, but the ups, they come. Listen to your parents 'cause they know. Parents are mostly always right. What they tell you is for your own good and not to hurt you. I don't see drugs and sex as a threat to me 'cause I know what's out there. Some girls they know, but they don't care. They just go out and they do it anyways. But I know what's out there. I know what I should be in and what I shouldn't be in. I don't see that as a threat to me. I just go on.

ADELAIDE, NINETEEN
ATLANTA, GEORGIA

I really wasn't planning on getting pregnant. I didn't know what was gonna happen to me after I left that group home. 'Cause you know, when girls go to group homes, they probably come from a bad background, being raped, mama don't love 'em. And love play a big role in the family, it really do. I don't want my little girl to be molested, I don't want her to become . . . I mean it, I really do. I really don't want her ever to be introduced to none of them things, because it stay with you all your life, it really do. You gotta have a strong mind to put it back. I just hope she grow up to be a good girl, and if I ever die or ever leave her, I hope somebody real good just take good care of her.

I was a virgin up 'til I was eighteen, when I left my group home. If I knew it was gonna be like this, believe me, I would have stayed back there. I had two roads to travel down. When you're in state custody, when you turn eighteen, if you're in a group home, sometimes you gotta leave. But if you're in twelfth grade, they let you stay until you graduate. I had two roads: leave, or just stay there.

I been knowin' this guy for like six years, and, I mean, I guess things just happen. I guess I just wasn't thinkin'. At the clinic, they told me I wasn't pregnant. But if you a woman, you know something's wrong with your body. So I went back. Then they said I was. I thought I was gonna lose my baby, I guess, 'cause, I don't know, I was just thinking all negative things. I was just thinking crazy things. They told me I was gonna have a little boy. I went out and bought all boy things. And I had a little girl.

My baby's father, he try to down me. My grandma, she said, "I done raised you better." I said, "Yes, ma'am." She said, "It's not good how that guy treats you." I said, "I know." But see, I was hurt, because I fell into the wrong hands, and I thought somebody loved me, but they really didn't. I came from a bad background. But it's really all a mind thing, to keep going on. I don't like to cry, but I do it every now and then to keep the pressure off.

I guess I grew up thinking that nobody really loved me. You know love, that word "love," I can't really say it ruined my life, but I really hate that I got introduced to it. If I say "love," everybody know, you and I know, that "love" means like sharing and doing this and that, but if you *don't* know, it's just one word. If you *don't* know what it is, you be like, "Golly, I wonder what is it?" But love was introduced to me wrong, you know? I know you don't know, but I'm telling you. Love, it was introduced to me wrong. But now, I'm trying to introduce it to my baby the right way. I'm trying…I'm trying to do it the right way.

Some people show they love…I guess they try…you think it's love, but it don't really be it. I gets mad and it hurts so bad inside that I hate that he even came my way.

I don't have no boyfriend. I don't have nothing but my child. But it don't matter no more to me. I guess when God feel that I need somebody, he'll send me somebody.

I have changed. When I was in state custody, oh, goodness, I used to cry all the time. I went to counseling every Thursday, and church every Sunday. I had a million, billion questions to ask, "Why me? Why couldn't I been one of the rich kids? Why my parents couldn't been a doctor or a lawyer, and take good care of me, and just discipline me when I need to be disciplined, and send me to school?" And you know that old saying, you teach a child in the way they should go—they'll go. I have that one on my wall at home. If you teach them love, they'll grow up humble, or something like that. Don't nobody really love me but my baby. I used to think my baby's father, when I first met him. But I been knowing him six years and he hasn't changed a bit.

In the back of my group home there was a big, nice beautiful creek, sand, everything. It was like blue water, it was so pretty. I'd go back there and just cry.

It's amazing, this world. I mean, it's not the world, it's the people that live in it, that you surrounded by, how they treat you. I'm a good person. I try to respect everybody. I come to you how you come to me. How you talk to me, I'll talk to you.

When I got five or six months pregnant, the doctor told me I had to quit work or I would lose my baby. I had no money. I had a bank account, but I spent it all. And so I prayed, I asked the Lord, I said, "I ain't got no money. I'm tryin' to hang on. If I can make it 'til my seventh month, then I'll quit work." So I stayed with my job 'til I was seven months, and then I quit. It was hard, it was real hard, 'cause my father sent me money every now and then, but I had to make it some way. I got really sick a lot, so I stayed in the OB clinic every day. That's when

I was starting to show. I just got fat. I was real big. I weighed, I think I weigh 150 now. When I was pregnant, I was like 285. I lost a lot of weight after I had my baby, 'cause I'm a size ten now.

I told my granddad, I said, "Granddad, I gotta get a car. I'm pregnant." I would beg my father. He kept saying, "You ain't got no license." So I taught my own self how to drive. I got in the car and didn't know what to do. But see, I've been in cars. I got friends who have cars. I went and took the driver test. The lady, I kept telling her, "I'm very nervous, ma'am. I'm real nervous." I had to parallel park. I messed up. She said, "You know what you need to do, Adelaide? You need to come up a little bit by that pole, and just come on in." And on the third time I got it. I did it, and I passed. I got my license, and my granddad was very proud of me. I went and got my license on my own.

I'm not gonna say I'm by myself, but it's my baby that keeps me going each day. My baby, she's wild, she's so nice. She has her days. She's teething right now. I love her a lot. Some days be bad, some days not, though. Her personality — she's so friendly. Sometimes she hollers and I don't know what to do. She makes me mad, and I deal with her. But see, I learned this: I don't cherish my baby, but I do love her. You gotta put God first in your life, and if you cherish something, he'll take it away from you. That's what I always learned; I know that from experience. And I know if nobody else loves me, my little girl does. She real crazy about me. Don't nobody else love me, but if you got a child, all the little things she do, you know for a fact that she do love you.

When I'm at school, I'm a kid, but outside in the world, I'm a grown woman. On the first of the month, everybody gotta pay bills. I try to budget my money. Don't nobody in this world give me nothin'. Unless, my granddad, he helped me out a lot, and my father. If I do have problems I just try to deal with it the best I can. If not, I just try to ignore it, just keep goin' on.

I'm here now. I'm doing good. I really am. I had my baby on Easter Sunday. Wasn't anybody there but Grandma and my niece. She was there. When I was pregnant, I needed help. My niece was there. And she ain't nothing but eleven years old. I went back to work when my baby was two months old. My niece kept my baby.

I didn't have nobody show me which way to go. But all that matters now is that I'm trying to do right, and I'm gonna do right. Every day

I try to accomplish a goal. They say some black kids don't know this, or know that, but I really am trying. I don't get no check; I'm not on welfare. I wish I was, 'cause they don't pay me enough at work. But I'm doing good. Right now one of my goals is to accomplish high school. I really wanna graduate. I really wanna be somebody! And I'm gonna do it this year, I don't care what nobody say. I swear, I'm walking down that aisle; I'm gonna get that diploma.

I get the blues every now and then 'cause my friends, they in college now. But I'm working toward trying to get somewhere, y'know, be somebody. I ain't gonna just sit around and not do nothing.

I done had plenty of jobs in my life. I done been a cashier, a manager so many times. I still don't know what I'm good at. I'm working—whoo! I'm trying. I would love to make some money! I work on a counter at the airport. I do domestic tickets. When a person's getting on a plane, I check their ticket. I wear a blue skirt and a white shirt. I like working with children and babies. I want to be a case worker, because I understand children.

Ain't nothing my boyfriend...he's not my boyfriend no more. I don't have a boyfriend. I'm kinda out there, just me. I go to work, I take care of my baby. He's my baby's father. He always said negative things to me. But it don't bother me no more because it's been going on for so long. I can't get him to do nothing for her, so I do it for her. I can't make him be a daddy. It don't bother me no more, as much as it used to. I done come a long way. I'm there for her, I don't care what nobody say, I am. I work two jobs. I got an apartment on my own. I pay bills every month. My baby's only six months old. I want her to live a good life. I don't never want nobody to molest her, treat her wrong. Can't nobody treat your child as good as you treat them. They say, watch out who baby-sits your child because they can do anything to them, 'cause at daycare centers, people have molested children. I wish that I could be there every moment of her life, but somebody gotta bring some money home, and that's me. I got a baby, I gotta eat, I gotta have clothes. I gotta work.

You know what, though? Sometimes when I'm at home, I still think I'm a little girl, because...I still think I'm a little kid, because...I went out on my own too quick. I left too quick. I was so confused, I really was, what to do? But now, I come to high school every morning. I go to work when it's raining, when it's cold. I just got my baby a coat, try to keep her warm. At first I couldn't get her one, but like I told them at the nursery, I was working on it. I got my check, I put a little in the bank, I take a little out. I'm trying to build it up. I try to keep me and my baby clean and nice. I try to keep my house clean. I feel like if I'm dirty, and my hair's not fixed, that's how I feel inside. I have hurted for so long, sometime that hurt inside me, it try to sneak back up on me. But you know what I do? I run away from it, I get up, I gone.

People don't really know you 'til they really get to talk to you. And they still really don't, because they ain't lived the life you live. I have my own style. I don't care what nobody says, I hold my head up high. I used to have low self-esteem, but I don't now. I love myself, I try to treat myself right. I meet different faces every day. I smile, I laugh. I try to keep going. I don't go to church every Sunday, and I don't go to Bible study, but I know there's a God. I try to whisper a little prayer every now and then to let Him know that I still love Him, and I thank Him for letting me do good. I try to let the blues stay off my heart.

I'm making it each day, I really am. I'm doing well. I can honestly say I'm doing well. I have a car, it's not much but it get me to school and get me to work. I know there's a lot of people out there that...some people lived worse than I done lived. I meet mean people each day, I meet nice people, I meet crazy people, but that won't stop me from making it. It really won't. I did...I came from a bad background, but...it's...it's all gonna change now.

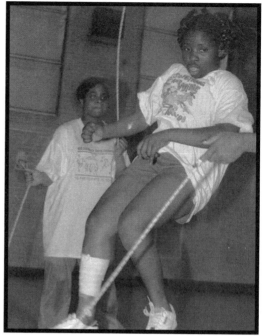

 AMBITION

S ome dreams of high accomplishment
are born in early girlhood. Felicia and April both
had big dreams as little girls. Now April speaks
softly, her voice swollen with longing. Felicia is
tentative, wide-eyed, eager to please.

Their stories show how being a girl can deter-
mine the shape of our dreams, and set our course
forever or knock us off our mark. They show how
delicate the aspirations of a girl can be, and reveal
deep needs for direction and devotion.

Their stories show what can happen when ambition lives in the body of a pretty little girl.

FELICIA, SEVENTEEN
WEST COLUMBIA, SOUTH CAROLINA

I had a good childhood, a real good childhood. I had a great family. When I was little, I liked to sing a lot. You know that thing you use to clean the toilet, to unstop it or whatever? That used to be my microphone. I had a little tiny guitar. I'd always be singing or dancing. I was happy. I got a Barbie doll every week. I was spoiled.

I wanted to be Barbie. Barbie was awesome, awesome to little girls. She seemed like she was kinda like a supermodel. She had the big huge house and she had the Corvette and all the wonderful clothes and all these great friends.

I always wanted to marry a real rich man, real great looking guy, kinda like Ken, and just have a great little family. I always wanted that. I remember I always wanted a little sister, but I never got one. I'm glad I didn't 'cause probably now we'd be at each other's throats.

The outfits that Barbie wore, they were so awesome. I was like, "Why can't *we* wear those?" Just some of the dresses that she had. I just liked the way her outfits fit. I liked her blonde hair and her blue eyes. I always wanted those and now, I like my brown eyes and my brown hair. I deal with it. I loved my Barbie coloring book, coloring in her hair and stuff. Sometimes I'd make her with brown hair and brown eyes to just see how I would hopefully look someday.

And here I am, kinda like, I guess, in a Barbie world sort of thing, just wearing all these gorgeous dresses that are outrageously priced. It's like you're in a dream world when you're in these dresses, because not everybody gets to wear them. Only if you're in pageants you get to. It's like you're in a whole other world when you're on stage, kinda like you're floating. I'm kinda in my Barbie world. I'm actually doing what I wanted to do. Except for the family, but that'll come along in maybe three, four, five years.

When I was nine years old, my mom and dad, they put me in Collins Models, a model agency. I was real, real, real, real shy. But that kinda built my confidence. They taught you basic modeling stuff. The lady had huge classes. There was all these little young uns and then there were some real older...there were a lot of older women. I guess they were in their forties. I just kinda watched them. I was real impressionable then. I watched them, how they walked, and I just kinda learned. Just by looking.

I really didn't pay much attention to my body, and then I woke up one day, and boom! I looked at it and I was like, "Whoa! Where did all this stuff come from?"

I learned how to put my makeup on at modeling class. For a pageant, I just kinda put a little bit more on. My mom helped me pick out the outfits and style my hair. It's just been my mom and I. We've really worked on it.

My mom was in like five or six pageants during her high school years. And the Miss Saluda, that's where she's from, Saluda County. She placed in about three or four of them, but she never really won one. I know she likes me bein' in 'em. It kinda feels to her like she's the one on stage and stuff. She gets just as excited as I do.

I think I was gonna...I know, yeah, I remember, I wanted to be a nurse. I was gonna be a nurse or a doctor. But then I had an awful experience as a candy striper. They put me on a bad floor, where I just pretty much saw people deteriorating before my eyes. So that kinda kept me away from my dream or whatever. From then on, I changed it, I wanted to start singing, possibly become a musical education teacher. That was when was I was fourteen.

My mom kept on talking about pageants. Every year when the Miss Peach pageant would come along, she kept on mentioning it. When I was fourteen, my mom was like, she and I were like, "Let's do it!" She got an application from a store down in Lexington. We filled it out and borrowed a dress, and I was in a pageant!

I won my first crown last year. I was Carolina Precious Sweetheart Valentine Queen. I really didn't have to make any appearances with that. My Miss Flame crown is the first one I've had to actually work with. You wear a crown if you're gonna go to a pageant and just watch it. You'll be one of their guests, or if you're gonna make an appearance, like at parades, or at a fair, or at the mall. It's really cool. I like walking around with a crown on, at parades and stuff.

These crowns are kinda hard to keep on, so you have to stick a lot of bobby pins in. I can put, like, twenty of 'em in, and it still feels like it's about to fall off. After a while, you kinda get used to having it on your head. But it feels like you have to tilt forward, it's so heavy. You kinda keep your head up, and it starts feeling normal. I like it.

At the parade that we were in, they stuck us on a fire truck. And every time it stopped, it would jerk, and I was like, "Whoa!" It felt like my crown was gonna fall off. I was like, "Oooh!" I had to keep holding on to it.

Everybody has a dream of winning Miss USA. I'd like to win Miss South Carolina USA, and go to Miss USA. I really think I have a chance. Everybody's got a chance, if they just go out there and work on it. But I really feel like I'm getting somewhere. I think I can achieve my dream. And hopefully I will.

I definitely plan on going to college. Starting next year. The Miss American system, they have a lot of pageants where they have scholarships, like five-thousand-dollar scholarships. If I win a couple of them, that will help me out.

First you get the application, and you fill it out. If you have an on-stage interview, you have to figure out what you want to talk about. Sometimes I talk about my Guatemala mission trip that I went on. My mom is like my coach. We have to go find outfits. If you have a cocktail number, you need to wear a cocktail dress. You have to figure out if you have the clothes or if you have to go buy them, if you need a new dress.

I kinda got blessed by the Lord with not being big in the thighs. I like to be in shape, and being in color guard helps me out with that. I mean, my legs are well defined. I don't like to look too white on stage, so I'll go to a tanning bed. I'm not gonna go every day, 'cause I don't wanna be like burnt. I'll go a couple of times just to give me a golden kind of look. Then you have to figure out how you're gonna place everything in the bathing suit. They have this sticky stuff for your behind, so your butt doesn't fall out on stage, so you have to get some of that. Firm Grip — it's fanny glue to spray on your tush so you don't get a wedgie when you walk on stage. It keeps all the fat and the stuff that jiggles in.

They have the roll-on kind, or they have the spray stuff. You have to pull the bottom of the bathing suit up and spray it on your behind. Then you place the bathing suit exactly where you need it. It's actually really good 'cause I wouldn't want to be on stage and have my tush hang out. Sometimes in a pageant, they'll make you do a little dance number in your bathing suit, which is awful to me, honestly.

One pageant, we did this little line dance, so we were all holding on

together. I was really self-conscious. I was like, "Please God, don't let me fall out." I was freaking out. I was just like, "Aaaaaugh!" I don't know how it looked to the audience, us up there dancing around, 'cause we were just kind of bare. So, you know.

My two favorite things are swimsuit and evening wear. My least favorite is probably cocktail. Just because you have to kind of dance around, and wearing high heels, it's not too fun sometimes. But swimsuit, I really like it, 'cause I'm pretty much comfortable with my body. As long as I have the spray that's gonna keep my tush in, I'm fine.

The only thing I'm worried about is taping. It's just because I'm top heavy. I'm real heavy on my chest. I have to tape a whole lot to keep me up, 'cause I really need support. God didn't make me with perky ones. I guess that's the best way to put it. I have to get a little help with the tape. We can't wear bras, so I gotta use tape. And I hate it, I hate it with a passion.

The tape — it's like having a bra. You know how a bra supports you? Well, it's tape under the bathing suit and you can't see it. Or you're not supposed to see it. And it keeps you up and supported so you're not like sagging. It pushes you up to give you cleavage. And, well, if you're not taped right, that'll hurt. I've seen it happen where they'll use the wrong kind of tape, and it'll tear the skin off.

Felicia and her mom in a motel room getting ready for the Miss Spartenburg, South Carolina, pageant, a preliminary for Miss USA.

Felicia: You want to try to be as perfect as you could possibly get. It takes every little thing. Taping, Firm Grip. Some people wear teeth thingies. And they wear pieces in their hair. People do a lot of things for pageants. They'll do all that they can to make themselves look the best that they can. And I mean a lot of people spend a lot of money, too.

Mom: One of the prizes for the girls who win is three thousand dollars worth of dental work, which would allow you six front crowns. You know, the smiling area. If you win, they want you perfect.

Felicia: If one of the state winners wins Miss USA, South Carolina itself gets so much publicity. And the people that they sponsor, they can say, "This is one of our customers." And they have pictures of her all over the place.

Felicia alone in her room.

In the Miss Bearcat pageant, my high school pageant, people would come up to me and say, "Oh, you know you're gonna win." People who don't even acknowledge I exist any other time. I don't really like hearing that, because nobody knows who's gonna win. Since I placed last year, the girls were all saying some rude and mean stuff about me behind my back. And when I won, I had people that hadn't talked to me since I was in middle school come up and congratulate me. It just kinda makes me feel weird, because it took that to make people talk to me. I just don't understand that.

You really need just to be your own self. Some people try to copy other people and it's not original. Have a good time if you're going to be in a pageant, because if you're all worried about the other person, you'll end up making yourself miserable. I've done that a couple of times. But when I have a great time and just enjoy doing it, that's when I do my best. You meet so many new and wonderful people. Pageants are a good way to build some confidence, also. I used to be a real shy, timid girl. Now I go to a football game, and I used to be like, "Oh my God, look at those people dancing with the band!" and now I'm one of the biggest ones dancing.

Guys, if they see somebody attractive, they hound her. I think every girl kinda sorta in some way has had a problem with guys. I've had boys I never met call me, and I don't know how they got my number. I've had rude comments at school. Every girl does. You just have to get on with it, and just shrug it off. I don't know if it's because I'm beautiful, or just because of my figure, 'cause I do have, I guess you would say, a voluptuous figure, with the top part. I don't know if it's that, or if they just truly like me for the person that I am, but some of them are going at it in the wrong way.

When I'm like just normal, I'm like, "Eeeeew!" Especially in the mornings. But sometimes, when I dress up, and I look in the mirror right before I go on stage, I'm like, "Whoa! Look at all this!" I mean it's really cool. I just love it, it's awesome.

I was kinda shocked when I put on that red dress. It's amazing that a person can really look like that. I know it's me, but your jaw just drops. It's a real...it's a normal person, but it kinda seems like you can't touch her, y'know, that it's just too perfect to touch. One of those

ladies that you just stare at, you can't believe God made something so gorgeous. It's incredible to think I was that person.

A lot of the gorgeous people, people think they're vain. I really don't think that I am. I hope I'm not vain. When I was a little girl, I was a little runt. And here I grew up...I'm growing up to be a really nice looking girl...um, lady. And I want people to see that I am a true person, I'm not just skin deep or whatever. I am a true person inside and out.

All in all, my pageant experience has been really good. I'm not one of the ones that busts up and wins every single pageant. I have to really work at it. When you do have to work at it, and you finally do win, it just makes it all the more special. Girls out there, don't give up and don't get discouraged because it's gonna happen. You'll have your day.

APRIL, SEVENTEEN
NEW YORK, NEW YORK

I want to be a pediatrician. That's what I've wanted to be since I was little. That's what I really want to be. It means a lot to me, and I don't want to let nothing stop me, nothing stand in my way. At one point I felt like, I should just be a nurse. That would be making money — but that's not what I want to do.

I know what I want to do, but I don't have a path on how to get there.

I'm pregnant and I'm seventeen and I'm having twins.

There's a lot of emotions, a lot of feelings that I don't think I'm ready for. I could have used condoms. I didn't want to take the pill because I was trying to lose weight. The pill was making me gain weight, too much weight. Now, being pregnant, I gained thirty-nine pounds. I wanted to lose weight, so that's kinda hard on me.

Now that I'm pregnant, I have a lot of mood swings. One minute I'm happy and I'm excited and I can't wait, and then the next minute I don't want to...I'm not ready for it. I made a mistake. I feel a lot of different ways. I feel like I'm gonna cry for no reason. I argue with my boyfriend a lot. But he's been there for me, and he says he's gonna help me. He's supposed to be buying the crib.

If I could do it over, I would wait. I'm not ready. It's not what I expected. It's gonna be hard and I can see that now. You have to buy everything, from the crib, the sheets, undershirts, pants, Pampers, everything, pajamas, everything. These babies come into the world with nothing. It's hard. I don't have a job. My boyfriend has a job, and he's planning on helping me. But there's no guarantees for the future.

The first time I had sex I was fourteen. That was a real hurting experience. I was young and I wasn't ready for it. I had a lot of feelings for the guy. I wanted to be his only girlfriend, but he had many other girlfriends. I thought since it was special to me, it was special to him. But it wasn't. It wasn't his first time. It wasn't what I wished it was.

When my mother found out that I wasn't a virgin, I was never treated the same again. I never got dolls after that or toys or ... and I still wanted to be a little girl. It was like I made a big mistake, but I couldn't go backwards.

I was stuck in the middle. I was changing. I wasn't a woman, but I wasn't a little girl. I wanted to play with dolls, but then I wanted to go out and meet guys. I wanted all these clothes, but then I wanted toys, too. I wanted slumber parties and boy-girl parties. It was a lot of changes. I really was stuck in the middle, that's how I felt. I don't know if my mother understood that or if she remembers how that feels.

Everybody talks about sex. Nobody talks about relationships. I don't have sex right now, to tell you the truth. We hardly ever and it's fine with me. I don't know how he feels about it. We don't discuss it. I don't know where he stands, if he wants it or whatever. Right now we need to get our lives in order 'cause we got two babies on the way. Sex is nothing to me right now. There's nothing it can do for me right now. It can't relieve me of my stress. I still feel a burden that a big responsibility is on the way. Discussing it with him makes me feel better than sex could ever make me feel. Knowing that he's gonna be there and him being sure that he's gonna help me ... He's buying the crib.

I'm having a boy and a girl. I kinda wasn't happy when I found out that I was having a girl. There's a lot of problems for girls these days, a lot of teenage pregnancies going on, and nobody wants that for their child. I'll raise my daughter differently than my mother raised me. I want her to be honest, and come to me and tell me about her experiences, even if it's bad. Even if it's about sex. I want her to tell me everything. And I would just have to deal with it and be understanding. 'Cause I couldn't come to my mother. I was ashamed.

I know I have to provide for them. I don't want them to see me as just another mother on welfare. There was a point where my mother

was on welfare, but she did move on and become something. My strength is gonna come from my kids. I want them to see me being a doctor. I want them to see that even though I had trouble, I still made it. Even though they came along, they didn't stand in my way. In a strange way it feels like they're gonna help me to be what I want to be. I know I can't just do it for myself. I'm doing it for two other people that need me. I'm gonna be what I want to be.

I'm scared, of course. What if I can't get a baby sitter? What if I have to drop out of school and get my GED? I'm scared, but I really want to be a doctor, regardless of how I have to do it. I'm gonna do it. At least by the time I'm forty, I'm gonna be a doctor. I don't care how long it takes. I think I'm gonna make it. Someday my name is gonna be known.

 DEVOTION

M onique and Aniela are called to self-
less service early on in life. They feel the press and
value of pleasing others and putting others' needs
above their own. Under very different circumstances, they diaper, bathe, and feed, rising to a
challenge that can strangle grown women.

These girls frankly voice their ambivalence about
the clash between tender service and attending to
their own growing selves. The complexity of their
stories shows that devotion to others is a persistent
burden on the slender shoulders of girls, whatever
their roots or dreams.

MONIQUE, FIFTEEN
EAST BRIDGEWATER, MASSACHUSETTS

I think it helps you get your name out there. I just think it can open a lot of doors for you, help you get noticed, and speed up your future, definitely. Because you'll no longer be, "Oh, that's just Monique Jones," but, "That's *Miss USA*, Monique Jones." Whoever wins, she's a big person now and I think that's definitely gonna help out whatever she wants to do in life. Hopefully it'll help me with my communications degree. I definitely wanna be on the news at some point in my life, hopefully not for doing anything wrong, hopefully for being a news anchorwoman. So I think that that would help me a lot, if I was Miss USA. Look at Halle Berry. She was a USA contestant, look at her now. She's got more money than God, so you know what I mean. It can only help you, it can't hurt you.

You could never catch me in jeans as a little girl. I never liked the concept. Jeans were for boys and dresses were for girls, that's just the way it was. I hated wearing pants. I just had this thing in my mind that Daddy wore pants, Mommy wore dresses. I couldn't tell you where I got that from. I mean, no one really taught it to me.

I had Barbie dolls up until I was twelve. I had the Barbie Dream House, I had the Barbie Corvette, everything Barbie — I used to make Barbie clothes when I was little. I was the most girly little girl. I used to go to parochial school and I loved it 'cause our uniforms were dresses. I never had to wear pants. We got to wear little sweaters and little shoes. I had really curly hair, little ringlets. My hair was so big, it was so curly and so thick, that they used to sit me in the back, because no one could see over my hair.

I have real dark, dark brown eyes. This is my natural eye color. I wear color contacts just for competing in pageants. I do wear them to school, just so I can get used to them. I have blue and I have hazel. It's not the hazel with the green. It's more goldeny-light, so it makes my eyes lighter.

My coach said these would be a good idea. Because my eyes are so dark, they really don't show up that much on stage. He thinks if I had lighter eyes, they'd be more exotic.

I just really always wanted blue eyes, ever since I was little. I thought it would be different looking. I never really saw dark-skinned people

with blue eyes. So I thought it would be . . . just to see. I think it would look good sometimes on stage.

They're actually not too hard to put in any more. The first day at the optometrist it took me an hour. I remember walking out and you'd have thought I just saw *Titanic*. Mascara all down my face, tears everywhere.

For fifteen years of my life I've had dark brown eyes. Ever since I was little I've always said, "Mom, I've always wanted blue eyes." When I was younger, she said, "You don't need blue eyes. You can't change your eye color." Back then, when I was like four years old, they didn't have color contacts yet. I'm kinda glad my mom made me wait until I was a sophomore to get them because I think now I can appreciate them more. I know that things cost money and if I wreck a pair or lose a pair, then I'm gonna be in trouble.

People may have a problem with me having blue eyes, because they think that's the quote-unquote white side of you. But I don't think of it as, I have a certain black side or a white side. Or that just because I'm half black I have to act black and be black. Correct me if I'm wrong, but if you look up the term "black" in the dictionary, there is no way of how to be black. That's a color. People always tell me, "Why don't you act your race?" Correct me if I'm wrong, but I do believe I'm half black and half white. I never understood that people thought you had to act your color. Honestly, do you know how white people act? Do you know how black people act? No, people act differently.

I want to get a nose job. If I win my state pageant for Miss USA, before I go to Nationals, I want to definitely get a nose job. But if I wait, I want to wait 'til I'm out of high school. I can never imagine going on Christmas vacation, getting my nose done, coming back and having different nose. This is such a small town and I don't know how people would take that. But I personally don't find anything wrong with it.

Not that I don't like my nose. I just think it doesn't fit on my face. Like this nose should have been on somebody else. I think it's fine when I'm serious, but when I smile, I think that, because of my background, because my father is, um, black, I got blessed with a really wide nose. I think when I smile it gets pretty wide. And I'm half Italian. Most Italian people have kinda large noses. I like Nicole's nose. I would love to have Nicole's new nose. But I'm just gonna kinda give my nose some liposuction. Just to make it a little bit thinner. Not a lot. I don't want a Michael Jackson nose or anything like that. But I definitely just want to make it a little bit thinner, so when I smile, it's not as wide. It's not really gonna hurt or anything. Nothing's gonna happen.

I would never get breast implants. I think that's kinda overdoing it. With a nose job, once your nose is fixed, it's not growing back. With breast implants you have the possibility of them leaking, or exploding. They can get hard. There are so many things that can go wrong.

I told my friend I think I'm going to get a nose job. She was like, "Monique, what are you talking about? Monique, look at you — you win all these pageants, obviously it doesn't matter to anybody else." Yeah, but I don't feel comfortable with it. That's the important thing.

I always think of what Ru Paul says. On every episode of her show, she says, "How can you love somebody if you can't love yourself?" And it's true. If I can't love myself, then what makes you think that I will love the next guy that walks down the street? I have to feel comfortable with myself and if I don't feel comfortable with my nose, then that's my prerogative if I want to change it.

Certain pageants, everybody there is blonde-haired and blue-eyed. There are girls that won't even talk to you. I remember there was a girl and I thought we were friends, we hung out. Until she figured out that I was in her division, and all of a sudden I wasn't there, I was invisible. I was so devastated. I was like, "Mom, why won't this girl talk to me?" She said, "She's your competition". At that pageant, I was a nobody. I was some little girl from Massachusetts. I had dark, dark skin and then I had my hair curly. I remember going down to Florida. My mom's like, "Lay out for a few days, but don't get too dark." I was in the pool every day for like twelve hours. I was so dark and I had a white gown. My coach later said, "I remember you — you were real, real, real dark. I thought you were completely black, I didn't know you were only half and half. And you had a white gown on." I was like, "Oh my, I'm not going back there, not if people remember me as a dark stick figure with a white gown."

Monique in her room, showing us her personal things.

I don't know where I'd be without Firm Grip. Especially during swimsuit competition. Basically it's butt stick. And what it does is, it makes sure that your bathing suit doesn't ride up on you. It's actually

body adhesive and it's used by people who have toupees. They stick it on with this and then they stick their toupees on. It's very, very, very, very sticky.

But the thing about this stuff is, you need to wash it off your butt before you put your underwear back on. I made the mistake of not doing that. I went to go to the bathroom and I couldn't get my underwear off. Thought I was going to cry. It totally didn't dawn on me: "Monique, wash your butt after you get out of your swimsuit." The butt stick stayed on and I had to go out with my skirt pulled up to here and wash my bum in the public bathroom.

In this picture, I look pretty busty. There's this thing called Pushup Cups and I don't know where I'd be without them. Actually, because the dress was tight, and then with the cups, it pushed my boobs up basically and that's why it's my favorite dress. Because every time I wear it I have the most cleavage I've ever, ever had.

My dad lives in Dorchester. I don't really see him. I really can't get out there a lot because I can't drive yet. I talk to my dad pretty often. He... right now he's not really involved that much in my life because he has other things to do. He called me after Teen USA to see how I did. He knows about me. He knows how old I am and stuff. And he talks to me a lot. It's hard because I don't see him that much. He's not always there. He was here for the first seven years of my life. And for the last eight, he hasn't been here. It was hard at first, but now I'm so used to it. I have school. I have pageants. I talk to him every once in a while.

My mom's boyfriend is really like another father. He's been here. I've known Toussant since I was nine years old. He's a great person. I don't know where I'd be without him. Sometimes if I can't talk to my mom, I can talk to him. He comes to just about every single pageant. People ask me, "Is that your Dad?" He might as well be. He's like a stepfather. I always call him Big Daddy T. He's always there to listen to me and stuff. I'll call him up and be like, "Toussant, talk to me." He calls me and stuff all the time. People always go, "Why does your mother's boyfriend call you?" 'Cause he was my friend before he was my mother's boyfriend. So obviously, you know, that's why he calls me. I kind of introduced them.

This is the grossest thing I own. This is my blankie. Yes, I know, I'm fifteen and still have a blankie. My mom made this and as you can tell it's pretty worn. It's pretty gross. For some reason it's just stuck with me for all these years. My mother had to trick me, fight me into washing it the other day. When I went to school she washed it. I come back and the first thing I do is I grab my blankie, get something to eat, and I go downstairs and watch TV. I came up here and the blankie was not here to greet me. And I flipped out. I was turning things upside down looking for it. Thought maybe I put it under my bed. Thought it was under my covers. Ripped them off. All of a sudden I said, "I bet she washed it." I went to the basement, opened up the washing machine, and there it is. I called out, "Ma, I can't believe you washed my blankie!" and she laughed. She said, "I forgot to take it out before you got home from school." She was going to dry it and put it back in my room so I wouldn't know. To me, this has its own sentimental smell. I don't know how else to explain it, but it has its own smell.

And I'm like, "Mom, someday when I'm rich and famous, when I'm Miss Universe, someone's going to have this somewhere and it's going to be worth trillions of dollars." She said, "Monique, no one's gonna wanna buy that. Look at it, it's disgusting."

I had to grow up kinda early because I had the responsibility of my brother. My brother lived at home for seventeen years and he's multiply handicapped and mentally retarded. I couldn't always be the center of attention, even though I was the baby of the family.

My brother was...he made a difference in our family because he wasn't normal. Unfortunately that's the way he was born. I always think to myself, if my brother was normal, imagine what he would look like. My brother would be hot if he was normal.

I always had to help my mom take care of him, and take him everywhere. I couldn't have people sleep over at my house. I couldn't have people over at my house while he was here. I always had to act more mature, because I always had to help my mom take him around, and cart him around places. He's almost three years older than me and I still had to help take care of him. He has the brain mentality of an eighteen-month-old baby. It's basically having a five-foot, eighteen-month-old baby. You know what I mean?

I think that when we took him to residential care, I think, in a way, in a sense, I kinda thought that it was a bad thing at first. I thought that

was the most horrible thing that my mother could do, have him in residential care. Because I thought, you're getting rid of him.

But it's good for him and my mom. Because it was a lot of stress on my mom. My brother didn't sleep through the night. So my mother basically had to sleep with one eye open. She was up every morning at five o'clock. My brother sometimes wouldn't go to bed 'til three in the morning. He was a big baby. If he had to throw up, he would just do it. He couldn't tell you. And my brother was still in diapers. If he had to go to the bathroom, he couldn't be like, "Mom, I have to go to the bathroom." He just went. And my mom dealt with it for seventeen years. And I had to help my mom, and cart around the big bag of diapers and pudding and pills. Clothes and pajamas and toys. I remember me and my grandmother and my mom trying to take care of him and because he's so strong, if he swung his arm we went flying across the room.

I always worried about what people would think if they would come over my house. That was a big deal to me. So, in a way, I'm kinda glad that he lives in residential care. I think it's good for him. He lives with nine other kids. He used to be a very finicky eater and he eats more now. My mother doesn't have that burden of my brother on her mind now. She knows that someone's going to be there twenty-four hours a day to take care of him.

I'm kinda glad in a way but I miss my brother. He was my wakeup call. At seven o'clock in the morning, my brother would be in here waking me up. I miss my brother. I only see him once a week, maybe twice a week. He's only been in residential care for two years. It seems like two days, two weeks. I miss him a lot. I love when I see him 'cause he's so cute.

Monique at a hotel for a weekend pageant. She's not competing; she's a returning queen, here to give up her crown and title to the new Miss Shining Star National Queen.

When you're a returning queen, you do try to look the part. You have thirty girls looking up to you saying, "This is a teen Shining Star National Queen." You have to dress the part. People see me, my banner, my crown, they know that *she's* the Shining Star Beauty Queen. People expect this to be a very glamorous pageant, meaning you have to dress glamorous. If you're a contestant, you want to impress the judges. When you're a queen, you have to impress the contestants and their families. That's your job, as the returning queen, to show everybody what this pageant's all about. You would never see any of the old queens prancing around in sweatpants and a T-shirt.

I feel very sad about giving up my title this year because I can't ever compete here again. I won queen of the highest age group, so I can't compete any more. I'm going to ask the pageant director to make me the Queen of Queens, so I can just be a queen every year. I can come back and help. I can judge next year. It's kinda, I don't know, it's not depressing, but, it's kinda...it's just really sad thinking that I will no longer be the Shining Star Queen. I'm just too old. I'll be nothing now. I'll be a has-been in the Shining Star system. Unless she makes me the Queen of Queens, where I can come back every year and still be a queen, I'm pretty much nothing after this. Just someone who won it years and years ago.

A lot of girls think of me as a role model. Not that I don't want to be someone's role model, but I'm fifteen, and there's not really a lot that I've done yet. I mean, I've survived two years of high school — that's basically all I've done so far.

When a girl looks at me, I want her to know that I didn't just get here, someone didn't just drop me off and I was this big winner. It took me a long time to get where I am today. It's taken a lot of time, a lot of practice, a lot of money to get here. If they really want to be where I am now, they need to learn that they have to practice. They can't just show up at a pageant and say, "Oh, I can win this pageant," because that's not the way it is. There's always gonna be someone out there that is either just as good as you or may even be better than you.

Some girls think that certain girls are born with this winning ability. That's not how it is at all. You really have to work at what you want to be. You have to have a positive image of yourself. You have to be comfortable with yourself in front of a lot of people.

There are girls I know, they get into pageants 'cause their mothers want them to. Well, that's not right, because if that's not what they want to do, it's gonna show on stage. That's true with any sport. If you really want to do something and you feel you can do well at it, do it! But if you don't want to be here, then you might as well take your mom and your clothes and go home. I know I can tell when a girl doesn't want to be on stage, when all she cares about is, "Oh, I hope I don't miss *Dawson's Creek*."

I love doing what I do. I mean, granted, on a Friday night I'm sure there are many other things that I would rather be doing than being at a pageant masquerade party. But this isn't that bad. This is part of my life. You have to want to be here.

I just hope that all the girls have fun and understand that this is one pageant. This is one judge's opinion, and they shouldn't take it personally if they don't win. It's not their fault if they don't win. It's not anybody's fault, it's just who the judges felt should have won that day. I just hope that everybody understands that pageants are fun. Granted, if I don't win I'm a little set back about it. But then I wake up the next day and I'm fine. No one wins every single pageant.

So, I'm getting ready for the pageant party. It's a masquerade dinner party. First I put on concealer. Usually for stage you're supposed to use like a pistachio-colored concealer and the reason is, it helps reflect the lights on your face so you look better.

This is my foundation. It's called honey-beige. Most foundations are easy if you use it in a stick. I just apply it over my face, and, I know this sounds gross, but I have to wait for it to dry.

It's corpse makeup. Like, you know, when you go to a funeral and they put makeup on the dead people and you can't see a wrinkle in them? That's what it reminds me of. It's not very good for your skin, 'cause your skin can't breathe. Look at the texture, look how thick that is. The way it sets in your skin, it doesn't move. Seriously, I could put this on now and wake up tomorrow and my makeup wouldn't change at all.

So when this dries, I can put on my powder over it, and once you put that on, you could like seriously, like *whoosh*, and pull off your face. That's why I don't wear it to school, because I don't want to look like Ru Paul with all this makeup on at school.

I was allowed to wear makeup since sixth grade. When I was younger, it used to be this biggest procedure to put all this makeup on. I didn't even need three-quarters of it. I used to do the foundation, the powder, the mascara, the eye shadow, the eyeliner—uggghh, I used to go the whole nine yards. And now that I think about it—to impress who? Who did I have to impress? The kids in my grade?

Now I'm gonna do my eye shadow. I start out with a translucent color. This is kind of the hardest thing 'cause you try to get both eyes to look exactly the same. I use four colors: a dark, dark brown, a light brown, I guess you'd say a mauve, and very light pink.

This is where I make my eyebrows. I lied, the hardest thing to do is eyebrows. 'Cause you don't want them to look too fake, but you want to make them look longer, but don't make them too dark 'cause then they don't look right.

I just put lip liner on and now I'm filling it in with lipstick. It helps so the lipstick doesn't bleed, like it doesn't run out from your lips and supposedly it helps it stay on longer.

Monique and her mom.

Mom: You know, today, to have a pageant gown made is a minimum of a thousand dollars. I mean, times are completely changed as far as the clothes and the outfits. That's why I think that the fun isn't there any more, like it was back when we first started. Those were the times when the mothers used to get together and sit down and have coffee and laugh and joke. That's not the way it is any more. It has become so competitive now and everybody is sized up. They're worried about this one or that one or the other who has more rhinestones or more pearls on their outfit.

Her first halter dress, she was fourteen. I had them put a long chiffon scarf down the back because I was really concerned about too much skin showing. I wouldn't let her wear the Miss America high heel shoes until she was fifteen. I see kids today, they're eleven years old, they're in three-inch Miss America heels. And they're in halter gowns. They grow up quick enough and soon enough they're going to be in halters and heels and all of that. Is it necessary to do it when they're that young? I guess to be competitive unfortunately you have to be extreme. I just have a problem with it being done at such a young age. As they're getting older, they have to become more competitive, so what are they going to do? Are they going to be having plastic surgery by the time they're thirteen? Since they're doing this at ten and eleven? What are they going to be doing at thirteen?

Monique: I remember how long it took me to get fake nails. That was the big thing with me. I always wanted fake nails. I remember I begged, pleaded with my mother. But I didn't even get fake nails until I was like thirteen, fourteen. I see kids that are like nine —

Mom:— nine and ten, they come to pageants with —

Monique: Fake nails. You know, not like Lee Press-on Nails either. No. Manicure nails, salon nails.

Mom: She'd say, "Ma, can I get these fake nails?" They were the ones with the paper sticking that never stuck. And she'd walk around the house with them. She always liked that girlie stuff. Barbies and that type of thing. It wasn't her schoolmates, but the girls in pageantry, they were showing up at pageants with fake nails. She'd say to me, "Mom, so-and-so has fake nails on."

Monique: And they won. Like that would make a difference. It made a difference.

Mom: Back then it was always the blond, blue-eyed little girls who won, who looked like little Barbies. You almost never saw a dark-skinned … you might have seen a brunette win every now and then, but never a dark-skinned brunette that won. So sometimes I think it must have been difficult for her, thinking, "Why am I practicing…"

Monique: … why am I here?

Mom: "… and doing all this, when I can't win anyway?" But she did persevere. My goal is to make her well-rounded and expose her to a lot of different things. So when she has that crown and banner on, they see a well-rounded teenager. Not somebody that's superficial or very into herself. Or "I'm better than you," anything like that. You can't ever lose sight of the fact that you're not ever better than anybody else. You may be prettier than somebody else, but somebody else is going to be prettier than you, too. That's the bottom line.

Sometimes you have to share some of that love and caring with other people that are less fortunate. And she does that. Pageants are a hobby, she just enjoys doing it. And hopefully we're going to go to college with some of that. That's what we're gearing for, more pageants where she has the opportunity to win some sizable cash or scholarship money. I've only got a couple of years to get ready before she goes off to college and try to figure out where the money is going to come from. Unfortunately, she hasn't named any cheap colleges that she'd like to attend. Unless in the meantime I hit the lottery or find a rich man, I'm in trouble.

Monique: Or I find a rich man, whatever comes first.

Mom: *(speechless for a second)* You're way too young for that. I thought you were never going to get married.

Monique: I didn't say that I would marry him.

Mom: *(speechless for three seconds)* You don't even have permission to date yet!

Monique: Ugh!

Mom: You'll thank me for it someday, when you're older and you get married and you have a daughter of your own.

Monique: I'm never having children.

Mom: Then you will realize, "Wow, I remember what my mother was like," and you're going to understand. You're going to understand someday. Believe me, because I never thought it was right when my mother did it to me. But it's true. It's true. That's the way it is.

In a hotel room, a hairdresser works on Monique before a pageant crowning ceremony. Monique's mother talks with us.

Her brother Shawn lived at home for seventeen years. She was very young. She always accepted and understood that he was special. She sacrificed for a very long time as a little girl, not being able to do certain things or go certain places or have certain things because of Shawn.

She...how can I even explain the responsibility? She learned how to change his diapers, feed him. She could give him his medication. She had to dress him. She would give him a bath. You had to keep him safe, because he didn't understand danger.

It was getting more and more difficult. Even though he's tiny, he's very, very strong. He needs one-on-one, twenty-four hours a day. Believe me when I tell you that was the reason I finally made the decision that I had to put him in residential care. I was having a hard time doing it any more. And she had all that responsibility for so long and she dealt with it. It was finally time to have her time. There's a certain amount of maybe attention that she didn't get, that she probably should have.

She always accepted it and never was rebellious about it. I'm not saying that she never got angry. There were times when she would say something like, "Mom, sometimes I wish I didn't have a brother like this." And I would say to her, "Well, you know what? You do. You do. And we have to live with it. We have to deal with it and we have to accept it."

You know, sometimes they'll ask a girl on stage who do you admire most and why. It's been her grandmother, it's been Rosa Parks, other black women that have made great strides in history. I don't remember what pageant we were recently at — they asked her who she admired and I was crying in the back because it was me. That was her most admired person.

And she said, "I admire my mother for her love and support for the past fifteen years." And it's really funny because many times I say, "Why am I doing this? Does she really appreciate it?" You wonder about those things. Not that she's not an appreciative kid, because she really is. I thank God once a day, every day, that she's a very good girl. I can't be with her all the time. I'm not positive that she's always sweet when I'm not around. But I know that she's basically a good girl. She has her moments, you know, she and I do have our moments. Most of the time I'm very, very proud of her. I think she does a good job.

ANIELA, SIXTEEN
NEW YORK, NEW YORK

My mom, I love her to death. She's a very strong woman. She has struggled. Her first sex partner was my father, and he left her. They had been together since she was fifteen. She got pregnant and he left. Then she married the person who I say is my father, 'cause he raised me. He drank a lot. My mom's trying to go to school, she works two jobs, raising four kids. We live in a bad neighborhood. She doesn't complain. When I was out there getting into trouble, I did a lot of things to her that I really wish I wouldn't have. Me and her got into a fight and I hit her. I regret it so much. I do love her. She's never given up on me.

When I was younger, my mom told me not to have sex. She didn't tell me why. She just told me not to do it. When she found out that I was having sex, it killed her. But, I mean, I already did it. Virginity is one thing that you can't get back.

When I told her I was pregnant, she insisted that I should have an abortion. But knowing that there was a life inside of me, I couldn't do that. In a way she understood, but I was still her fifteen-year-old baby. I was the one who was gonna go to college first, the one who was gonna get married first, and I was the one who was gonna have children while being married. It crushed her world to find out that I was pregnant, because she wanted so much more for me.

I'm sixteen now and my son is a month and a half. I put him in bed with me and we'll just stare at each other. We could just sit there for hours and hours and stare at each other. I talk to him and I sing to him. He smiles at me.

My son is my whole world. It would crush me if someone would do anything to him. I'm not comfortable leaving him with anybody, not even my family. Not that they're bad, but sometimes I don't like the way they treat kids. I don't want them to do to my son what they did to me. So I stay home with him. Wherever I go, he goes.

I love him, he's my whole world, he's everything to me. When I first got pregnant, not that I didn't want him, but I wasn't sure if I could handle it. I was scared. Now, I take very good care of my son. His father's in jail and I'm basically by myself.

His father is twenty-seven; he's a lot older than I am. He's a good man, he's really, I mean, he's got...his heart is genuine, but he's made a lot of mistakes. In certain ways he's still young. He still tries to act young. Before I got pregnant, he was going in and out of jail. Now he's back in jail. He was caught selling drugs. I had already broken up with him. Because he's so much older, he tried to tell me what to do all the time. He loved me a lot. He always wanted to be there. I mean always! Everywhere I turned, he was there. The only way I could get a break from him was to break up with him. Even that didn't stop him. My mother, she loved him. She'd call him to the house to come fix things. It drove me crazy. This is my ex-boyfriend! I'm trying to get away from him — but he's at my house!

Now he's in jail. I got a card yesterday he wrote to my son. He apologized, saying he was sorry that he wasn't there when he was born, but he's gonna try and be there from now on. I think he's gonna make a good father. Unlike a lot of other men, he didn't just leave me. He's still trying to be there with me. I can never say that he doesn't love me. I mean, I'm lucky. A lot girls don't have a guy like that. They get pregnant and the guys leave 'em. With me it was the other way around! I wanted to leave him, but he wouldn't go away. But now I'm grateful. It's really hard being out here by myself.

The whole time I was pregnant, I was really scared. Not that I didn't want to be a mother, but I had hoped for a lot more for myself. But my son has actually straightened me out a lot. I was really doing a lot of

things that I shouldn't have done before I was pregnant. If it wasn't for him, I'd probably be in jail right now, or really, really...messed up. I thank the Lord, 'cause he's really straightened my life out.

When I was pregnant, I was sick a lot. I got really heavy and it was hard for me to walk. My asthma really acted up. I was out of breath.

Those pains—those pains are no joke. They hurt! Anybody who tells you that they don't hurt, they're lying. It *hurts*! I mean, it's indescribable, it's really, it hurts. I made the mistake, when I was pushing him out, I reached out and I felt his head. I freaked out, I started screaming. I never thought something that big could come out of something that small.

After I gave birth...they usually try to put the baby right on you so you can have skin to skin contact. But I was mad at him 'cause I was in so much pain! I kinda took it out on him. As soon as they put him near me, I was like, "Get him away from me! I don't want him!"

After they cleaned me up and I rested, I was dying for them to bring him back. I kept calling the nurse. When they brought him in, I was scared to touch him. I just looked at him for a while. Then I picked him up, and I started counting the little fingers and toes. It was amazing, to think that he was actually inside me just a few hours ago. And now he was mine. He's somebody that I could love forever.

Sometimes I know what I'm doing. I know that my son's healthy and that I'm raising him OK. But there are times when you're unsure of what you're doing. Especially when they get into these crying moods and you don't know what's wrong and you don't know how to stop them. If you truly love your child, it hurts you if they're crying and you don't know how to make it better. My son...when he starts crying, he starts screaming, and I gotta figure out what's wrong, it kills me. I'm like *ohhhhh*! I get frustrated, I get really stressed out. I would love to have him just shut up and I would love for him to just stop and be quiet. It kills me! Every time he starts crying, I rush to him and I try to make him feel better. I hate hearing him upset! It hurts me too much to hear him cry. I have to make him stop.

When I was pregnant, I thought, "Oh great, I'm having a baby. I get to dress him up." Yeah, they may be cute sometimes, but they're only cute when you can return them. Once they're yours to keep, they stop being cute. You have to feed them and change them. They're not gonna let you forget, and it's gonna drive you crazy. If you're not ready to give up your life, then you're not ready to have a baby. Your life is over, once you have a baby, your life is over. Now you have to live for your child. It's a job. It's a hard job.

When I was younger, I would think a lot, and I would imagine what I wanted my life to be like, and then...I stopped. I saw where I was living, and I saw the people I was hanging out with. I didn't think I was ever gonna make it any better than they did. Any better than my parents did. What's the point of dreaming if it will never come true? Then I got pregnant and I had to think a lot. I just think if I could get my son away from this neighborhood, maybe he has a chance of not ending up in jail like his father. Maybe that will give him a little more hope in life.

I was a really smart student. I went to school for gifted and talented kids. I was always on top of my class. Now I'm struggling to make it through high school. I have to repeat ninth grade. That's something I never expected for myself. I come to school, pick up my work, take it home, do it, and bring it back.

It's all 'cause I was in such a rush to grow up. If somebody would have taken the time to sit down with me and show me what my life was worth, show me all the things that I could become, then I probably wouldn't have started having sex. I would have paid more attention to my school work. My life would be much different now.

I'm gonna raise my son that it's OK to enjoy being young. You don't have to grow up so fast. After fifteen years, I'm an adult. I have that responsibility. There's nothing I can do about it now. I can't put him back! He's here to stay.

All through grade school, girls hated me. I was so hated it was not funny. Girls picked fights with me because I couldn't afford to buy the new clothes or the new sneakers. They made fun of me. I used to go home crying. I got along great with the guys, but the girls couldn't stand me. I never understood why I never had friends. It was like everybody I knew just left me. And that crushed me. So I was like, "Forget it... my life means nothing." I gave up and I stopped caring.

I started acting the way people wanted me to act, instead of the way I wanted to act. I became totally fake. I became obsessed with what people thought I should be. I followed the crowd, and all it got me was trouble.

I was in something we call "The Nation," which is really a nice form of saying I was in a gang. Cops went to my mother's workplace, saying that they were gonna arrest me. I was really messed up. I really didn't feel I had anybody to live for. What was the point of me trying to save my life when, who was gonna care? A lot of things were going on that weren't right.

My teachers were scared of me. They wouldn't say a word to me, because I had my own gang chapter in my school, and they knew if they were messing with me, they were messing with my Nation. I had power. People looked up to me, and my teachers knew that. I had a lot of friends in school, and they would listen to me. Not that I could boss them around, but when I spoke, they listened.

Last year, my first year of high school, it got worse. I really...I was bad. By then I'd become a leader in The Nation. I had people under me who would take my orders. It was kinda like I was the president. I had my vice president, then I had the cabinet.

To me it felt great. I finally had friends. Everybody knew who I was. It made me feel so good to be popular. That was what I always wanted. But I risked my whole future for that. I put my education on hold. I became very disrespectful. Instead of being this sweet girl, the sweet, quiet girl that I was, I became loud and obnoxious. I would talk back to adults — which was not me. My mother raised me to have respect for adults. All that went away. I did a lot of self-destructive things. I got involved with things that I knew were wrong and illegal. It didn't matter to me, because that was the cool thing to do. I would get high, just because my friends were doing it. They never asked me to do it. I volunteered myself to do it. I drunk like I was a fish. I would go to school drunk. If you got in my way, I was gonna tell you off. 'Cause that was the cool way to be. To be careless, to be free, to be rebellious. I did it, and it cost me a lot.

For a long time I thought The Nation really was my family. I thought they were the only people that loved me. I got into fights with my mother because she thought it was wrong. I loved my Nation so much, I refused to let anyone talk bad about them. I refused to give it up, because that was my world.

They taught me a lot. Before I joined The Nation, I wasn't proud to be an Hispanic woman. I didn't know the difference between Spanish and being Hispanic, but they showed me about my heritage. They showed me the way to be proud. There were a lot of things we did wrong. But they did show me how to love, how to love myself, how to love my people. I give them thanks for that.

I'm no longer a member. My son is more important. My life doesn't belong to me any more; it belongs to him. His father's in a gang. We can't impose that on him. When he gets older, if that's what he chooses to do, I can't stop him. It's gonna hurt me, of course, but my mother couldn't stop me.

Adults, honestly, they don't pay attention to girls. They still think that guys are the ones who are gonna make the money, guys are the ones who are gonna get ahead. It's more important for guys to go to college. The woman can stay home. They've been doing it for so long, hey, who cares if they do it for a couple more centuries?

If you start paying attention to us, before we get pregnant, then we probably won't get pregnant. Then we will have something to live for. But schools, everybody, they have to make more things open to teenagers, especially girls. We have it the hardest, especially when we come from inner cities. People ignore us, they think that we're all gonna end up on welfare, so what's the point wasting the time, wasting the money on us? They have to realize we're still people, and we deserve the same chance that people in Minnesota get, that people in Idaho get.

Girls are looking for love. They have babies to find love. I try not to, but even I go, "Say you love mommy, say you love me." He doesn't know what love is! Right now, all I am is a human feeding machine. I take care of his needs, I change his diaper, and I feed him. That's all he cares about. He couldn't care less who I am. He doesn't know that he's supposed to love me.

Girls have to realize that maybe you don't think you're being loved, but if you're being taken care of—then you are loved. Buying you everything you want, that's not love. If you're sick, and they lie in bed with you, and just make you feel better, then they love you. If they don't just say, "Go take some Tylenol, get over it," then they love you. If they take the time to be with you, then they love you, and you'll be able to love. As long as people love you, you'll know what love is. You'll figure it out on your own and that's when you'll be able to love. When you figure that out, then you can open yourself up to let people love you.

I was nine years old when I got my period, and it scared the life out of me. It was like, uh oh, I'm not a kid any more. I thought that meant I was grown, and I had to catch up to my body. It scared me, because I wasn't a baby, but I wasn't yet grown. I was stuck in the middle.

Once I made that change, from being a child, I got boy crazy. Boys were the most important thing to me. I thought if they paid attention to me they loved me, they cared, and they would be around.

For the guys, I had to start doing my hair, doing my makeup. I had to start fixing up my clothes and all that stuff. I used to see these women in magazines with all this makeup on. I tried to do the same thing and I looked like a clown. I would go outside like that. They looked nice, so I figured, I look nice, too. Maybe I don't like it, but I must look nice.

I was really, really, young when I started having sex — sixth grade. It wasn't like a choice that I made. I mean, it happened so fast. I was in such a rush to grow up, that I just kinda did it.

I really wish I would have waited. Maybe now I wouldn't be a teen mom. I love being a mother, but I wish things could be different. If I didn't start having sex so young, if I wasn't in such a rush to grow up, things would be really different. I didn't realize how precious it was to be young, and be able to do what you want. I didn't value that, and now I do. I can't even go out. Everything has to be planned. I have to make sure that the weather's OK. If it's not, he can't go out, so I can't go out. I have to pack his bag and make sure that he's dressed properly. It's a lot of responsibility. Sometimes, I think I pushed myself into it, and that maybe I wasn't ready for it. I kinda forced myself to be ready for it. It's a big thing.

It felt strange, making that transition from being a child to a teenager and now to an adult. The transition is like a jump. It happens so fast, that you kinda miss everything. Teenagers should not be in no rush to grow up 'cause once it's gone, it's gone, and you can't get it back.

 CONNECTION

Cheri Antoinette is classically, quintessentially twelve, clinging to her mother and shoving her away. Tracey marvels and balks at her own daughter, in whom she sees her mother and herself. Lindsey tries to keep her lonesome soul afloat while she builds and breaks bonds with her friends and her mom.

We long for close connection but bristle at interference. If we are moons to our mothers' Earth, we have to find our orbit path. Too distant and we drift, silent, into deep black space. Too close and we crash and explode.

CHERI, TWELVE
GASTON, SOUTH CAROLINA

Cheri and her mom.

Mom: Cheri is developing, filling out.

Cheri: A thing that I really don't want to do—

Mom: —which I don't think she's ready for. But it's gonna happen. It happens to everybody.

Cheri: Noooo!

Mom: She will not wear a bra.

Cheri: *(laughs)* I hate them, they itch me.

Mom: I don't know what we're gonna do about that 'cause that's gonna be a problem. We've been through about six bras, but they disappear. I don't know where they go, but they go.

Cheri: *(laughs)* The dogs eat them!

Mom: Cheri doesn't want to wear a bra at all.

Cheri: Wheee! *(laughs)* I'm free!

Mom: Her Granny won't wear one, so that's probably why. Because of Cheri's surgeries, I think she's probably gonna be a really late developer. She's twelve and she's not where the rest of the girls in her class are as far as development. But they all do it at such a different rate. Some of them start at eight, some of them don't start 'til they're twelve. Who's to say?

Cheri alone.

My past has been OK, but most of the time it's been terrible. When I was two or three, we had to go to the hospital every weekend because of my heart. And now we don't have to do that any more. I've had my last open heart surgery and I won't have to have any more.

I've had seven open heart surgeries and the reason is, I was born with a single ventricle, a single atrium, one pulmonary on the right side and none on the left. All that inside me is plastic. Half my heart's plastic. *(Pause as she considers this, as if for the first time.)* Whoa! *(laughs)*

I can't run with the other kids. If I do, I'll collapse. I have to sit down and I have to go inside. I can run a little bit, but not like the rest of them can. But I can do a lot of stuff. Used to, I couldn't do anything.

After I had my fifth open heart surgery, I didn't go to sleep for three years. I did not get any rest. None whatsoever.

At school, I'm really behind because of my heart. I get sick most of the time. And when I get sick, like when I had that dizzy spell, I don't get a lot of my work done. It gets really frustrating when you don't get this done and you don't get that done and your teacher's screaming at you because you don't have your homework.

When I was five, they froze my brain. And ever since then my hands, they get really shaky. When they do that I drop things.

When I'm waking up from my heart surgery, 'cause they put me on a lot of drugs, I'm going through these tunnels. I can't wake up until I reach the top of the haunted house. Things are popping out at me and I really don't like them. I can't wake up unless I get to the top. Sometimes I wake up before the dream ends and sometimes I have to finish the dream out. And get up to the top.

At the fair they have this haunted house every year and I can't even go over there. I really wanted to ride the Spaceship 2000. It's goes around in a circle and then it feels like the floor drops out from underneath you. I really wanted to ride it. But I was afraid to go because of that haunted house over there. I can't even ride the best rides because I freak out. It feels like, when I start to walk over there, my heart stops and I can't move. I'm too scared to go over where the haunted houses are. I have to stay with the baby rides.

Cheri and her mom.

Cheri: The needles still aggravate me when they come in and draw blood and stuff. I just kick and scream. One time I kicked a nurse right in her nose 'cause she was gonna stick me. I hate them big long needles.

Mom: Let's just say that when she goes in there they have to get the right nurse. There's just certain little things that Cheri doesn't like to have done. She doesn't like to have IVs put in or removed. The worst thing was, she had to have a chest tube. She got really irritated by that.

Cheri: I still have that mark where that chest tube was. I still have it.

Mom: She was just real aggravated about the chest tube because —

Cheri: I hated it.

Mom: — when they put this one in, they didn't knock her out. I had to go in there with her and hold her down —

Cheri: I hate it.

Mom: — and he shot four tubes of anesthetic in there but it did not have time to work. He just cut her right there and water shot everywhere and then he stuffed that tube in her. She's kicking and screaming. Two days later, they say —

Cheri: *(laughing)* — we gotta take it out, it don't work!

Mom: — it's not in there right. We gotta —

Cheri: — take it out and put another one back in her!

Mom: — put another one in her. She got really frustrated with them 'cause they couldn't get it right. There's really not too much we can do besides be with her and comfort her. And try to let her know that everything's ... it is gonna end. You are gonna get to go home sooner or later. You are gonna get to go home.

Cheri: I have a scar going straight down the middle. One on both sides and one going all the way around my back. From one side all the way around. I have one that goes all the way down my front. I have two chest tube scars. I have one like right below my belly button.

Mom: Well, pageants have helped her get back on her feet after surgery —

Cheri: — and they help me get confident. We do a lot of beauty pageants and this year I tried out for cheerleading. And I didn't make it. And I really wanted to. And I didn't. But it really didn't matter to me. And this year I'm gonna try out for basketball and probably color guard. And maybe next year I'll try out for cheerleading also. And maybe next year I'll make cheerleading or color guard or basketball. You never know.

Mom: But pageants is something that she can do —

Cheri: — it helps me get my confidence up for a lot of the stuff that I want to do in school.

Mom: It also teaches them how to speak in front of people.

Cheri: You can get really nervous.

Mom: The biggest thing I think pageants has done for Cheri is, it has give her something to do to keep her going. Gives her something she can be involved in without having a whole lot of stress. I mean, it tends to be stressful at the moment. But it takes a very minute effort to do that beauty walk! If she wasn't doing pageants she'd be sitting on the couch, stuffing her face, watching cartoons. I just think she needs to get out and do something.

Cheri: 'Cause if I don't when I'm fifteen or sixteen I'm gonna —

Mom: — be hanging around with the wrong kind of people. People that don't have anything to do. I think that all kids need to be active in something, their community or dance or theatre or some type of activity where they can feel good about themselves.

Cheri: When I get in high school I'm gonna go into drama acting. And one day I might be able to be Juliet. Someday I'm gonna go to Hollywood and be an actress or maybe even marry a rich husband and send thousands of dollars to Granny and Mama and everyone else in my family. And head to Las Vegas —

Mom: — and have a big house —

Cheri: — and have a big house and send money to Granny and Mama. And build them a house on the lake so they can go swimming. That's what my fantasy life is gonna be like.

Mom: That'd be a good one. Oh, and you've gotta have a red convertible, too. Their granddaddy bought one so they could ride in parades.

Cheri: When we go to parades, we put the top down. And we sit on the little hump in the back. And we just sit there waving and smiling at all the people. My crown keeps flying off! Least it didn't fall in the road like it did in the Christmas parade one year. We use that car so much, last year we had to get a new top put on it.

Mom: And a new motor —

Cheri: — and a new motor in it.

Mom: I just want her to be healthy and stay well. That's what I worry about. When she gets away from me, is she gonna stay healthy? Is she gonna take care of herself? That's my main concern.

Cheri: That's why I stay with my mommy all the time.

Mom: That's why I don't let her go very many places, because she's not supposed to be in cigarette smoke. And just that she'll stay out of places that she doesn't need to be into. And keep herself healthy.

Cheri: I'd like to go to college. It's just that it's really hard 'cause you have to get up. But you don't have to go in the mornings —

Mom: — if you don't want to.

Cheri: You can go in the afternoons.

Mom: You have to do something that you really, really like. And I don't think she's found something that she really, really likes yet. What do you want to be when you grow up?

(Cheri shrugs her shoulders.)

Mom: You haven't even thought about it, have you? Ever.

Cheri: Yeah, I have. I wanna be a doctor.

Mom: She says she wants to be a doctor. You have to go to a lot of school for that, Cheri.

Cheri: I know.

Mom: Cheri doesn't like to go to school. Cheri's very one-way. It's her way or no way. Just the way it's always been. She stayed in bed for the first four years of her life watching TV and that's what she thinks she's supposed to do. That's one of the reasons why we got in pageants, to get her out of the house.

Cheri: Me and my mom, when we go do pageants, we get along really well 'cause we're not all grouped up in a car, or humped over in a house. We're free. We go do them 'cause they're fun and we like them and they're possibly the only thing I can do.

Mom: And we get to spend time together.

Cheri: That's one of the main reasons.

Mom: That's the basic thing. That's our time together.

Cheri's mom, alone.

When she's sixteen...I hope she gets to be sixteen. But I don't know what happens to them when they get to be teenagers. They go crazy or something. I really don't know. They get to start thinking all kinds of things. It's just totally different. You don't know what to expect. Because they're learning so much at school that they shouldn't learn. Cheri's twelve, her friends are older. A lot of kids at her school, either they've stayed back, or they've failed, and they're all older.

They probably don't have mothers who do what we do. I take Cheri to dances, to football games. We go skating. I play Nintendo with them. We play cards. We have parties. If we're at home, we're sitting in the living room doing something together. I never leave my child with somebody else. I'm overprotective. But I know I'm gonna be there to make sure nothing ever happens to her if I can help it.

I hope that she doesn't have any more heart problems. Because they've done all the surgery they can do for her. That's it. They can't do anything else, other than a heart transplant. And they didn't do a transplant when she was a baby because she did not have the hookups for it. She didn't have any pulmonary arteries for them to take another heart out of somebody and put into her. They had to reconstruct her heart and her pulmonary arteries.

And it'll fool you, too. She can be well one minute and be just near death's door the next.

It used to be worse when she was littler. She was very, very ill. She couldn't walk very far. We had to carry her a lot. Now, since she's had her constructive surgery, she's pretty well under control. She knows better than anybody else when something is wrong with her. She takes a cold real easy. Anything that takes us a week to get over, it usually takes her four weeks. Her immune system's low.

We just take one day at a time, 'cause that's what we've had to do. One day at a time. When she was five and she had surgery — it was her first reconstructive surgery — her brain froze. They froze the cortex of her brain because she was in surgery for eighteen hours. And when she woke up and came out of the anesthesia completely, it was like she was retarded. All her fine motor skills were gone. She had to learn to walk. She had to learn to eat again. Every time we'd sit down to the table she'd spill her drink. Knock her plate over. Her hands shook. Her head hung, her tongue was out her mouth. It was terrible. It was the worst time in our life. And pageants helped her get back. They really did. I would still put her in pageants and her hands would shake on stage.

The doctor told me that if she was going to get anything back, it would come back in six months. And she basically, everything but the hand shake came back. There's only ten surgeries that's been done like Cheri's. One of them didn't get anything back. They told me we'd just have to wait and see how Cheri was going to do. But she got everything back. She got, well, everything except that handwriting. It's tedious for her hand-eye coordination. Like playing Nintendo. Before she went to surgery, she could play that Nintendo. She could shoot that duck. When she came out she wouldn't touch it for about five years. She didn't play Nintendo. She wouldn't go near one.

Cheri and her mom.

Mom: There's a pageant a weekend. You can pick whatever style of pageant you want to be in. Festivals, local pageants, nationals. But you've got to spend some money. If you're in it like we are, to compete, then you have to spend a lot of money. You can't just go out there with a hundred dollar dress. You've gotta have a good dress. And you've gotta have good hair and makeup. You've gotta have your pictures if you're gonna compete with the big girls.

You've got different categories in your pageants. Some pageants just have beauty. Some have beauty, sportswear, photogenic. Some have fifteen different categories. Some have...I mean, down to rainwear. Rainwear, costumes—

Cheri: Really weird.

Mom: We usually just do five events.

Cheri: Beauty, sportswear, Western wear, photogenic, and portfolio. Just enough to qualify for the overall title.

Mom: That's what puts you in the overall—your pictures. That's what wins you the money. Beauty's fine, but everybody's beautiful. All these girls that compete, every one of them is gorgeous. The modeling, you've gotta have the modeling to put you into overall, and you've gotta have your photographs. Your clothes have got to be good to get you into overall, too. And that's where the money's at, is in the overall.

Cheri: One picture won me five thousand dollars. In my pictures, I look like a twenty-five-year-old.

Mom: See, that's how I see her every weekend since she's been four, so it's not that bad of a shock to me.

Cheri: It is to me!

Mom: I guess when you're doing it every weekend, that's what they look like. This is bad to say, but I don't make Cheri take her makeup off and so sometimes when she gets up on Sunday mornings she still looks like that!

Cheri: My hair will be done exactly like that and so will my makeup.

Mom: And it stays. It'll stay for days if you don't brush it out and take it off.

Cheri: My mama will tease my hair so tight that it'll just stay for three days. And she'll spray it. She uses like a half a can of hair spray on me.

Mom: Some pageants give cash on stage—

Cheri: Cars, too.

Mom: And cars. Even little local pageants now are giving fifty dollars for overall, a hundred dollars for overall, twenty-five-dollar savings bonds. People like to compete for the money. When they give that five thousand dollars cash on stage—

Cheri: —it's been our winning picture—

Mom: —it's an investment. It's like a dress. We don't buy a dress that we can't wear for two years. I get her clothes made to where they can be let out and she can wear them for two years. And we do pageants all the time.

Cheri: We go to them every weekend that we can get a chance to, to get away from the house. That's the only reason we go to them, is to get out of the house.

Mom: We started pageants because Cheri has a bad heart. And a friend of ours kept saying, "Well, she don't have to do anything but walk across the stage and that's it. All she's gotta do is walk across the stage." 'Cause when she was little, she didn't have any breath, 'cause she hadn't had her corrective surgery. She said, "All she's gotta do is walk across the stage." Well, it turned out to be a lot more than just walking across the stage!

Cheri: We go out and eat—

Mom: —after every pageant—win, lose, or draw—we go to a restaurant, the whole gang. Sometimes there's twenty-five of us.

Cheri: Sometimes we have pageant bashes where people bring videos and we talk about the pageants that we didn't like.

Mom: We do that a lot. We have friends come over and we just sit down and talk about what we need to do to change things for each one. Like with their modeling routines.

Cheri: I'm like that a lot. I get out there and I mess up and then I catch it up and then I do something else.

Mom: The basic thing that I try to teach them—

Cheri: I'm like, "My mama's gonna whip my butt!"

Mom: —is when they go out there, if they do mess up, just cover it up. Nobody knows. I can fix this.

Cheri: Nobody knows what I'm doing. I can do it all over again.

Mom: That's right, that's the key. That's what you've got to instill in them, that they can go out there with confidence. If they mess up, if they forget, just do something else. I tell them, "If you mess up, do step, flick, step, flick, cross, turn," and then get back on track. So that's what we do.

Cheri gained just a tiny bit of weight. I don't know. It comes with the territory. You grow up, you gotta decide what you're gonna do. You gonna do pageants, you gotta keep that weight down. One of the older girls has put on — well, she's really thin, I mean, severely thin, but she's got a big butt. And one judge told her that her butt was big and she really took offense to it. I don't think she's won a pageant since. Really did something to her self-esteem for him to tell her that.

You can get injured. You can slip on your high heels and break your foot —

Cheri: I did that.

Mom: — break your ankle. They get leg cramps at night after being on heels all day. It's like — that's their job. That's what they do on the weekend. I do the hair. My sister does the makeup. Somebody steams the dresses. My mama does all the pinning.

Cheri: We're just like a big old happy family.

Mom: We do it to spend time —

Cheri: — together —

Mom: — with my mother, my sister, my niece. Sometimes, her dad goes with us. We all get in the van and we go. Mother and daughter, that's... it just depends on how everybody's feeling that weekend, you know? Like if she's tired, she may not even want me to touch her and we may have a big argument.

Cheri: We did that one time and —

Mom: — I'll let her, if we're at a big national pageant, I'll let her get done by somebody else. Like if I'm doing ten girls, I'll send her to somebody else to get her hair and makeup done and then that way we don't argue.

Cheri: Me and my mom, we get along OK. When we go do pageants together, that's how we get to know each other. When we go off and we spend a weekend together, we get a little bit of each other. She'll tell me about her life and I'll tell her about my school days.

Preparing for the Chitlin Princess pageant. Cheri's mom holds up hanks of disembodied hair.

Mom: This is hair, 100 percent human hair. These are extensions and everybody uses them. This is hair glue. It just glues in, then you VO5 it to get it out. If you use the glue release they sell with it, you'll lose your hair. *(To Cheri)* Tilt your head. *(She glues the hair to Cheri's scalp. Cheri bleats.)*

It's to enhance their hair, to make it fuller, or longer, or whatever you desire. It's getting dressed up, it's costume. It's just like fake fingernails, or paddin' your boobs. If you don't have a whole lot of hair then you have to make up for it. You can't stand up there and compete against girls who have tens tons of hair. That's like standing up there with girls who have ten tons of boobs, and you don't have any, you're flat-chested. It makes a big difference.

Cheri: I hate this! It itches! It's terrible. I like my own hair.

Mom: Now, last weekend we didn't put Cheri's hair in when we competed. And what'd we get Cheri?

Cheri: Nothin'!

Later, Cheri's teased hair swallows her head like a crazy flame. She tears at her nails with her teeth. The air sticks and stinks with hair spray.

Cheri: *(hollering)* Ow, Mama, that hurt my head!

Mom: I'm sorry. We got one more row.

Cheri: *(screaming)* No! You are hurting me! Mama, please!

Mom: You're just tender-headed. Scream all you want.

Cheri: I can't, 'cause if I scream I'll ruin my make up!

Mom: Not screaming, just crying. Go ahead and scream. *(Cheri's mom creates a sculpture of spun-sugar hair.)*

Cheri: Mommy, no! That looks stupid!

Mom: Well, just what do you want tonight? You don't want me to tease it, but you don't want it flat, so take your choice. I'm either gonna have to tease the heck out of it, to get the height, or we're gonna go with a flat head. It's up to you. I'm not gonna listen to you whine!

Cheri: It hurts, Mama!

Mom: Well, just grin and bear it, grab on to the chair.

Cheri: No, it hurts!

Mom: That looks pretty there.

Cheri: That hurts!

Mom: It looks good.

Cheri: It hurts!
Mom: Well, that's just a little bit of life, ain't it?

Cheri alone.

In first grade, we had our Christmas party and this boy asked me to slow dance with him. And I didn't know what to do. I mean, what was I supposed to do, you know? And I was like, "OK, sure, whatever." Then I was like, "Oh, no, I just made a fool out of myself." 'Cause he was one of the not most popularest boys in the whole school.

Some boys act crazy. I know this one boy, every day of the week he'd always act stupid. Or either weird or something. He'd be over there thomping people and stuff and I'd be like, "uh-uh, no way." And I'd just walk away. I'm not gonna hang around people that thomp people. He didn't hit me 'cause he knew if he did I'd slap his head.

I was popular down in elementary school but now I'm out of the crowd, you know. No one likes me. I don't know what it is, they just don't like me. They would sit around in class and talk about me and stuff. It would really hurt my feelings. They write notes and stuff and they'd be passing it and I wouldn't be able to read it. And it would just tear my guts up. A lot of the time I feel left out. Not like all of the time, but some of the time. Like when my friends, they go off. I feel like they know that I'm there, but it's just that they don't even notice me. I just feel like I'm left out. I only have one girlfriend and the rest of them are boys. Girls are, I don't know, they're not attracted to me. But I'm OK with it. It really doesn't bother me.

One minute I'm mean and the next I'm really sweet. But at school, I'm always sweet. It's just when I get in that car, I gotta let it out. I gotta let it go, 'cause some people would just get on my nerves. And I can't say anything about it at school. And it would just eat away at me. So when I get in the car, I just gotta let it go.

I get feelings in my gut. It would tell me, "This person doesn't like me, I better stay away from them," or, "This person really likes me, so I better hang out with her."

I have a very best friend. Her name is Marcy. We've been best friends since kindergarten until now. I'm in the seventh grade so I've known her for a pretty long time. We just get along. We're not popular, we're not anything in the upper crowd. We're like kind of in the middle. We hang out with people in the band 'cause we're both in the band.

I was actually four years old when I started in pageants and they were really fun in the beginning and now they're getting even more funner. The parts that I really enjoy are when you get to go out there and you just get to stand there. Most of them, they have parties. We like to swim in the hotel pools when they have them. I've been doing pageants for about seven years now so I think I'm really good at them.

Cheri and her mom.
Cheri: Some of my titles, I've had Calendar Miss. I was Miss Ambassador for Calendar Miss Nationals. And I've had Miss Frog Jump, Young Miss Fire Prevention. Miss Catfish Stomp. Chitlin Princess.
Mom: *(laughs)* You know what they are, don't you? The intestines of a pork, a pig. They fry them up.
Cheri: A pig, the insides of a pig.
Mom: —the intestines of the pig. And they clean them and they fry them—
Cheri: —and they're nasty and they stink!
Mom: I think it's like pork skins that you eat.
Cheri: And they stink.
Mom: They do stink.

Cheri alone.
I feel very excited when I win. I go home and tell my daddy and he's all happy for me and me and my mom and my dad and everybody else in my family, we go out after a pageant and we eat. Usually when I don't win, I go over and I hug the winner and I tell them "Congratulations." And I go back and I stand in my place and I smile.

I think of all the girls as equal, because all of us are beautiful and all of us are winners in God's eyes.

LINDSEY, THIRTEEN
LAFAYETTE, CALIFORNIA

I always wanted to be like a star or something. I told my mom, "I'm gonna go to the Olympics in synchronized swimming." Y'know, I hadn't even started and I had no clue what it was like or anything. I was like six years old. But I told my mom, "I'm gonna go to the Olympics." So that's sort of my goal. I don't know if I'll make it, but I'm trying.

Sometimes I think about quitting, when it gets too hard, or I get scared. I get scared that I'm gonna drown. I feel like I'm out of breath, and my lungs are gonna explode. I gotta come up, I'm gonna die! But then the other part of my mind's saying, "You gotta stay under or your coach is gonna get mad at you. You're gonna get in trouble!" So I stay under. And when I come up, I, oh, I'm dead, I feel so tired.

I have two sets of friends, my school friends and my synchro friends. My school friends, they don't really understand quite what synchro is, y'know. They tried out once for it, but none of them really liked it. They thought it was too hard. They didn't feel like they were strong enough to do it. It made me sort of sad, because I knew they'd never really understand how I feel about it. There's just so many things that other people can't understand, y'know. You have to be in there and doing it.

There's been many times I wanted to quit. Two years ago, there were girls that picked on me a lot. Like, when I'm with close friends, I just talk, talk, talk. But with them I felt like, I can't really say anything, or they'll tease me, and I'll be embarrassed. They all go to a different school than me. A lot of times what was in style at my school wasn't in style at theirs. So they teased me a lot about what I wore. My mom would shop for me. I'd like the clothes she picked out, but my synchro friends would say, "That's gross, why are you wearing that?" And, "Oh, what are you doing with your hair? That's pretty ugly!" Me and my friend put on makeup and we thought it made us look gorgeous. They said, "You look like a clown!" I was like—ugh! That hurt.

You try to look like everyone else. If someone says, "Oh, you have your own unique style," it's sort of like an insult. Some other time, like in a few years, it might be a good thing. But if you're different, it seems very strange. It's like, "No, I don't want to be different, I want to be like everyone else. I want to wear the same things."

At school it wasn't a big deal what we wore, 'cause lots of people wore different things. But at synchro it was a big deal. Sometimes I had to change my school clothes on the way over here, in the car, so I could fit in with the synchro girls. At school it was fun, I was comfortable, it didn't really matter what I wore. But at synchro I had to watch out.

My coach, I don't know if she was trying to make me better. That's what the coaches always say, y'know, "I'm not picking on you, I'm just trying to make you better." But it sure felt like I was getting picked on! I was the youngest, and I was pretty immature. I got teased a lot. It was really hard. I would come home every night and just cry. My mom would say, "You gotta keep going, you're gonna go to the Olympics!" And I would say, "I can't go on, Mom, it's too hard, I just can't do this!" Then the next day at practice we'd do something fun, so I'd get back into it, and, "Oh, I like synchro again!" But there are days when I just can't do it. I'll be really tired and I'll go, "I can't do this. I can't do this. But I've gotta do this. So I'm gonna do it."

Our coach always talks about the center of your core. You have to tighten your center. When she gives you a correction, like your leg is over your back, you need to move it *slightly*. Otherwise, if you move it, BAM! You're gonna totally lose control. Everything has to be slow and still and careful, otherwise you're gonna lose it all. I have to count to myself and go, "OK...I'm gonna hold this for a few counts...a little slower...and move on..." I have to keep a tempo going so I don't speed up or slow down, so I can stay under. You have to keep control. You know you're strong enough to move faster, and you could do it quicker, and you could just keep going. But you can't do it fast, and you can't do it as strong as you'd like to. You can't throw yourself into it. You have to take it slowly and sort of calm yourself and control yourself. Make sure you're sturdy, and don't go all out.

We do things over and over again, to perfect each move, even if it's only an arm stroke, where you just put your arm in the water at one count. It feels so great when you know it's perfect now, it's the best, you can't get it any better than this. Other times you can't get that move synchronized. One person's putting their arm somewhere different than someone else, so it doesn't look right, it looks sloppy. If you're having a bad day, like at school you fell down, everyone's teasing you, if you're feeling really bad, then sometimes you'll just sort of drag through the water. You'll try to get through the practice, and your coach will yell at you, and everyone will pick on you. Then there's days when you just get out there, and, "We can do this! We're gonna do it perfectly." Then there's other times when you're having a bad day and you come to synchro and it's like, "Yeah, finally, away from the world. I'm with my team, and we can do anything."

I usually do my homework when I have free time. I like to draw. I like going shopping with my friends, even if we don't have money to actually buy anything. Just going out to the mall, sitting down at McDonald's, eating lunch. Looking around. Sometimes I like to write poetry. I'm not very good. I get in moods, like I'll feel really strongly about something and I'll want to write about it.

We have practice at night from five o'clock to eight o'clock. Sometimes it just...I can't...I don't have time. I'll get home and I'll be so tired, I'll fall into bed and go to sleep without any dinner. I just get so off track. Then there's nights when I'm up and awake and I just want to write something. I'll write to like a person, not really a person, someone that...you could write to.

My friend Casey, she quit the team. We were like best friends, and when she quit it really hurt me. She went to speed swimming, so I felt sort of dumped or ditched or something. I tried writing letters to her, but I never really sent them.

Lauren had always been my really close friend. I'd sleep over at her house and we'd tell secrets, you know, or we'd gossip — like, "She's really getting on my nerves," you know. But now it seems like we're sort of drifting apart. We used to be duet partners, so we were pretty close. We always worked together and stuff, but not any more. Now it feels like she's getting more friends. If she has a chance to invite someone over, she'll invite...she might invite me...but she might invite someone else. So it's sorta like we're drifting apart. I could invite any of them over, but I'd rather invite Lauren. But now she's sort of spreading out through the team. It's selfish, but I feel like I'm losing her, you know? And so it's sort of sad.

Routines, they can be so hard they get scary. Our team routine really scares me. At one point I stay underwater and then I get lifted up, but I don't breathe. This one girl, her head goes on my stomach while she lifts me. And it feels like she's pushing on my lungs, like I'm gonna explode. I came up and I was crying and my coach just kept saying, "If you break again, Lindsey, you're gonna have to swim it all the way through by yourself." I was really tired and nervous. I just kept getting scared. Then I broke again, and I had to swim it through by myself. I couldn't...I kept...I did a really bad job on that. There's just days where it's like, "Aw, I can't do this, it's too scary, I'm scared." You just go home and you cry, "Mom, I wanna quit synchro." And she says, "But you gotta keep going, honey, you've come so far. Six years of your life. You can't just throw it down the drain. Gotta get somewhere." So I say, "OK, I will, I'll try it again tomorrow." All this week I've been scared. "Oh, not this!" you know. Then we get through it and it's like, "Whew, I'm done, I did it, I'm done." It's a good feeling. It's a hard routine.

Sometimes my mom says, "OK, quit," like a reverse psychology sort of thing. And I'm like, "But I don't know if I could leave my friends." When I feel like I want to cut my relationship off from synchro, the last little string is the friends. They all go to the same school so if they quit they'd still see each other. But if I quit I wouldn't be able to see them. I think that would really hurt, because this is where I spend all of my time. We always complain about how we have no life because we're always swimming. But I think it would cut a big thing out of me. A big six years of my life has been on this. I get so strong from this and I'm in shape because of this. I could be like a fat old woman because I don't swim any more.

I try hard. My coach always says that I'm never focused enough. It's really hard for me 'cause I try to stay focused but there's other things like, "Oh, who's that man walking by the pool?" or something. And my coach is talking. "Lindsey, Lindsey, are you listening?" "Um, yeah." "What did I just say?" "Um, I don't know." I get in trouble for that.

I'm pretty good at practice. But during the meets I sometimes freak myself out. I get nervous and I get all shaky and I'm like, "I can't do this." I get worried and I start crying. And then I have a really bad swim just to get through it. That puts me low down on the team. Sometimes you just go home and you cry 'cause you know you're like the lowest on the team and everyone is better than you. I have to remember that I'm on one of the best teams in the world. Five of our people went to the last Olympics. You just have to think, you're not really the lowest. And if you are the lowest, you just have to think, "Well, I've got to get better."

The judges score you really bad and it's like, "I thought that was good. It *felt* good." At this past meet, I thought I had done pretty good. Then I saw the results and I was dead last. I just went home and into my bed and I cried for a while and then I went to sleep.

I woke up in the morning and I said, "OK, I'm gonna be better this time, I'm gonna do better. I'm not gonna let anything get in my way. I'm not gonna be last." It's hard, but you just gotta keep going, to work yourself harder.

You have to work together with people in the world. You can't just go out and live your life without any help from anybody. It's all a team thing. Your team's gonna help you get better and you're gonna help your teammates get better.

You can't give up that easily, especially with synchro. Like my school friends, sometimes I think they're wimps. They gave up too easily, they didn't try hard enough. It's sort of sad because they'll say, "I'm spending the night at Susie's, do you want to come over, too?" And I'll be like, "Ugh, I got practice the next day. I really can't." Friday nights, I can't have sleepovers because I'll just be too tired for Saturday practice. If I wanted to maybe miss a Saturday practice 'cause my friend was having a birthday, I couldn't. I had to miss so many of my friends' birthday parties because I had practice. And it really hurt when my friend... she didn't invite me to her birthday party because she figured I wouldn't be able to go. So I wasn't invited. And it hurt a lot, because even if I couldn't go, just to be invited is sort of a special thing.

A lot of times my school friends bug me, "Oh, you should quit synchro and then you'll have more time with us." Then I think, "That's selfish. This is my life. I'm not gonna give it up just for you." But other times I think, "I'm not being the best friend in the world, because I could be with them, and I just don't have the time."

My friends, they can just go home and play games with their brother and sisters or watch TV and then have a snack and maybe a few hours later decide they want to start their homework. But I have to get home, do my homework, go to the pool, come back, take a shower, eat dinner, do the rest of my homework and go to bed if I want to have any sleep whatsoever. It's really hard.

You have to be dedicated. You give up a lot of things and you have to be ready for that. You have to make that big commitment, that, "I'm gonna be there for my team." You can't quit in the middle of the year. What is the team gonna do? They won't have enough people. You have to stick with it. Get used to it.

We put Knox gelatin into our hair to make it stay back in a bun. It's sort of fun. Well, it's not really fun, 'cause it's really smelly. It's really

smelly and sticky, and it's gooey, and I really don't like it most of the time. When I just started synchro, I was pretty young, like in third grade. I was telling my friends, "Oh, I got to wear makeup at the meet this weekend." Makeup was pretty big back then 'cause none of our parents would let us wear it. But at the meet, you got to put on lots of it, and it was sort of special. When your friends would come, you'd be like, "Guess what? I'm putting on makeup!" They'd watch you put on makeup, and you'd be like, "Yeah, I'm doing this." And your hair's all up and all Knoxed in a bun, or sometimes in braids. And the hats and suits, sometimes they can be really pretty. It depends on what your music is and how much sequinning your parents are willing to do. Sometimes they can be really ugly, too.

I think it would be really cool to tell my kids, "I went to the Olympics and I got the gold," or that I was even *in* the Olympics. Just being able to tell people that would seem like so amazing. And you get the Olympic bags and Team USA stuff. My coach was the Olympic team manager. She had these suits from the Olympic team and we were like, "Wow," you know. It would seem cool if you got those things, like a hat or something, you know.

This guy at school, he's like, "No offense, Lindsey, but synchronized swimming is nothing and it should be taken out of the Olympics." And I'm like, "What?!" I blow up when people say that. I wish they could get under there. I'm like, "You should try it sometime," and I just want to kill him. There's so much more to it than just what they see. You just see smiling faces going up and throwing your arms up and putting your legs up. But really it's like, "Oh! We're gonna drown!" "I gotta be tight, gotta get higher," "Oh no, oh no, oh no." They just see a smiling face and sometimes it's sort of — I feel like, well, it's just not fair. I want them all to know what we're going through! But if you want to swim good, you have to make it look effortless. Make it look perfect. Make it look easy. No one ever really knows what you're actually going through, what you're doing under water to get yourself up and how you're working to move your body. It's impossible to explain to people. This guy at school, I just felt like I could kill him. You can't really say anything. There's nothing to say.

Lindsey's Mom.

I was a synchronized swimmer, years ago. I was in junior high when I started. You have to start at six or seven now to be competitive. For those days, it was pretty intense, but nothing like what they do now. I got so much out of the sport. I got to travel. I had wonderful friends. I learned about responsibility. It was great for me. I hope it will be for her, too.

We try to make sure she still has fun in her life, that it's not just all struggle. It is a worry whether she's too focused. She's only thirteen years old and she can't do a lot of things... she can't experience a lot of different sports. She used to enjoy soccer but it got to a point where she had to make a choice. She couldn't do both. It seemed like it was an awfully young age for her to have to make that decision.

It was really hard for me to quit synchro. I stopped when I was eighteen, when I graduated from high school. I kind of hit a plateau. I probably wasn't gonna go any further in the sport unless... I probably just was at that point. Plus I didn't really have the support from my parents. They felt it was time for me to get out and get a job and get on with life. I always wished I had been able to continue. I didn't... I wasn't really ready to leave the sport, but that's how it happened.

The highest goal, I guess, would be for her to get to the Olympics. I'd love to see it at least get her through college. There's a lot of girls that get scholarships now. If she was good enough, she could stay with it and go to school locally. But because it is so intense, if she decided down the road that she just wasn't getting anyplace with it and it wasn't fun any more and it wasn't worth all the time she put into it, then of course we'd support that.

There's only so much you can do with it. This year they started in Las Vegas, there's a Cirque du Soleil and Olympic athletes all over the world were asked to try out for this show. It's like the first time ever that there's professional synchronized swimming. Otherwise, coaching is all you can do.

She says she wants to be a teacher. That's fine if that's what she really wants. But I want her to know that there's lots of other opportunities, lots of other things she can do. Not just be a teacher. Because that's a female profession, and there's so many other things she could do. She has a real math ability. We've heard so much about girls and math not being encouraged and I keep trying to think how we can encourage her. What career would be really good for her to use her math skills? Will she have that opportunity? She's very intelligent.

TRACEY, NINETEEN
CARROLLTON, GEORGIA

She is extremely outspoken and highly intelligent. She's red-headed and orange-headed and blue-eyed. Pale-faced, with curly, natural curly hair. She is my world. She's my little version of myself and my mother, my grandmother, and her mother. She's my little best friend. She's always been with me. She'll be with me 'til death separates us. Her name is Raven Cheyenne.

In the beginning, I resented her. I loved her with all my might. I never knew that I could love anything like I love my little girl. She did not ask to be born. In ways, she was not an accident. But she's a little soldier.

She kinda backs away 'cause I used to be strongly temperamental. I never hit her, but I resented her because I had so many problems. Sometimes I could just say, "Raven, hush! Don't talk!" 'Cause her little voice can ring on my nerves like nothing else. She is my strength, but she is a burden sometimes. She hinders me from doing a lot that I would probably do. College, my life, my career, my goals.

But I love my baby, I love her with all of my heart. And when I feel alone, I have her. She knows. She reads me very well. She kinda knows when Mama's mad. When I'm crying, she pats me on my back like I would do her. She tells me everything is gonna be OK. She's my world. She knows it's wonderful to me to have somebody love me so unconditionally like she does.

My mother was young. My father was killed when I was fifteen months old. He was my mother's young love. My grandmother pretty much raised me. She is very particular. You have to take your shoes off to ride in her car. I didn't have your everyday, typical, run-of-the-mill childhood. My mother was strung out on drugs. I had a stepfather, briefly. He was very hostile. The only way I knew how to deal with things was violently. My mother, she just, she's only known one way of life and that's living in an abusive relationship. She's thirty-seven years old. We're more like sisters. She has come around, but with her, everything you do, there's a string attached.

It was the day before my prom. I found out I was pregnant and from that moment on, there was fear. I knew my mother, and I knew how she would react. I was afraid to confront her with this. I didn't tell her 'til I was nearly six months pregnant. I had not had any medical care. I was showing a little bit, but I was always real small and I hid it real well. I would go back behind the house and get sick when she was getting ready for work.

My mother finally came around when I was nearly eight months pregnant. She kinda took over. The baby I was gonna have was gonna come home to *her* house. It was *her* grandchild. I was *her* daughter. I was a possession, was the way she seen it. It was constant chaos my whole pregnancy. Even the day I was in labor, it was constant chaos.

I was extremely hostile. I was very aggressive. You couldn't tell me anything, 'cause I knew it all. I was Raven's mother, you don't tell me how to raise my child. I was hardcore. I used to fight worse than anything. I'd rather hit you than try to stand there and reason with you. I have jumped on people for doing things that I thought wasn't right to my daughter. I have been to court because I have drawn knives on people at school. I got arrested for having a concealed weapon. My little girl was six months old, and here I was, carted off to jail, looking like a fool. Now I see I was. Back then I thought I was tough because I toted a knife.

I watch other girls. I am kinda envious. Sometimes I wish I could be that girl, who could live at home and not have to worry. Sometimes I can feel myself falling back into a rut of wanting to be that schoolgirl and I'm not any more.

I live from week to week. I would have never thought in a million years that I could settle for anything less than what I wanted. But as a parent, and as poor, financially, as I see myself, I've had to settle for less a lot. I used to want only nice clothes, nice things. Now that Raven's here, she's my first priority. I do the best I can and we get by. But I'm tired of just getting by. I want to live!

I got my first job when she was a month old. This is the road that my life has taken. I deal with it.

I was twelve years old when I lost my virginity. He was black. It was...not very memorable for me. Painful. Not any meaning there. No love. I was twelve. It was something to do. I don't know if we were bored, I don't remember the setting we were in. It was just a thing to me. I know now that sex isn't something that you should be just doing. It should be something that you share with someone you love. But, in reality and everyday life, it's not. It happens. People do it all the time.

Sex education in my home, it wasn't there. You didn't speak of it. Sex was nasty. You didn't have it. I knew how girls got pregnant, I knew how you get STDs. I knew all those things. Since the birth of my child I have been tested for AIDS four times. The first time was the hardest thing I've ever done. I was scared because I knew that the people that I had been with were very promiscuous. I didn't want to be a victim of AIDS, and leave my daughter here, motherless in this world. I didn't practice safe sex, but now I do. Out of concern for her well-being as much as mine, I haven't been overly sexually active. But now when I am, I'm protected. Every test has been negative, thank God.

When I was thirteen and fourteen, I *never* thought that by the time I was fifteen I would be pregnant and by sixteen I'd be a mother. My life has swung around in the opposite direction from what I had it planned out to be. My dreams and aspirations...I wanted to go to college, I wanted to be a college cheerleader.

I went to a very small high school, three-hundred-some-odd students. Everybody knew everybody and everybody knew what was going on with everybody. I was extremely lonely. I was fifteen years old. I was popular. I was a cheerleader. I was very active in the school. I was just very well known. A lot of girls, they wanted to be like me. I used to be really mean to them. I've made fun of people that had less than me, but as I have grown up and matured, I've given people a chance.

When they found out I was pregnant, it kinda shocked everybody. I had teachers that felt sorry for me. They shook their heads. I didn't drop out of school. Big as a barrel as I was, I went. I sat sideways, sitting in chairs anyway I could get in. I was on the honor roll.

My pregnancy, it was kinda expected. I done it because I needed somebody to love me. People loved me but I didn't feel it. People in my family just don't come up and say, "Oh, I love you. I love you just for being you," they just don't do it.

When reality hit, I was confused. I was in a daze. At times when I was pregnant, I walked around and I was proud, because I had kept my baby. Other times I was ashamed. People would try to glance at me, and I seen it. It made me feel inadequate. But I learned early on, I had to hold my head up high.

I knew I would keep her. I needed somebody to love. I just felt like she was mine. 'Cause I loved my mother unconditionally, despite...I have a lot of hard feelings. But I knew that when I needed strength, I could pick that little baby up and hold her and comfort her and have her depend on me. That was very important to me then.

A lot of times I think she was the answer to my problems. She stopped me from going down the wrong road.

Raven's father, he is a redneck. I'm not! We were as different as night and day from day one. We were the last two that anybody ever expected to get together. If I walked down the hall and seen him years before, I'd never have dreamed I'd have his child.

He was very immature. He was the baby of nine. He was spoiled rotten and petted. He got whatever he wanted. His mother forked out money, bought him new cars. When I met Brad, in a way, he was security to me. I wanted a boyfriend with a car. He always had money on him. It was for all the wrong reasons, why we got together.

His three older brothers all got girls pregnant very young. So his family kinda expected it.

He loves Raven, but he doesn't take responsibility as being her father. He likes the idea of her calling him "Daddy." It gives him power. He gets her every other weekend. He supports her financially, so to speak, in some terms. Brad, he's a good person. He's just very not me. He's country. He's prejudiced. That was one of the things that broke us up. I'm not prejudiced. If I believe in something, I'm gonna stand up for it. He didn't want our child to be raised around black people. I, on the other hand, had left him and dated a black guy. That 'caused a lot of ruckus and controversy. I have no prejudice. I think that was the main factor that broke us apart. He's not willing to change and I'm not neither.

We broke up this year. I was dating one of his friends behind his back. Me and Raven's father, we really hadn't had a relationship in some time — sexual, friendly wise, in any context of the word "relationship," we have had none. The only thing we have in common is Raven.

The guy that I dated, I thought he was really wonderful. He was intelligent, he was kind of a rebel, a "bad boy," he stood up for what he believed in. That attracted me to him 'cause I thought that I wanted somebody like that. He's been in a lot of trouble, and I've been in trouble, and I just felt like we had a lot in common.

This (pointing to her purple-yellow-blue-black eye) happened Friday night. We just got into a fight. Raven was with her father. We just got into a fight and he blacked my eye. He was arrested. I pressed charges. He stayed in jail three days, and I get to walk around with this. It's the first time he'd ever hit me, and it's certainly going to be the last.

I don't think I want a man at this point in my life. I've got to concentrate on myself and school and Raven and bettering ourselves. I don't foresee myself living from paycheck to paycheck for the rest of my life. I want a good, stable, comfortable... I like nice things. I like interacting with all different kinds of people. I'm not gonna do it staying where I am. I don't plan on living in this little community for the rest of my life. I can see myself in a big city. She's gonna have the life that I didn't. I'm gonna move forward from this point on. I don't want anybody stopping me, hindering me, pulling me down.

My life is gonna be good when I get it the way I want it. I just want to be able to provide for her. I don't want to cater to her every want and need. She won't appreciate it. I just want to give her a lot of love and a lot of support. I want her to know that home is safe for her. If she has something that she wants to talk to me about, I want her to say, "Mom, this is what's up with me. Please sit down and talk to me." I'm not gonna lash out and grab her and beat her or kick her out. There is nothing she could ever say or do that's gonna make me turn my back on her, like my mother has done to me time and time again.

If I had it to do all over again, if I could have the same little baby... that's never gonna happen. I can't turn back. There's nothing I can do to change the things that I have already done.

I am no longer a teenager. I am a mother now. That's what's gonna differentiate me from everybody else. If you're gonna walk this walk, you better be able to put up. It's not easy. It has never been easy. Some days are easier than others, but every day is hard.

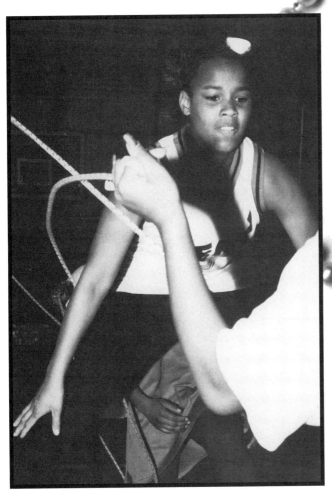

 BATTLE

I von is swift, small-boned, and battle-
scarred. She speaks for the girls who told us they
had been hunted and hurt.

Ivon battles to break the spiral of violence that
swirled in her family even before she was born.
She is wrestling down the choking ghosts of her
painful past.

Willonda talks about the big black gaps between the way things are and the way things
ought to be. Between words of hope and frustra-
tion she reveals her own potential for playing
with fire.

WILLONDA, EIGHTEEN
DULUTH, GEORGIA

It didn't seem like it could be me. Getting big, carrying a child, having a baby. It didn't seem like it could be me. I'd look in the mirror, and say, "That's not me," in the mirror, "That's not me." It's amazing. It's really hard to believe that I'm, me, pregnant. It's real hard to believe. Before I was pregnant, I looked like a little girl. I had a little innocent face. Now I'm looking my age, probably older. I couldn't really believe it.

I never thought about it, when I was twelve, thirteen. Some girls have babies around then. It never once crossed my mind, to have a child. As a matter of fact, I was still thinking the little birds brought the babies, you know.

I always said I wanted to go to college and be a lawyer. I did feel strongly about coming of age, graduating high school, and going to college to be a lawyer, study law. I felt strong about it. But the being pregnant part, I don't know. It's something that came about. Plans just changed. I really don't know how that changed. I still feel strongly about getting a higher education and going to school to study law. I still want to do that. When this came about, it was something that just happened. It just happened.

The first time I had sex, I was fifteen. I didn't like it. I didn't really know what I was doing and it scared me. The only reason I did it was because I had a crush on this one particular boy. He was popular and all. I was crazy about him. I wanted him to like me. He already had a girlfriend but I just wanted to draw his attention to me. He was like, "Well, if you do this and you do that..." I was like, "I like him, so I'll try it." So I tried it and then...it scared me. It didn't work out how I wanted it to, so it wasn't worth it. I waited a whole nother year and a half before I did it again. I still didn't like it. It's not enjoyable. It's not what people say it is to be. It's mostly peer pressure, the reason you first want to try it, anyway. You got that temptation, because of that person you like, and you hearing about it from everybody else, it's this and it's that. It's really not. It's not cracked up to what people say.

It's easier for a girl to find that particular boy, and want to be with only that one boy. With the guys, I think it's different. They don't care, they go from this girl to that girl, no matter whose feelings are involved. The only thing they are out for is the sex, most of 'em, from what I see.

You should wait to get to know that person, 'til you a little bit older so you can understand it better. And be with a person that you know you gonna be with for a while, and you feel like you love and you can share that with them. 'Cause once you lose it, you start to regret it. Then when you meet that person that you gonna marry, you be wishing you could have gave that gift to them, instead of to the other person.

I think that what I'm going through, being pregnant, it's really difficult. They say it's difficult after you have the baby. It's also difficult while you carrying him. Your emotions change and hormones get about. I have got softer than what I used to be. I used to be able to take a lot more than what I can take now, 'cause I'm real sensitive now. Anything you say, you look at me the wrong way, I might break down and start crying. It's funny how your whole body changes because you carrying a child. It's really amazing to me. My face got fatter, my nose got fatter. I'm used to being a real thin, small person. I'm not happy with my body, the way it's looking. My breasts got bigger. I never had a butt, my butt got bigger, and I have a lot of stretch marks on my stomach. I gained a lot of weight since I got pregnant. I probably gained like forty-seven pounds.

The thing that I most like about being pregnant is that I get to feel him move inside me. He's moving now, his hand or something is just right up here. He makes my stomach get lopsided. He's real busy. I can just feel a little knot or something that curves like that. I'll watch it move and make little funny shapes. It look like a little alien or something, trying to get out.

My boyfriend is in South Carolina and when he calls me I put the phone to my stomach and let him talk.

I'm eighteen now. In June, I graduate high school. After I graduate, I'll start back working. I hope I can give my baby what he needs and not have to worry about not being able to get nowhere 'cause I don't have a high school diploma. My plan is to make it so I won't have to struggle. I want to raise him as comfortably as I can. I'm hoping he won't go needing for anything. I'm dependent on my boyfriend 'cause I'm not working. He's working and I'm dependent on him for everything.

We have a good relationship. We still together. I plan on still being with him after, now and after. We planned on getting married and after the baby's born, I had planned on going down there, to stay with him in South Carolina. But things don't always go how you want, so you can't really picture the future. I'm hoping that everything will go how I want it to go. I can't really say. I would want, well, me and my boyfriend, my fiancé, we engaged, we still be together, no problems. Most teenagers, their baby's daddy and them not together no more. Hopefully we'll still be together and I can provide for my baby like I want to, and still do what I need to do for myself, and for him, when we married and together and we all one little happy family. I'm hoping it'll go like that.

My life is not as complex as other teenagers that I hear about, but to me it's real difficult. There is so much going on in the house that don't nothing go how I want it to go. I stay with my mom, my step-dad, my older sister, and her son, he's one. There's my little sister, she's two. And now my aunt and her daughter's living in the house. Nobody in the house respect other people's things. There's a lot of attitudes and tension, just a lot of stuff that I want to get away from. It's difficult to cope with it. Nothing is working out.

I go through a lot of stress, cussing, arguing with somebody, going through battles. I think if you are pregnant you don't need to go through all of that. What you feeling, your baby also feels. Then you sit and worry about, "Is he gonna be OK? Is something wrong with him? Is he gonna be healthy?" That already, and when somebody come and picks an argument with you, all of it balls up together and you can't do nothing about it.

I'm having a boy. I wanted a girl 'cause with a little girl, you can dress 'em up in lace and do their hair in little barrettes and they can be real dainty and cute. A little boy, you give them a ball, and they kick the dirt up and play. You try and keep a little girl nice and neat. A little boy, they just like to get dirty.

My mom, she's supportive of me. She don't like my boyfriend. She's quick to do something when she knows that it's not involving him. She says she'll watch the baby while I'm going to school. If I want to go out and party, she says she give me three weekends out of a year to do that. I said OK, I respect that. Because it's my child. So she's there to help me. I don't know too much about his parents. I met his mom one time. When I call there, she don't have anything to say. This gonna be her first grandchild. His mom, she doesn't say anything to me like, "How are you doing? How's your doctor's appointments?" It's like she

don't acknowledge the fact that I'm gonna have her grandson, so I don't know if she's supportive or what. I don't talk to her, or none of his side of the family.

My boyfriend, he's one of the...when I met him, he was one of the little doggish-type boys. He was messing with this girl and that girl, then trying to talk to me, too. But I was like, I'm gonna break him out of that. I hope that I have. He's big and he's bald-headed — you look at him and you be like, he can't be a father, he's not gonna amount to anything. It's surprising, because he's there for me. He's real supportive. Whatever I ask him, he tries to do it if he can. I really look up to him for that, because he's helping me a lot, being there for me. When times get rough, he's there to comfort me and give me the attention that I need. You can't really find a lot of teenage boys, especially black boys, that does that — that be there to stick beside 'em. 'Cause they make a baby here and a baby there and they don't care. So I really like him for that.

I don't really think that much of him going out and messing with somebody else. He act like he so devoted and dedicated to me, by his actions and his attitudes. But he always leaves room for doubt. He's in South Carolina. He goes out and he stay out for long periods of time. I'm trying to feel like I can trust him 'cause he has a son on the way. I give him the benefit of the doubt. I'm hoping he'll always be there for me, while I need him. I always told him, if he wanted to leave me, do it before anything like this happens. I'm pregnant now. I told him, I threatened him, he better not mess around. It's my attitude towards him. I try to make him scared of me by doing some of the things that I do to him. He hasn't messed up so far that I can see.

We used to fight, like arguments, but I get violent with him. Just to scare him. I don't like to be predictable, 'cause I don't want him to get that comfortable with me. Because when somebody get too comfortable, they try to run over you. So I'm not predictable, I'm just, I do little vicious stuff to him when I get mad at him, just to scare him.

I got violent with him, you know. We got into a fight. He didn't hit me or anything, but he pushed me. I was like, "Don't touch me like that, don't push me, I don't care how mad you get." And anything I gets my hand on, I hit him with it. I made a blowtorch out of an aerosol can and a lighter, and I aimed it at him. I made the torch come out, but I didn't get so close to where it would burn him. So I let him think he don't know what I'm capable of doing or what I might do. So don't try me. I try to scare him like that. I'm pretty sure he got an idea that I won't do anything that will put him in the hospital or hurt him like that. I don't want him trying me, 'cause I'll give him something to think about. I wouldn't never do anything to hurt him, though. But he don't know that. Keep him, keep him guessing.

IVON, EIGHTEEN
NEW YORK, NEW YORK

It was happening with my mother and my father. If I wasn't there to stop it, my father would have really hurt my mother. I was always in the middle. When they see me cry, or catch all type of things, they stop the argument. My father just gets up and leaves. My mother just stands there crying. But if I'm not there, my father would have caught her good. I know it was happening before I was born. My mother still got permanent marks, scars, from my father. My mother had seven kids by him. So they were going together for years.

My father loves me. Even though he's with another woman now, I'm still close with my father. He calls me on my birthdays. He's in California now, and he calls me. If he's in Guatemala, he calls me to say happy birthday, late at night. We keep in touch. He knows that I'm gonna make it. When I was pregnant, everybody was getting on me, my sisters, my brother, my mother. My father got so mad. He said, "You don't know if she could become a doctor or a lawyer with that child." He was really on my side. He gives me confidence. That's why I love him. He didn't drop me like some other fathers drop their kids, only 'cause they're with another woman. He never dropped me.

I was a little tomboy. I used to play with boys. Basketball, kickball, baseball. I was the only girl on my block with holes in my jeans. I used to climb fences, trees, anything. Whatever boys did, I did, too.

Now, when I think back, I can't believe it was me, knowing that I got a son now. People can't believe I had a baby. The way I dressed... whatever, they were thinking I was a lesbian. I'm not saying nothing about lesbians, but they really thought I was with the guys, you know. I think my mother thought that, too. I guess after I was pregnant, she was like, "OK, my daughter's not...the other way." A lot of people thought I was a lesbian. But I proved them wrong.

I turned into a woman when I was fourteen. That's when I had my first...you know, sex. That's when I thought I was grown. I was scared, that first time, that first time I had sex. I was scared. I didn't do it again for like a year.

My mother was strict. When mothers are strict, girls act wild. I kept on cutting school to be with my boyfriend. I was running away. I wanted freedom. Not freedom, but a little freedom.

I didn't tell my mom when I got pregnant. I was too scared to tell her. I was only sixteen, just turned sixteen. She thought I was her little girl, still. But I wasn't. She thought I was gonna be a sweet sixteen, but I wasn't sweet.

She was upset that I had a child even though that's not my first pregnancy. The first one, I got pregnant by my ex-boyfriend. He was an abusive boyfriend and I couldn't have it. I feel bad that I had an abortion. I got pregnant again, and I'm glad that I had it, but I still feel bad that I had an abortion. I don't believe in abortion. So in a way I do wish I had that one, too, because I be feeling bad. Especially when I heard what they do, what happens, with the abortion...everything. Before I had the abortion I had a sonogram, and I could see a little something. 'Cause I was like four months going on five. They told me when they suck up the baby — they do something — that the arms fall off, whatever, I don't even know. There are a lot of things I heard.

Oh, my God. I met this guy. He was my first, and things was going good. But after his mother died, I guess he got stressed out. I was the only one there for him. Stress was coming and he was taking it out on me. I couldn't leave him, because he always kept saying I was the only one there for him. Nobody was there but me and his friends, and you can't really count on your friends, especially guys. I was there. He was just...beating...he sent me to the hospital two times. He did a lot of bad things to me and I should have left him. 'Cause if he did love me, he shouldn't have hit me. I got a lot of marks, I even got permanent scars on my face. He did a lot of bad things to me.

His family kicked him out of his house. My mother felt sorry for him and let him stay with us for like nine months. I didn't tell her he was beating me that whole time. I was in love with him. I didn't want her to hate him or kick him out. I was sixteen then.

He was getting money after his mother passed away. He was doing things for me. He took me off my mother's hands. She didn't have to put out money to buy my clothes. He was really there to help me. I think that's why he thought he had control, 'cause he was buying me things.

I think after his mother died, he had to take out his stress on somebody, but why it had to be me? Why it had to be me?

He was beating me like a man in the street. Like he was beating on an enemy. Like if he ain't had no sympathy. I was black and blue. He cut me. He rearranged my jaw. You can still hear it now, if I yawn, you can hear the *"kkkkk click"* like it tries to go back together. A busted lip he gave me, he almost opened me inside, I almost had a second mouth, that's how bad it was.

Oh, my God, there was one time. You know the movie theaters, right? When you go down the hill, you know the parking lot? He took me there. It was . . . we were supposed to be in school. And um, he took me down there. And um, he was, um . . . he was beating me like . . . I thought I was gonna die right there. *(Fighting tears.)* He was beating me. *(Crying.)* I was screaming. He was hitting me with um, the Club, you know, the Club? That car thing? *(Whispers.)* Man, that hurt. So, um. I was screaming, and I guess the security guards were coming, like . . . looking . . . and I went to scream some more so they will come, but then he says, "If you scream and I get arrested, I'm gonna kill you." *(Whispers.)* So I didn't scream no more.

At the hospital, they wasn't thinking of my boyfriend. I lied. I told them it was some girls who jumped me in a train station. I even made a report, and I was describing, like, one had braids, one had a ponytail. I was making up mad things. But I wasn't saying that it was him.

I didn't really want to break away from him. I didn't know what I really wanted. I was blind, probably. He just kept on telling me I was the only one there for him. When I tried to let him go, I was in pain, I would cry, cry myself to sleep. But when I was with him, I was still in pain. I didn't want him to leave, I just wanted him to change. I'd rather for him to be there, then we could work it out. We work it out for like a few days then another fight comes on.

There was a point, I went to talk to my school counselor. I couldn't take it no more. I was seventeen. I spoke to her, and she talked to the other counselors. They threatened my mother, and told her if he don't leave that house, they gonna put the blame on her. So my mother

hurry up and kicked him out. And if I knew, I wouldn't have told my counselor. 'Cause I didn't want that to happen to him.

He was even cheating on me. After I broke up with him, I found out he had been with some other girl. If I knew I wasn't the only one there for him, he would have been gone. He would have been gone. The sad thing is, sometimes I think on it, all the time, not just some times, all the time. Before when I used to see Ricki Lake or something, on abuse or whatever, I used to look at it and be like, "Them girls is stupid, why she didn't leave him?" I don't talk no more. I don't say nothing no more. I just look. Nobody knows until it happens to you.

I think my father would have killed my old boyfriend if he knew he beat me up. When he lived there, it was happening, but he didn't hear it, and no one told him. We was trying to keep in on the low. He used to take me on the roof, or outside, to beat me up, but not in front of my father. I guess he knew better. 'Cause he knew I'm my father's little girl no matter what. I could have ten kids — I'm still my father's little girl. He wouldn't want no man beating on me. I think that's how Guatemalan men are, they swear they got control of their women. When he found out I was pregnant, he really didn't want the father to be a Guatemalan man. 'Cause they hit, they cheat, then they . . . like my father . . . whoo! He was a Casanova back in the days.

My baby's father, it's going good. He treats me better than anybody ever did. But me, I'm treating him bad. Probably 'cause I think of the things my ex-boyfriend did to me. I take it out on him. My now boyfriend, he play-hits me, sometimes he likes to yell at me, like my ex-boyfriend used to do. I just . . . react . . . my reaction is to hit him quick. When I was with my ex-boyfriend, I was too scared to hit him. So them things I'm doing to my boyfriend now, I wish I was doing to my ex-boyfriend. I'm trying to change that. He's treating me good. He's a real good man. He's taking care of his son.

I'm raising him to be a happy little boy. I don't want him to be ruthless, or nothing. When I do get out of school, I'm gonna go to college or something. I want to get out of here, that's the first thing. A lot of bad things happened here. I graduate high school in June. I wanted to be an electrician, like my baby's father. He's an electrical apprentice. But if I can't make that, I'm gonna try to do something, 'cause I wanna make money. I gotta help support my child.

I love that little boy like crazy. I miss him now, I wish I was home with him, but I'm in school. I'm in school for him, really, for me, too, but really for him. I was really messing up in my old school. I was skipping school, smoking pot, drinking. But now I don't do none of that. I just take care of my own.

My mother has always been there for me, no matter what. She never kicked me out. She hated the things I did but she was still there for me. She's getting old now. She's gonna be fifty-six. I want to help her. I wanna do a lot of things before, God forbid, my mother pass away. I want her to see me graduate high school and college. She has high blood pressure. I think I'm the main cause. When I used to run away, she had to cry herself to sleep, that's what my sister told me. And she has a drinking problem. Ever since my father left.

Now I'm nice. I'm not... I can't say I'm nice. I'm trying to get along with people. Before, anything that any girl say, I flip on them. I just start trouble with them. They don't have to say nothing. The way they look makes me wanna hit them. Now I don't think of stuff like that 'cause of my baby. Anything can happen, you could go to jail, or they could catch you later. I never want them to catch me when I'm with my son. I hope I don't see them girls now. You know when you hear about what comes around, goes around? What I was doing to them girls back in the days, that's why I got it from my old boyfriend. I got what I deserved, that's what I think. I'm trying to get along with everybody. That's the best thing. That's what I should have done before. But I was out there acting up. That's what smoking pot and drinking does to you.

Every day, I talk about my son. I miss that little boy. In school, I sometimes don't pay attention to what I'm doing. I think on him, what's he doing now, or what he did yesterday that was so funny or so cute. I think about him all the time. When I get home, I drop my books and run to him. He sees me, he starts laughing, jumping up. He misses me, too, I guess.

When he was born I didn't feel like no mother. I just felt like I had a hard responsibility. It is hard, but I'm glad that I have him, now that he's more active. I feel like a mother now. Before, I was just like — damn, I can't go out. No more parties. Now, I don't care... sometimes I don't care about parties. I just be home with my baby.

If I had a second chance I wouldn't have had him now. Not until I'm twenty-five, thirty, when I'm financially...I'm glad I have him, but... at first I wasn't glad, 'cause he was just...I had to do things for him, there was nothing he could do for himself. Not that he's walking or nothing, but now I know him more. I know what his cries are. I know when he needs diapering or whatever. I got everything down pat.

I just want him to have the things I never had. I'm gonna spoil that little boy to death, we gonna spoil him. I want him to follow in his father's footsteps, 'cause his father is a smart man. He went through school, he wasn't messing up like I messed up.

I think God gave me a baby on purpose. The way I was acting, I was really into smoking pot, drinking, fighting, breaking night, like never coming home at night, stressing my mother. Plus, summer was around the corner, and a lot of crazy things happen in the summer. People don't know how to act when it's hot.

My mother couldn't trust me no more. She wasn't giving me attention no more, since she thought I was a woman already, you know, sex and all that. My father wasn't here. It's like I needed attention. That's why I went to my friends. What my friends was doing, I was doing. Drinking, smoking pot.

It happened. It could have happened at the right time. I wasn't mad that I was pregnant. I thought I couldn't get pregnant, to tell you the truth. I was trying to see if I could. I was unprotected. I wasn't using no condoms, no birth control, no nothing. When I did find out I was pregnant, it was unbelievable. I just kept it, 'cause I thought that if I get another abortion, I'm gonna go crazy. I was always thinking on the baby that I did abort.

In the future—I want to see myself in a house. I want a car and a jeep and seeing my little kids running around in their own yard—not other people's yard, their own yard. I'd like to marry my baby's father. I don't want to have kids and they all got different fathers. I want my son to be with his father. I don't want him to come every weekend, or come every month, or he move out of state, he comes every year. I want him to be there every day. Go to work, come back home. I'm gonna stop treating him bad, so he don't have to leave me for a good girl. I'm gonna try to keep us together, so they can be together.

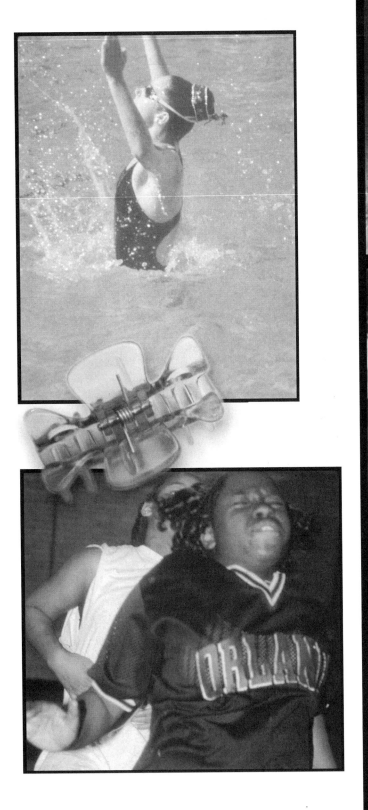

 STRUGGLE

Alison and Stephanie Lee are warrior girls, with smiles for their shields. They compete against themselves, other girls, and cultural ideals. Alison wants her African-American beauty recognized by judges who tend to honor blue-eyed blondes. Stephanie Lee creates an anti-oppression, anti-apartheid performance for judges more accustomed to Tchaikovsky and show tunes.

They both know the judges are fickle and subjective. They suspect they're biased and cruel. But they work to perfect their performance and struggle to win respect.

ALISON, THIRTEEN
CAMBRIDGE, MASSACHUSETTS

I'd like to take it as far as I could. Miss Universe would be great. Miss USA. Miss America. Miss Teen. I wanna become a supermodel and be on TV a lot. It's just something I love, something I enjoy. When you love a sport, like football, you watch football, you wanna see the Superbowl. When I watch pageants, since I do pageants, I wanna see Miss USA, Miss America, Miss Universe. It's the same thing.

People come up to me, they're like, "You spend so much time on pageants." But it's really probably about an hour or two at night. I'm an everyday person. I like doing outdoor stuff, hanging with my friends, going to the mall, spending time with my family, traveling. Look at ice skating, and look at pageants. You spend a lot of time ice skating. You have to wear makeup, you have to have costumes, costing as much as the gown would cost, which is pretty expensive. There's a lot of hard devoting time. If you say stuff about pageants, you should say "Why do you spend so much time on baseball, or ice skating, or basketball?" It's the same thing.

For me, and probably for a lot of other girls, it's competitive also. "Let me see if I can beat her." It's not really like, "Ooh, I gotta beat her." It's fun because some girls win a lot of titles, and when you finally beat them, you feel real good 'cause you're like, "Wow, she's real hard to compete against, and I finally did it, I finally beat her." It's not competition, we wanna be all as one, but we wanna be competitive more. That's the fun of it.

When I was little, I'd line my dolls up and pretend those were people. I'd perform for them, 'cause I like to be in front of people. My little sister, she'd pretend like she was a judge or a person that could watch me.

For the beauty competition, you have to have a gown that's really glitzy with diamonds, broad shoulders, high collars, chiffon. For sportswear, you need a jacket, 'cause in most pageants, you have to take off the jacket in a routine. You have to do a lot of dance modeling and a lot of turns with the jacket. For swimsuit, it's freestyle. You can do anything you want, as long as it has some kind of modeling to it. I made my routine to the Macarena. I have a beach ball, I have a swimsuit, I have a shawl. I fool around with the ball and do modeling. It's freestyle. You have a routine, it goes with the music. That's the fun part. It's not

like Miss USA when you have to walk around in a circle and everybody does the same thing. Everybody's different.

Alison with her mom.

Mom: Basically, we shop. We look in pageant magazines. We get ideas by going to pageants. We have a lot of pageant sisters and they'll say, "Oh, come on, my daughter's gonna be at this pageant." We'll go and it's like, "Oh, they changed the outfits this year." They've gone away from the rhinestones and the furs down to that ice cream frosting cake type of look, that lollipop look. One season they could be on all fur, then it could be really glitzy, then they could be real plain. You have to see where it's going, and follow that. It turns around. It goes through a cycle.

When we go to pageants, we bring a crew of eight. We all travel together. We get to do her hair, we get to do her makeup. We meet different people, and we sorta socialize. We have a legitimate excuse to go somewhere.

Alison: My aunt does real good makeup. They have makeup artists at pageants, and they're real expensive. We just have her come along and do my makeup. It comes out just as well as the professionals. Like, when I have makeup on and when I don't have makeup on, I'm two different people. It's like night and day. My cousin will help me out and take care of my little sisters. My grandmother comes along. My other aunt comes. She helps me pay for the expenses. My sisters, they have to come, just to travel as a family. That's the eight people.

Mom: I keep her in line. I make her practice, practice, practice. I give her a little pep talk. I say, "You're here to do your best, and don't add anything, don't take out anything. Just do your routine and that's that."

Our family thinks we're crazy spending all the money on gowns, sportswear, Western wear. She likes wearing those expensive clothes. I think that's the real main thing. You're out of the everyday jeans. You get to wear some nice-feeling silks, and you get to be in a gown that's got all rhinestones on it. Then you get to show it off, and if you're good enough, they'll call your name, and you get to go up there, and there's all the excitement. The adrenaline gets going. Gives us an excuse to dress up for a day and have fun.

Alison has a goal. She wants to go to college. She would like to compete in Miss Teen USA or Miss USA. We use pageants for her self-confidence. She has no stage fright. She can get up and do anything and not even show that she's nervous. We're really not in it for the money or the prizes. We're in it for the experience, so that when she does get ready to compete in Miss Teen USA, she's ready.

Alison: I'm thirteen now. My ambition is either to be in technology or to be a registered nurse. At the same time, still doing modeling. That's nothing I probably will ever give up. I'd like to have kids. Get married, live in a nice house, be in a nice environment. I live with my mother and my two step-sisters. My grandmother lives down the street, a ten-minute walk, so I'm always over there. I just met my father two years ago. I found out I had two other step-brothers and a step-sister.

Mom: We met in college, and he went to Haiti. When he came back, he thought I had already left, got married, moved away. Lo and behold, he didn't realize I was in the same apartment. My mother was still here, the phone number was still the same. We were trying to find him, 'cause she said, "I want to meet my dad." She wrote a letter, and then we got a phone call, like, "Oh, my God! I been thinking about you guys and didn't know how to get ahold of you." So we went to Atlanta, and we met him, and he's family, we're close.

Alison: It's not like I get to see him every day because he's moved to Alaska now. Just him. His wife and his three kids are in Atlanta.

Mom: It's hard for black African-Americans to compete in pageants, there's not a lot of us who compete. Some of us don't have the hair length, so we have to add extensions to give us that long beautiful length which they look for in beauty pageants. Some girls try to look like the Caucasians, blue-eyed, tall, skinny. Us African-Americans, we go out there as we are. We don't have to wear a lot of makeup, we have the beautiful eyebrows and lashes, we have the perfect lips, you know some girls have to go and get their lips done. We have the beautiful eyes, just as well, even though we're brown-eyed. There's plenty of models out there, Naomi Campbell, Tyra Banks. There's a lot of them that are dark skinned. Short hair. From Nigeria, Ghana, and Ivory Coast.

Alison, alone in her room after the Shining Star National pageant.

This is a score sheet. Every judge has one. Not every pageant gives them back. I like doing the ones where you get them back so you know what you can work on. These are scores for Appearance, Beauty, Poise, and Overall Impression. Appearance is makeup, facial appearance. How your eyes are, nice and wide, or your smile, very wide. That's probably what appearance is. Beauty, I really couldn't tell you what that is. It could be the gown itself. It's probably not really judging you on how pretty you are. It's probably not on your facial beauty. It's probably on your gown.

They write comments and scores. I got "very striking gown color" and "very poised." But one judge scored me a lot lower than the other judges. She went down a whole tremendous lot. Beauty 15, Poise 16, Appearance 15, Overall Impression 15, Total Score 61. Her comment: "Gown is great color, but too short. Slip is showing." Where that comes from is beyond me. I've done so many pageants with that dress, it's brand new. I've had no problems with it, I mean, I don't know.

In the Fashion category, they have Appearance, Modeling Ability, Personality, and Overall Impression in the total. We come down to this very disappointing score sheet. Ugh, this is terrifying for me. Appearance, 17. Modeling Ability, 15. Personality, 17. Overall Impression, 15. Total score, 64.

I don't understand. This weekend, I thought I did so good. I thought I might win Superior, Supreme, Overall. I'm sitting there, I'm all excited. But, these scores, I don't know what to say. Whether she was having a bad day, or she just had a different opinion, I really don't know.

It's not like I did anything to her. I just wanna know what I did. I wanna know, what do I need to do to get you...to impress her, to get a high score? Because, I had Overall — or Supreme — Superior. I went to this pageant and people say, "What did you come back with?" Nothing.

Those scores, it's terrifying. I'm still recovering over it. I talk about it every day. I sit down with my mother, and I'm like, "What did I do? What did I do to deserve this?" I never did nothing to her. We went out to eat after and that's all we talked about. The phone's been ringing off the hook. They're like, "What happened?" It's the first pageant ever where I walk out with nothing. All because of one judge. And that's what they do. One judge can really tear you up. She can tear you up.

Everybody's scared of her now. Hopefully she won't be at the next pageant, 'cause I know she does a lot of judging. Or maybe she'll think, "Wait, look what I did to her last time. Because of me, she didn't get what she deserved." Maybe she'll think of that. I don't know. My mother swears if she sees her at another pageant, she will walk out. I mean, that's not a good attitude to put forth at pageants. But you see scores like that, it pretty much adds up. All I can do is just look at those scores and be devastated until the next pageant. Until I win a crown, which will be soon, hopefully.

STEPHANIE LEE, FOURTEEN
ALAMO, CALIFORNIA

I just love to compete, whether I win or lose. I think I just have this obsession, almost, with competition.

It starts as soon as you get to a meet. When it's a national meet, it's something really big. You get totally excited before you go. You walk into the pool area. You see other girls warming up. You dive into the pool. You see girls from around the country who work as hard as you do, and practice as hard as you do. You know that out of all these girls, only a couple of them are gonna win. I love that feeling. If you do well, then it seems to be all worth it. It's such a great feeling of success.

Everything is better when it's challenging. Things that are too easy are boring. At school, people are like, "This is easy — good." I'm like, "What? It's easy? That's bad!" I like things to be hard. Everything is more fun when it's difficult.

OK, so this is the whole feeling: you're about to go underwater. You know you have to stay under for a really long time. I think that's half the difficulty, knowing that you're consciously forcing yourself to die. It's like, "OK, I'm gonna go kill myself now." So you're up there and you're like, "In less than three seconds I have to go underwater and be under for a really long time." Underwater, sometimes I say, "if I can't handle it, I'll come up." But that'd be really bad. And this is only practice, of course. At meets, when I can force myself, this is what I tell myself, "If I pass out it's OK, somebody will save me." I kind of have to tell myself, if I die, it doesn't matter! Because I know I'm not going to, but it feels like I'm going to. Like, "OK, it doesn't matter, it doesn't matter." And so then I just keep going.

It's the weirdest thing because as soon as you come up and you get air, you're completely revived. You're all excited and you're really happy because you completed this. I feel like I don't even remember that I was tired when I was underwater.

I haven't died yet. I haven't passed out yet. I hope that I won't. I think I owe it to my team — I know it sounds kind of corny, but — I owe it to my team to stay under. Because if they can do it, I can do it.

It's kind of hard for me. I've never been one of the people on our team to be able to swim the best. Always, sometimes, I'm never like the best person on the team. I'm always like the person who just barely made the team. Something that seems really easy for some of the other girls isn't easy for me. At practice, our coach says, "Swim the routine all the way through, and if you mess up, you're gonna have to do it again. If one person comes up, everybody's gonna have to do it again." And I've come up, and I've broken figures, and I've made the lift fall. 'Cause it's really hard. I always try not to break because I know that my team is counting on me. That's part of the incentive to stay under.

We swim three hours a day, five days a week. I come in extra sometimes. Truthfully, I have no idea how I do it. This definitely takes up more time, even more than schoolwork. I'm involved in Speech and Debate and I play piano. I'm in Chorus. Everybody wants my time. It's really difficult. It may seem that I'm not committed to one thing, but I really like a lot of things. My schoolwork never gets easier. I just do things as fast as possible. Every spare moment I have to be doing something. I always have to tell my friends, "No, I can't go to the movies," "No, I can't go shopping," "No, I can't go over to your house," "No, I can't do anything, ever." Almost — it's like they've given up. My friends never call me any more. They're like, "Oh, Steph probably can't come."

Everything conflicts all the time. I was supposed to go and sing at Carnegie Hall with the rest of my choir. I couldn't go because I had a synchro competition. Last year my chorus went to a children's festival in Prague. They sang with children's choirs from around the world and they toured Vienna and Salzburg. I couldn't go again because I had a synchro meet.

I, on the other hand, am never bored. It's my first year in high school. At my middle school we had no problem with drugs at all. Now it seems like, "Wow, this is actually happening in my school." I definitely think that extra-curricular activities get you out of doing drugs or smoking or drinking or whatever. I have friends who don't do anything at all and they sit home poking themselves and they get really bored. I always have to do something, even when I'm not at synchro practice or chorus or piano lessons or debate, I have to be doing my homework.

I live with my mom and my dad and my brother and my dog. We have this traditional American family except for we're not American. My parents came here from Taiwan. My grandparents went to Taiwan from China during World War II. My parents are Chinese, my grandparents are Chinese. I guess I could say I'm American. I was born here. "Whitewashed," they say. My parents, especially my dad, has this big obsession with doing really well in school. I do, too; it's not like he's forcing me or anything. My brother, he plays baseball, basketball, soccer. He does tae kwan do, he plays the clarinet, he plays the piano, and he plays tennis. Our whole family tries to be good in everything. I'm a freshman in high school and I'm already starting working on those SATs! I work really hard to do well in school. It seems like it's a Chinese thing. You have your traditional Chinese parents. We eat rice, we use chopsticks.

My parents, sometimes I feel bad 'cause they're completely devoted to driving me and my brother everywhere, and nagging, "Don't forget, you have to practice piano today." "Don't forget that you have to study for your SATs." They make dinner especially early so I can eat in the car and get home and start working on my homework. My parents do a lot for both me and my brother. It's a lot of work for them. I guess we just work a lot in my family.

I've always known I'm on the bottom half of the team. When I was twelve, it was a big realization point for me because of what happened in tryouts. There was an A-team and a B-team. I wanted to be on the A-team so bad. I think even now, that is the thing that I've most wanted in my entire life. I worked really hard during tryouts. I didn't know if I would make it. Sometimes you know if you're gonna be able to do it and sometimes you don't. Coaches weren't sending me any clues.

Finally, my coaches told me that they decided to put me on the B-team. And that hurt me a lot. Sometimes when you win, you're happy, and when you lose, you don't really care. But this time it's like there's only two places you can go. One would be really good and one would be really bad and there is no in-between.

I've never really had talent for synchro. It's just something I always wanted to do. I have to work hard to be where I am now, which is not nearly as good as some of the girls on my team. I don't want to bring them down. I want to improve myself. I feel like I'm doing everything right and then we'll watch the video and I look wrong.

Everything seems to be magnified eight hundred times. You think you're off vertical a little bit but it turns out you're off vertical *a lot*. You have to tune into details. Every little tiny . . . one arm is out by like a centimeter too much . . . it makes such a huge difference and you wouldn't think that it would. It's like never perfect ever. You can always be better.

I want to prove to everyone else, but mostly I want to prove to myself, that I can make this happen. All these years I've been on the bottom half. I wanna be able to show myself that, yes, I can do it. That you don't have to have talent to be a good swimmer. That working hard is good enough.

I'm not gonna say that I know what real courage is. I think people face stuff that's way harder than what I face. But for me, in my sheltered little life, it is a lot of work. It takes a lot of courage. It's hard to come to practice knowing that the other girls are better than I am. I feel like I have to work ten times as hard to get to the same place. It's always like, "No, Stephanie, you're doing it wrong. Do it again. Do it again. Do it again. Do it again," while everybody else can get it on their first try. I guess for me it seems like a lot of courage. But it's probably not.

This weekend will be the first time I've ever done a solo. It's really important to me. All these years I've been in synchro, I see all my teammates progressing with their individuals and I haven't. I've never done a real solo before. When I was ten, I was in a trio, and I was real excited about it. But my coach told me, "Well, I think I'm gonna switch it to a duet, because I don't think you're ready to do it." And that really hurt. When I'm swimming by myself, it only depends on me. It's a lot of pressure, but it's not like I'm catching up to anybody. I'm starting the level and I'm building it from there. I've always wanted to write a routine the way that I want it. I want a theme. I want a story. When you have to work with other people, they're not always gonna agree with you. Sometimes I'm not satisfied with the way the idea comes out and sometimes there's no idea at all. But with the solo I'm able to do whatever I want. I can make the theme, I can make the story.

I think my music isn't like smiley, happy music. What really bugs me is some of the routines, they have this totally dreary, sad music and then there's people like, *(flashes big showbizzy smile)*. And you're like, "OK, whatever."

My routine is not a big smiley character. My music is from the movie *The Power of One* and it's from a book about apartheid. I'm really inspired. I really want to express this because I feel so strongly about what the story is and all that.

What I'm basically trying to convey is the idea of oppression. Trying to break through people's prejudice and that kind of thing. And it's like kind of supposed to be inspiring. The story goes, first you're being oppressed, then you decide to go to war, then there is actual war, then you decide that war is bad. Throughout the whole performance there's never like, the person never completely breaks through. The oppression is always there still. But they know they have a chance. Just knowing that there's even a chance is incredibly exciting and so just at the end, it's kind of like they're inspired. So they get smiley.

It's kind of like a synchro thing. It's like how to make yourself exciting. In synchro, you're either a robot or you're happy. Those are your choices. You have to show what you're trying to say through those expressions.

I want to be like, *(breathes hard)* but instead you're supposed to be like happy and smiling. It is really hard, especially when you're about to go under and you want to take a breath but you can't 'cause you're supposed to have this certain facial expression. It's difficult to stay happy when you're about to die.

If there was no reality, then I would want to swim at World Championships, swim at the Olympics. But they say it only gets harder from here. I come home at night and I'll start my homework at like nine o'clock, and I go to bed at eleven. Of course, in our family schoolwork comes first. I've never put synchro above school, even though I really love it. I've been able to keep up straight As, but I don't know how much longer I can do it.

If there was no reality, then I would take synchro to the highest level, because I love it so much. But I know that that's not necessarily gonna be possible. There's a lot of people on our team who, after getting to high school, they just can't take it any more.

I don't know how I do it. It's like a drug, I have to have it! I really want it, and I've been willing to do whatever work it takes to be able to have this experience.

I can sort of say that I kind of love to be tortured! I know that you don't get success without working hard. But then working hard is what makes it half the fun. I guess you could say it's fun. It's something that I love to do. And even though it seems like I'm about to die when I'm underwater...I mean, out of my whole day, how long do I have to be underwater holding my breath? Like two minutes? So, when there's twenty-three hours and fifty-eight minutes of reflection, and two minutes of dying, it's definitely worth it.

Sometimes we come in at six in the morning. Last year we had practice on Wednesday morning at 5:30. Pool looks freezing. There's steam coming off. Have to get in anyway. But once you get in, you're like in a different world. You don't have to worry about how cold it is outside 'cause the pool's warmer than you think. Winter or summer it's always there. It's kind of a relief.

I've always liked swimming around underwater. Sometimes you lose that feeling because you're running out of breath. But when you go underwater and you look up and you see the sky, but there's water there, it's like the sky is water. I wish you could see.

I go under and try to blow perfect circle rings. When you're on Earth, you have to listen to everybody else. But when you're underwater, you don't have to listen to anybody. You can just do whatever you want. You can't talk. There's no noises, there's no smells, and there really isn't much to look at. You can reflect very easily.

When it's raining, I love to go under and look up. You're used to seeing rain come down. But when you're in the pool you're looking at it from a completely different perspective. It's also different from looking at rain hit a window. Instead of the water coming down and sliding off, it actually comes in and then it becomes a part of the pool.

In a corny metaphor, it's like swimming a team routine. You have individuals, but collectively you are supposed to act as one. That's what water is like. You can take it apart, in individual drops, but then when you put it all together, it gels, it works together. That's what synchro is about. I mean, it's being able to move, feel, and express things — together.

Stephanie Lee's mom.

I grew up in Taiwan, the youngest of five kids. The whole country was poor at the time. So I always dream about doing this and doing that, but I could never do anything. For my children, I want them to do as many things as they want, for a lifetime of relaxation, to enrich them spiritually. I never expect them to be a superstar. Just to let them try different things.

In Oriental culture, we are very disciplined and work very hard. Family is very strong and supporting and we are very bonded to family. From outsider it may seem like it's a pressure from family; you do things just to meet the family expectation. Sometimes it seems like you are really trapped. But it's mutual. They care for you and you care for them. I come to this country and it's different. You learn and you become more creative here because you don't have as much worry around you. You just do what you like.

COMMITMENT

 COMMITMENT

Adolescence can be a journey to another planet, far beyond the moon and stars of childhood. For Lily and Tamara, the trip is cultural as well as spiritual. Lily's mother is from China and Vietnam. Tamara's is from Trinidad. Both came to the United States determined to raise their daughters in security and freedom.

Lily and Tamara are committed to the cultural ideals they were born to: strong, close families, hard work, discipline. They see the freedom and license of American youth as a blessing, a temptation, and a threat.

LILY, SIXTEEN
SACRAMENTO, CALIFORNIA

I live with my mom and dad and my older sister and my younger brother and sister. And my grandmother. We speak Chinese in my house, because my parents don't speak English fluently. We have a good family. We don't communicate a lot but there's a lot of understanding and support. Like whatever decisions we make, my parents are always there to support us. Something funny about my family. I don't know if it's all Asian families. They don't seem to show a lot of love — like passion. Like, "I love you, honey," affection and stuff. It brings me down a little bit, but I know deep inside they love me. Once in a while it's a sad moment. I'm not sure if all Chinese families are like this. But that's my family.

I had a very fun childhood, because we lived in a neighborhood with a lot of Chinese people. I was a little tomboy, honestly. Very playful. I would play Superman with my little brother. We would be hitting each other, climbing trees. I got a lot of scars from my childhood. We used to go out every day, out in the front and play swords and imitate kung fu fighters.

I don't play like that any more. I grew out of it. I'm very calm now. I miss it. It was so fun back in the days. I had all my old friends. I always wonder where they all are now. I'm sure they have their own lives. I miss it. I wish I could go back.

I don't know how it changed. I think it was in sixth grade when the popularity thing hit. I had this friend who was very into clothes and fashion. It's kind of peer pressure, but it wasn't bad peer pressure. Now I'm more involved in clothes and shopping. I do love shopping now, but up until fifth grade I was still a tomboy.

I'm still not a big fan of makeup. If I'm in a hurry, I'll just run off. If I have time, I'll do my eyes a little bit. I don't like it too dramatic. It makes my eyes kinda look like a raccoon. It looks like I just got punched out. But lipstick, I like a little maroon, brownish color. And then some powder because I have a T-Zone right here, combination skin. That's about it.

The Miss Chinatown pageant is not based on looks. It's based on your personality and how you represent yourself. It has nothing to do with looks. Basically the judges will mainly judge you on your appearance, how you walk and your poise.

I really want to represent my culture, the Chinese culture, and spread my culture 'cause it's not widely known in America. That's why I'm here. Traditions are very important. In my family there's a lot of knowledge and values that are passed down from older generations. Like how we celebrate Chinese New Year. We have a lot of superstitions, like during the New Year, the number eight is important. In my language, when you say eight, it means lots of money. It's good for the New Year. And our religion. I'm Buddhist. It's a big religion in the world and not a lot of people understand it. We keep the ancient culture. We give prayers and thanks to our ancestors, then we burn paper money and clothes so when the smoke rises, they can receive it, the spirits can receive it in heaven.

Lily wins Miss Chinatown.

I'm looking forward to being Miss Chinatown 'cause I want to do a lot of great things like volunteer within the community and do performances. The Pacific Rim festival is coming up. Dinner with all the pageant contestants at the Happy Garden restaurant. Should be fun, we get to meet a lot of rich people, lawyers and doctors and politicians.

We are doing a candle dance and a ribbon dance for our school, for our cultural performance night, so we're really excited about that. I do the ancient Chinese candle dance. The point of this dance is to keep the candle flaming. It takes a lot of practice. You have to be very graceful with your hands. I got my nails burned right here from the flames during practice! You have to be very slow so the candles won't blow out. That's the trick of the dance.

Kids will look up to me. "Oh, yeah, Lily did positive things, I just want to be like her," like a role model. Like Michael Jordan sort of, everyone wants to be like Mike. I just want to be a positive role model — that's my main goal this year as Miss Chinatown.

Lily and her mom (Lily's older sister translates for their mother).

Lily: My mom was born in Vietnam, somewhere in Vietnam, and she grew up there. It's much different from America. She has learned the American ways, but it's different. When she went to school, my grandma was very strict. When Grandma says, "You stay home!" you stay home. We're living in America now, so I want to make my own decisions.

My mom, she knows what's in our community. There's a lot of gangs and teen pregnancies. I'm sure that she's aware of that stuff. I think she thinks that we have a little too much freedom and we tend to take advantage of it. But I don't like people telling me what to do. I feel like I can take care of myself. I know she's my mom, she worries for me. I just have my own opinions.

Mom: I do believe that American teenagers have lots of freedom, sometimes to the extreme. The environment plays a role in how we develop only up to a certain point. The major factor is our own, our own identity.

I hope that all my daughters will be successful in life. Get an education, that's the key to life. Above all, always be a good person. I'm really proud to have three daughters that are poised and pretty. But beauty fades and disappears.

I hope my daughters are able to find good jobs. I hope they marry good husbands, someone supportive, a nice, understanding husband. The most important thing is to marry to a good husband who can support her, care for her for her life. Women in Chinese culture are not looked upon as being in dominant roles and men are. I hope they'll marry into good families. And also represent America well, as citizens of the United States.

It's very different here, from Vietnam where I was born. When I was a little girl, my daily routine was go to school, come home, help out the family, cook, chop wood, and basically just do family chores. Nothing more — no freedom, no hanging out with friends. It's really, really different. Here, people are encouraged to be independent, to be yourself and enjoy youth at least for . . . basically enjoy being young.

I had never seen lipstick or makeup before. But I learned when I came here, I learned what lipstick was, eye shadows, eyeliners, moisturizers, the whole beauty regimen. It's really different.

There is conflict because I was raised in a very traditional Chinese family. I know that there's a lot of temptations out there as my kids are growing up. I try to control things, but I know I can't control too much. I have to let go, because otherwise it will create a conflict between my daughters and me.

In Vietnam the culture is very different. There's no transportation, there's no running water, there's no heat or electricity. Life there is really difficult. You have to live with nature and whatever nature gives you. You have to grow your own food, make your own clothing. Sometimes when you want to see your relatives, you can't, because there is no transportation. I feel lucky for my daughters who are growing up in America where we have everything: running water, electricity, transportation, clothes piled up in our closets. I'm happy that they are growing up here. I'm happy that I brought them to the United States.

We are Chinese but we're from Vietnam. We are considered outsiders. We came here because of the war in Vietnam. After the war was over, the United States allowed relatives that were over here to petition us over. We were sent to China first. On the journey from Vietnam to China, we were all packed in a little boat. A lot of people were seasick. It's a long journey, and the boat leaked and there was a storm. We were on the verge of death. It was a really, really bad experience.

From China, we went to Hong Kong. We lived at a refugee camp. It was really sad there. It's like hundreds of people stacked up in one warehouse with bunk beds, three-tiered bunk beds. There was curfew time, we had to be inside the gate by a certain time. Many people lost all their money, their fortunes. They usually did not carry bills, they would carry gold or jewelry. There was a lot of theft. People lost all their possessions. After Hong Kong, we were stationed in the Philippines. From there we came here and settled in Sacramento.

Through it all, I traveled with my family and the people of my village. They gave me courage. As a village, we live. We are in the same boat, to live or die. We are going through the whole thing together, whether it's good or bad. That's what gave me the courage to go on.

Lily: She never really told us these stories. She won't really say, but she hints. I feel like she doesn't want to talk about it, so I don't want to bring it up. I'm just surprised — some of these stories I've never heard. The journey she took, she never actually told me about. I knew it was a hard struggle to America, but I didn't realize it was that hard.

I feel so bad when I don't listen to her or I make her upset or so mad. To know what she would do for us. Her commitment to America was actually for us. She gave us this opportunity, this land of opportunity.

TAMARA, FIFTEEN
DORCHESTER, MASSACHUSETTS

I'm from Trinidad. I live with my mother and my father and my brother and my grandmother. I live with my whole family. They interesting, they funny. We all grew up in Trinidad, and moved to Boston eight years ago. All of us are together, my aunt and my cousins. It's a three-family house and we live together. I came up here when I was six.

It's different here. If you be bad in school, the teacher got to tell you six thousand times, "Stop, don't do that." And you have chances to go to the principal's office. In Trinidad, you either get a whuppin', or you get sent home and you get in bigger trouble from your mother. And if your aunt find out, you get in trouble with your aunt, it keep going on and on.

Up here people don't really care. She'll get suspended or expelled and she just go home and stay.

Trinidad is like an island and everybody knows each other. Everybody's together, your whole family is together. Up here, everybody is separated. One person might be in New York, one's in Boston. In Trinidad, everybody's together. They're always together.

They don't have social workers, Department of Youth Services, in Trinidad. If you disobey your parents, you get a beating, you get in trouble. I don't think in Trinidad there's high teen pregnancy and stuff like that 'cause everybody knows if you do this, your mother's there to say, "Why did you do that?" and "Why did you do this?" Up here, it's totally different. Everything is scattered about. Kids say, "If my mother hits me I'm gonna go get DYS on her. And I can get pregnant at any age." They don't know how they're feeling about themselves, so they not sure. They don't have a high self-esteem about themselves.

I know a girl, she's sixteen, and she's pregnant already. There's another one, she's seventeen and she had the baby already. Another one that lives down the same street, she's sixteen and she's pregnant. Most teen fathers say, "It ain't my baby, I heard you was with some other dude."

My grandmother is very strict. She's like, "If you don't do this, then something gonna happen to you." So you got to be on point. You can't be slacking off, watching TV. You spend like two hours in your book reading, be very smart. That's one of the things that she drilled into my head, get off the phone, you got to get into your books.

You have to be positive about yourself. Don't say, "I can't do this, I can't do that." I'm willing to try this and I can do this. To the best of my ability, I can do this.

When I first started double dutch, I was about eight years old. I started jumping on my street with the girls.

I never knew how to jump. Everybody was like, "Oh, she can't jump, I don't want her jumping with me 'cause she can't jump." I was like, "If you teach me I'll know how to jump." They finally taught me how to jump, how to jump in the rope, how to get out the rope.

Double dutch, when you doing freestyle, you can be real with yourself. You can be free. You don't have to be so uptight, you have to be loose to jump in the rope. You can handle yourself in the ropes. You can be what you want to be, if you keep at your goal.

You feel happy, you feel like you did something good for yourself. I came a long, long, long, long way, to have somebody actually say,

"You did so good—you can teach other little kids how to jump." You can pass it on. I feel happy 'cause of that.

You can get a scholarship through double dutch. Like most sports, like basketball, you can get a scholarship. It can help you go to a good college. But it's different from any other sport. It's mostly girls doing it, you never see any boys doing double dutch. I asked some boy to jump, he's like, "No, no, no, no!"

Tamara and Chantal talk about competition.
Chantal: You just gotta be perfect.
Tamara: If you not smiling, they take off points for that.
Chantal: You have to smile.
Tamara: If you have a mean look on your face—
Both: That's points, definitely points.
Tamara: No matter what you do, you got to remember, be happy. It's supposed to be a fun sport and not taken seriously. You should take it seriously in order to succeed. But you got to be happy for what you doing. Don't be mad or anything like that. Some girls came in third place and they started crying.
Chantal: We came in last at the Worlds, but I didn't cry.
Tamara: A whole bunch of teams was crying because they came in seventeenth, sixteenth place.
Chantal: They just take it too seriously. You supposed to take it serious, but enjoy yourself.
Tamara: Have fun. That's what double dutch is mainly about, is to have fun.

Tamara with her mom.
Mom: She just can't sit still. She loves to dance, she loves to do everything that has motion. I guess where we came from, it's part of the culture. It's like calypso. If you know the beat, it's constantly moving around. She has the rhythm, she has a lot of rhythm.

She's been a pretty good girl, I mean, for fifteen years old. She keeps her room clean. Top prize for that! And she listens, you can talk to her and she listens. Sometime she says, "Mom, I'm tired of hearing this," but I can't help it. I just keep drilling stuff in her head which I think she needs to hear. Pregnancy is one thing I'm always telling her about, you got to be careful. Drugs is another one. And just trying to be yourself and be somebody that's good. Respect yourself, people will respect you. She's right on a middle line. She sees what goes on in the house and she sees what is out there, so it's left up to her to make that choice.

In Trinidad, it was very much family-oriented, grandmothers, aunts, uncles, everybody was just right there. You couldn't be, how the kids are very flip with their mouths right now. At least if there was an adult around, you would never hear any obscene language coming out of a kid's mouth. Because they're gonna go tell your mom! But up here, the language and the television, all the things the kids are picking up, it's totally different from my time. I guess time changes, so.

Tamara: Sometimes it's like I wish my mother was here right now, to comfort me right now. But then again, you in school and you got to face the fact that there's other people and some of them's gonna be real bad for you. There are bullies out there that's gonna be like, "You better give me money right now." I learn from my mistakes. Everything will fall into a place that I know I feel comfortable in.

Tamara on her front porch with two friends. They're braiding extensions into each other's hair.

Sherel: I love working with kids, worrying about what's going to happen to them.

Sheeana: I think I might break a kid's neck.

Tamara: That's a lot of stress.

Sheeana: That's just like a probation officer. I think I break the kid's neck if they keep doing the wrong thing. "I'm tired of you, you're getting locked up. Bye!"

Sherel: You can't do that. That's what you go to school for, to learn how to deal with it. It must be hard to keep it away from your personal life.

Tamara: Imagine that kid threatening you.

Sherel: Not even that, but worrying about the kid out on the street and alone, getting abused and stuff. That's gonna be hard to keep away from your personal life. And not worry about him or her.

Tamara: I'm having *no* kids.

Sheeana: I don't want any kids and I'm not getting married.

Tamara: I'll get married when I'm fifty, sixty.

Sherel: Yeah, you say that now, but when the future comes, you'll hear those bells ringing. *(Hums the wedding march.)*

Tamara: It's too much commitment. You can't do things like you used to. Before you married, you can go to parties and...

Sherel: You just saying that now, you don't know. You gonna find a guy.

Tamara: We only have two or three boys in this whole neighborhood. The majority of them that used to hang around on my street are locked up. They got locked up last summer, for some stupid stuff they shouldn't have did.

Sheeana: Those boys, they robbed someone and kidnapped people. The oldest one was seventeen, the youngest one was thirteen. They're gone! For at least five or six years. I think the boys, they gang-bang. I think they do it 'cause they don't know nothing else to do. They see that fast money, instead of working for something. If someone gonna give you all that money just to stand out in the street, just to sell something that you not using, that's fast money. Why not?

Sherel: They too lazy to get a job, so they think that's the only way they can survive, by selling drugs.

Tamara: Yeah, there are a lot of girls that do the same thing. That's fast money. Fast money get them locked up.

 DESIRE

A young girl's desire for love has the magnificent, selective force of Mother Nature, hurtling down a hurricane.

Her brain is washed in hormonal surge and whatever magical mix that clicks in chemical, electrical attraction.

Liza, Janice, and Regina wade into the stormy surf and forever change. They survive, wounded but wiser, to warn younger girls.

Tameika is lost in a bitter wind. Feeling betrayed and abandoned, she turns slowly from her old beloved to the new boy in her life.

For Madeline, desire is danger. She walks to school past gang girls whose hungry eyes are lined in Cleopatra kohl. They scream for her brother at night in the street. Madeline's tough for twelve. She beats boys back with her fists. But Madeline's mother feels the charge in the crackling air, and she lies awake at night.

LIZA, SIXTEEN
LAWRENCEVILLE, GEORGIA

I don't know what it is that attracts girls to the guys that get in trouble. It happened with all of my friends, every single one of them. It's just the guy that everybody is like, "*Ooooo...*" We really didn't pay attention to the goody-goodies. They were boring, I guess. We just wanted somebody that was exciting and stuck up for us all the time. Somebody all the guys liked to be around. All the girls wanted him.

When me and James were together, I thought that he was great and he was wonderful. Now I know he was a total jerk. His friends were number one. I was just there when he wanted me there. I wasn't important to him like he was to me. But I didn't see that at the time. I pretty much ignored that.

Girls, when they're young, they're thinking about their first love, their first kiss, and falling in love. They just want that so bad, and I don't think they take the time to pick the right guy.

I'd tell other girls, don't just feel all the love. You gotta *think,* too. Don't just use your heart, use your brain. Really take a look at your boyfriend and see how he's treating you. Is it the same way you treat him? Is it how you want to be treated? I know it's hard. You really don't want to look at that stuff, but you should. You need to.

Some warning signs are like, if he's not interested in meeting your parents, he's always into his friends, and he doesn't care to get to know you. You're just there when he wants you there, and things just move too fast. Girls think that can happen, that you can fall in love within a week. But it's not really love, it's not. It's more like lust. I don't think girls know the difference when they're that young. They've never felt it before so they think it's really love.

Girls are looking for a boyfriend, somebody they can fall in love with. Guys, I don't know if you can say they're just looking for that one thing. But falling in love is just not as important to them as it is to girls. She should be more into school events and doing things that she likes, having her own things, instead of being so dependent on a guy. I was never into any of that stuff.

When we were together, I felt like he was everything. I really can't remember ever doing something that I liked, going out with my friends when I wanted to. It was just going out with his friends or sitting at

home with him. I mean, if he asked me to do something, I did it. I dropped my friends but he kept all his.

I would tell younger girls, just be careful. Don't think that just because you're young and naïve that you're not gonna get pregnant, that sex isn't gonna change your life, because it will.

I was eight, eight or nine when I got my period. I was like, "Mom, Mom, help me, what do I do?" I couldn't believe that I got it so soon. That's the age that people get it now, though. My mom told me that I was a woman now and that I'd get it for the rest of my life, until I was a lot older. I was like, "No! Please take it away!" I had already started to wear my bras and everything. Them I didn't mind, but I didn't want to get my period. I wanted to start shaving my legs. My mom told me no, but I snuck it sometimes. I started to wear makeup, and I did my hair every morning before I went to school. I felt like a girl when I did that, you know, like, older and — pretty.

I met James through one of my best friends. I was always over her house. We were really close. Then I met him. It seems like all the girls are attracted to the quote/unquote bad guys. She got mad and we stopped being friends because I started hanging out with him too much. She didn't like the things we were doing, like spending the night at his house and lying to my parents. Drugs, 'cause he was doing them. She couldn't believe that I had sex with him.

I was always with him. I was stuck on him. Nothing else mattered but him. I just wanted to be with him. I thought it was special at the time, but I know now that it wasn't.

I was fourteen when I lost my virginity. The first time we had sex we were at his house and his mom was home. We were upstairs in his room. I felt weird with his mom there. I lied to my parents that night. I told them I was staying at a girlfriend's house. I always felt like, "God, I hope I don't get caught this time." Every time! "God, I hope my friend lied for me."

I was just, I mean, I was scared, but, it just felt right at the time. And every time afterwards, too, I guess!

The first time that he came inside of me, I felt like, "I can't believe I let him do that, I'm gonna get pregnant now." And I didn't. So every time after that, I was just like, "I guess I can't get pregnant." Sometimes it seemed like he was more scared about it than I was. Sometimes he would say, "Liza, why don't you get on the pill?" Or, "We need to start using a condom." I was like, "Oh no, I'm not gonna get pregnant. If I was gonna, I would have already." And then we'd drop it again.

We were together a year, and that's when I got pregnant. And we sort of grew apart. He was more with his friends and getting into trouble with the law. I was at home getting bigger. I was going to Lamaze class, and he was going to jail for aggravated assault. Then he was on probation, so anything he did wrong, he went back to jail. When I had her, that's what he was in jail for. He violated his probation. He had to be in at eight every night. If an officer came by and he wasn't there, he'd go to jail. He'd stay there until somebody bailed him out, which would always be his mom.

It really hurt me that he was in jail when she was born. We broke up two months after that.

Now he doesn't see her, he doesn't come around. He called on her birthday, but he doesn't come over. I want him to be in her life, but I can't force him. He tells his friends that he pays child support, but I still won't let him see her. He spreads lots of rumors that aren't true. I want him to make the first move. I know that she needs a father, but I can't make him do it.

I never thought that I would have a baby and the father would be in jail. When I was little, I first wanted to be married and I wanted to have time to spend with my husband before we had children. I didn't want this to happen. I thought about being stable, having my own home, being older, and being able to take care of everything on my own. 'Cause I mean, I really do need my parents now.

I had always skipped around on my period. I didn't even go to the clinic until I had missed it for like two months. When they said, "You're pregnant," I was like, "No way, are you sure?" I just ignored it for another month, thought it would go away, sort of. Then I started to show.

I thought, "Well, I can't keep her. What am I gonna do with a baby?" I went to try and get an abortion three different times. I got all the way up to where they took my blood. But I couldn't go through with it. I thought, "God, how can I kill, kill one of my, you know, something that's inside of me?" I just couldn't do it.

So then I went to adoption. I was like, "If I could give her up for adoption, why not? Why take that life from somebody else who would really want it?" So then I was really set on that. I had the people. I signed all the papers.

As soon as I had her, they set her on me. I looked at her and she was perfect. It's just a feeling that I have never, ever felt before. You just love her, just like that. I mean no matter what she did, she's just, she was mine. Holding her and seeing her, I changed my mind again. There's no way I could give her to some stranger. I wanted to keep her myself.

Well, I'm a Mormon, and they really don't believe in sex before marriage. I had to go to kinda like a church trial. My parents had to be there, the bishop and higher up people. It just really hurt me that they were gonna kick me out of the church, because I made a mistake. They didn't want to help me. They just wanted to punish me. I felt like I was already havin' enough of that. We don't really go to our church any more, 'cause so much happened.

My parents didn't react the way I expected at all. They were calm. They wanted to talk about it. They wanted to know what I thought and what I wanted to do. We talked about my options, like school and getting a job. I had to ask my mom if she could watch her while I worked. Now she watches her all the time.

Me and my father are close. My parents are still married. They're like the only ones out of all my friends. He works and he takes care of us. He's a good husband and he's a good father. When I tell my daughter about her father, I don't know what I'm gonna say. I don't know if he's gonna be in her life by then. If not, I'm just gonna tell her that he loved her. I don't know why he didn't stay in her life like he should have. I know it's gonna be really important to her.

I haven't even had a relationship with anybody since me and James broke up. I can't deal with a relationship right now. I want a break from them big time. It's just me and my daughter right now. I'm not saying I don't like guys or anything, 'cause I want to get married still. But now when I choose a boyfriend, I have to think about how he's gonna be with her. Since I've become a mother, I feel like I just need to take a break from guys. James really put me through a lot. I just want to spend time with my daughter.

I'm not attracted to the same kinda guy any more. They just seem really immature and they just don't know what's going on. They're just more into partying and getting in trouble. Most of 'em don't even have a job or money or anything like that.

I've been working at Domino's part-time for almost a year. I make pizzas and answer phones. I'm a junior in high school. I'm in the first year of cosmetology, learning how to do nails and hair and makeup. I want to get a job at a good salon and move out of my parents' house. I don't want to have to live from paycheck to paycheck. I want to be able to buy her things that she wants, she needs. I don't want to have to be broke all the time. And I want to find somebody that's good for the both of us — not just me and not just her.

Now she's number one in my life. I just have responsibility twenty-four–seven. It doesn't go away for the rest of my life. I know that I've changed a lot. People just see the mother in me now. I'm not into partying and all that. I don't hang out with my friends as much, I'm home more. I have like four really close friends. Two of them have babies themselves, so they know how I feel.

I thought my parents, the way they raised me, was really good. The only thing I would change is maybe being able to be more open. I want her to be able to tell me everything and anything. I want to be able to talk to my daughter. I'm gonna tell her what happened with me and most everybody else I know.

It's kinda like she was a blessing 'cause there's no telling where I'd be now. I was getting kinda rebellious until I got pregnant. Before that, I did what I wanted to do. I talked back more to my parents, and I didn't respect them as much as I do now. Me and my mom get along a lot better now 'cause she didn't like James. A lot of our fights were about him. Spending too much time with him. She figured out some of the times that I had spent the night over there. But now I know she was just lookin' out for me. That's what a mother does. I know the feeling now.

TAMEIKA, FIFTEEN
SUMTER, SOUTH CAROLINA

Tameika at home with her mom. Tameika rolls her eyes and shakes her head, exasperated, behind her mom's back, as her mom speaks, softly, dead serious.

Mom: We talk about anything. She talks about her little boyfriends. I tell her there is no such thing as boyfriends. Just associates, who she talks to. Just an associate. We talk about sex. Sometimes I get nerv-

ous talking about it. I try to answer her the best I can. I was brought up, I didn't have nobody to talk to. We wasn't told nothing.

Her getting pregnant, that's my main concern. I talk to her and I trust her. But kids, you trust 'em and they go out there and . . . peer pressure, that's my main concern. But it's gonna happen, it's gonna happen.

I was a teenage mother, eighteen, not married. I don't want her . . . that's why I try to talk to her and tell her, at her age, a baby, that's her life . . . her life is finished if she go out there and . . . that's the end of it. All your privilege, your freedom, is out the window. She got to find out for herself, but I don't want her to go through that pain. If I had to do it again, phew! I wouldn't want to make the same mistake. Nope.

Tameika alone.

My cousin, she was trying for a cheerleading scholarship and she almost got it. But she got pregnant and she had to get off the squad. That kinda threw her off. She was upset about that. But that's what I'm trying for, a cheerleading scholarship. Keep my grades up, hopefully get it.

People think cheerleaders are just cute little girls in short skirts. They're Miss Popularity, Miss Prissy, and they have lots of friends. But that's not really what it is. They don't see the real picture. They don't see how hard we work to be as good as we can be. You have to have a lot of strength and durability to do the stunts. It's not about being cute. It's about doing what you like to do, and working at it. I'm driving for a cheerleading scholarship, hopefully.

We just had a big state competition. I looked through the newspaper, but they didn't write about it. I don't think girls get enough attention in sports. People think cheerleaders don't do anything. They don't think we're athletes. Cheerleading is basically an all-girl sport. Basketball, football, those are basically boys' sports. They get attention. People don't think girls can do the same things boys can do. They think boys are more important. Boys are better.

We had a game two weeks ago and we lost. But that was the first time after a game that the football players said, "Good cheering, you all did a good job. You looked very pretty out there. You supported us and we thank you for that." We smile. Even though we're losing, we smile. We smile through it all. It helps support them, makes them think they're doing good.

The girls on the squad, we call each other sisters. If you have a problem, you can come to one of your sisters. We'll never turn our backs on you. We call each other, "What are you doing this weekend? We can go out, we can go eat pizza." It's like they're like real sisters. I call you tonight, we talk on the phone for a while, you just talk about a lot of things, you talk about boyfriends and stuff.

Cheerleading, squad practice, competition camp, you're with your squad more than you are your friends. I think they're closer to me than my other friends. They understand me more, they know me better. I can talk to them about anything. I talk to them about their boyfriends or their break-up. You lean on my shoulder, I'm gonna cry with you. That's why we call each other sisters. We can depend on each other. They gonna help lift you up and you uplift each other.

When I was a little girl, I think I was like a silly little girl who had high expectations of everyone else. I had these thoughts in my head. I was a dreamy little girl. You get older, you get people who don't support you, those dreams kinda go down. I was a bad little girl. I was bad. As a little girl, I was kinda like a dreamy little girl with high expectations, you know.

In fifth grade, the teacher sent all the boys out of the classroom. They were looking in, saying, "What are they doin' in there?" The teacher says, "I'm gonna talk to you about periods." We were like, "First period, second period?" She said, "Menstrual cycle," and we acted like we knew what she meant. Then she started explaining it, and when she said, "blood" we just freaked out! Like, "Eewwww, this is sickening!" And then I thought about it, and I thought, "This is kind of neat, I'm gonna be a woman! Can't wait to be a woman!" Older, you know? I don't feel that way any more!

Cramps, I can't stand it, I just have this hate towards it, it's like, "Do something, surgery, take it out! Give it to someone else, they want it, they can have it." I'm in a little circle on the bed, just laying there, trying to make it go away. When I got my little training bra, I thought I was the bomb. I was like, "Yeah, I'm a woman now, I'm a woman now," you know? I was excited about a lot of things I didn't understand. Now I'm just like, go away, leave me alone.

I live with my mom now. My mom and dad separated a year ago.

When your mom and dad fusses a lot, it's like, in your head "Stop!!" Then if they separate or divorce, you're like, "I didn't want this to happen, I just wanted them to stop fussing." When you go to court to get a divorce, they try to put you in the middle of it. "OK, who do you want to stay with?" Then it's like, when Dad calls, what should I say? What should I do? He's like a stranger. You're a stranger. I let my dad pick me up from one of my games. I don't even know who he is any more. He's a total stranger.

As a little girl I had high expectations, as far as family goes. I thought my dad would always be there. I was Daddy's little girl. I was the spoiled little brat who got everything. It seemed like all that started drifting away as I got older.

I started seeing that they weren't getting along as much as I thought they were. I was like, they don't look as happy as they used to be. They was always fussing and fighting. I tried to be asleep and I hear a fuss and think, "They're not fussing, they're not fussing, it must be in my dreams." I put my pillow over my head and I won't listen to anything. OK, I wake up the next day and everything is quiet, OK, everything is back to normal.

Maybe the week after that I hear them fussing, maybe in the morning. I'm going to school, I don't want to go to school, 'cause all I'm gonna do is think about them and I might cry. That's when my grades started dropping, because I'm thinking about my family instead of schoolwork. I was like, I don't know what's wrong.

Then one day they had a big argument and ever since then, I have this sort of hate towards my Dad. I don't want to say hate, but like, dislike, you know?

I tried to go on with everything. My grades, they were improving. I was doing good and then they separated, and then I like dropped. I just had to think to myself and I prayed that something would lift my spirits and I'll get better. My grades started improving, and I was like, "OK, OK, I'm doing good. I'm doing good. I put it behind me."

Ever since then I'm trying to put it behind me, put all the good excuses, why he didn't come over on the weekend. All the little excuses, why he didn't call, try to put them behind me and worry just about the big stuff.

Daddy's not all that I thought he was. Everyone else saw it. But I was just a dreamy Daddy's little girl who always got her way. Now I see other people's point of view, who tried to tell me for so long, "Well, don't depend on your dad."

I was Daddy's little girl, so I got everything from Daddy. When they separated, me and my mom got in an argument, "You can't have this right now, 'cause I don't have the money to get it for you."

So I called Daddy, thinkin', "Daddy will get it for me." But you see the thing is, I called Daddy and Daddy didn't call me back. So I'm calling Dad and Dad doesn't call me. I thought about it for a week. I was like, "What's going on? Daddy's not calling me, I never talk to him."

Then I want to go somewhere. "No, you can't go." "Well, Daddy would let me go if he was here, I want to go stay with Daddy." That kinda threw me and my mom's relationship off. I didn't like that so I kept trying to pull it back together. But it's like every time I want to do something, she tells me that I can't. I don't like being told no. I was a little spoiled brat, and Daddy always told me yeah.

So I called Daddy. I was thinking, "I want to go here, I want to go there, he'll take me." But again I called Daddy and Daddy didn't call me back. It was kinda weird.

I've just learned. I'm not gonna call Daddy until Daddy calls me. If Daddy doesn't call me, then we just won't talk. I'll just have to do without, won't go anywhere, so...I've kinda learned to accept that.

He used to always come to my cheerleading games. This year, Daddy wasn't at any of my games. I got upset on the way home and Mom kept asking me, "What's wrong?" I finally told her, "Daddy wasn't there, it's just not the same, I'm not happy cheering without seeing Daddy there." But I'll get over it. I thought maybe I'll get over it.

Sometimes I don't smile. We'll be cheering at a game and I think, "Daddy should have been out there, Daddy's not out there." They all say, "Meeka, why aren't you smiling?" I put on my little smile, "I'm happy now, see?" And they think that's a smile. I put on the smile that they want to see. It's not really a smile. Inside I'm like, it's hurting me, inside, it's killing me. Daddy's not up there, that's Daddy's spot. Daddy is gonna sit right there and wave to me and tell me everything's OK. But he's not there.

I don't have anyone to talk to. The house is all quiet. Mom's at work, brother's gone. I'm sitting there thinking and I start thinking about

Daddy. I start crying. I can't have him any more, and I get mad when I can't have what I used to have.

Then you fuss with Mom and that throws the relationship off and you try to put it back together and you fuss again over something stupid, but it's all because of Daddy.

I think it's gonna be a long, long time, but eventually, hopefully, I'll get over it.

I want him to come to my competition, but I couldn't get in touch with him 'cause he wasn't home over the weekend. He didn't let me know that he was leaving. I called him like a million times. No one answered the phone. So I was like…OK…I see…OK.

Every time it gets real quiet and I sit there and think, he's the first person that comes to my mind. I try and think…over him, just try to think about other stuff. Like, "OK, game next week, competition next year." But it all comes back to him. Is he gonna come to the game? Is he gonna be there next year?

I want him to be in my life, but he's pushing me away. I try to pull him towards me and he just keeps pushing me away.

It's hard, just smiling through it all, and he's driving me home and I'm sitting in the car and he asks me, "How's school?" and it's like… it's just school, you know? We have nothing to talk about, it's just quiet. I don't think he really cares, it's just something to make conversation. I'm just sitting there smiling, putting on my little fake smile.

I'm not Daddy's little girl any more. Daddy doesn't tell me he loves me any more. Daddy doesn't see if I want to go and get something to eat, go and get ice cream. We used to go to the zoo a lot. Daddy doesn't want to go to the zoo. We always went shopping. Daddy doesn't want to take me shopping. I just try to put on the biggest smile through it all and then it's like I can't smile any more, I can't take it any more, it's killing me inside, and I get real sensitive and I cry all the time.

But I was trying to get over it. I started praying before I went to sleep, and hopefully that's helping me, hopefully that's helping with my spirits. I try not to bring my troubles to school with me and I try to wait until I get home, but it's kinda hard. I can't take that pressure worrying about them and then school and then practice and then come home.

And then I'm like, "OK, well maybe I should stop cheerleading."

And then I'm like, "Oh my gosh, are you crazy? You know what cheer-leading means to you?"

I'm not gonna stop cheerleading for him, because he wants to do something stupid, he wants to go be with somebody else or another family, and then it's Christmas coming up. I'm supposed to get every-thing for Christmas and now he's buying someone else everything for Christmas and not me? It just tears me apart.

I try not to let that bring me down. I can never have down days at school. 'Cause I don't want them to see, "She's unhappy, she's not happy." Then everyone will start asking you questions, and it's like, well, I don't want to talk about it.

Mom against Dad, Brother against Dad, Mom's side of the family against Dad's side of the family. Dad not communicating with me or Mom, not caring about Mom, doesn't think about her. I'm in the mid-dle. Me and Mom, we just gonna live in our own little world and Dad just somewhere else in his own little world.

It's a weird feeling inside. You messed up, you don't know what to do, you don't know whose side to be on. Me and my mom always fight because of Dad. You love Dad so much that you don't want to see her hate him.

You don't want to tell him how you really feel. I think I'm kinda scared of my Dad.

Next time he calls I'm gonna hang up on him 'cause he hasn't called in two weeks, and I'm gonna hang up when he calls. I should be mad that he didn't call me. I should say, "You hurt my feelings, you need to start doing what you say you gonna do and stop breaking promises." But I can't seem to do that. I'm always just so happy to talk to him. It's just that reaction that I have to Daddy. I tell myself I shouldn't be that way. It's hard to be myself and hard to do what I'm telling myself to do inside, instead of being Daddy's little girl. I'm a big girl and I'm still Daddy's little girl, but I'm not Daddy's little girl no more. It's tearing me up. I'm trying to get over it.

I don't want to see my mom and dad get back together, 'cause I know that they're not gonna get along. In my head they might get along, 'cause it's through my eyes, through a child's eyes. But I don't think they gonna get along. If they split up, that's OK with me. As long as Daddy still comes and sees his little girl. As long as Daddy's celebrating birthdays, Christmas, Thanksgiving. To me, I just want all of that to be the same. Daddy can be with his little family. Dad, just like come over every now and then and see how I'm doing, ask me if I want anything, take me places. I don't want to be like one of those girls who live in California somewhere and don't know where her daddy is, hasn't been in touch with her dad for years.

I think he's neglecting me. He seems to, like, try to, well, not forget about me...I don't really know what he thinks. He's just pushing me far, far away. I think he thinks, "She's staying with her mom, let her be with her mom, I don't have to do for her any more," and that's not true.

You don't feel loved by that parent. And the other parent, you two don't get along. You have no one to love you and if Mom loves you, you don't feel that, 'cause you always arguing. So you have your boyfriend, you turn to your boyfriend. You got to talk to somebody. I talk to my boyfriend. He listens and everything. If my dad pushes me away, my boyfriend kinda brings me close. He says, "It's gonna be all right," and he talks to me about it.

I turn to him for a lot of love and support. Cheerleading, he supports me a lot. I tell him my problems and he tells me his in turn. It's like, "OK, I'll be by your side. For Christmas, what do you want? If your dad won't give you this, I'll try and get it for you." He's like trying to be my dad. I sometimes call him Daddy. "If your dad doesn't want to love you, then I'll love you. I'll tuck you in. I'll call you before you go to sleep, make sure you're safe in bed."

I have been with him for like six months, and that's a long time in a relationship with one person. You're really serious about the relationship.

If I do have sex with him, it will be safe sex. I think I could get pregnant, but I hope not. I don't want to get pregnant. That would hurt my mom a lot. Me and her have talked about it. Hopefully it won't happen to me. I don't think I'm able to support a child right now. I'm trying to graduate so I can go to college. I think if you have a child, that child will bring you down. You can't be a teen any more. You have to be a mom. Like, cheerleading is out. You can't go to practice, you got to go home and take care of your baby. Mom's not gonna take care of the baby all the time, Mom's gonna get tired of it. Boyfriend might leave you. Boyfriend might not be there like he was. I think about those things and I'm like, no. I don't think I'm ready for a child.

Tameika's mother.

She has two cousins who are in college, real smart. She always talks about how she wants to follow in their footsteps. We start talking and she start bringing up boys and sex and that makes me wonder, you know. I remind her, I say, "What about your dreams? And all you want to do?" I tell her these things. I keep a check on her, make sure she don't stray from that. That's what I want for her, too, that she go to college.

But me, a single parent...people, they want to see something bad happen to her. I tell her, I say, "They looking to see us fail, 'cause it's just me and you. We can't let that happen."

Kids always want, they always gotta have. She knows that it's hard, me working. I help all I can and she helps me. We keep each other going. She found out what I can handle and what I can't, so she try not to put too much on me. She helps me out a lot around the house. We do things together. Every time I go somewhere I ask, "You want to ride?" She comes along so I won't be by myself.

The boys now, they're so...fresh! I don't believe in a whole lot of touchin'. I tell her when you let 'em touch you, that giving them permission. If you tell them to take their hands off you, they'll have respect for you. But if you let 'em hang all over you, that's not showing no respect. I took her to the movies with her little friend. I told the guy, "Hey, don't worry about it, ain't no bootie call here, so don't think about it." I like him, he's a nice guy. But he gotta stay in his place.

If her dad was here, it'd be a different story. He won't let her have none of that. He said he'd pick a boyfriend for her, and she wouldn't have one 'til she's thirty.

She knows that if she let me down, it gonna hurt me somethin' fierce, she knows this. I'm countin' on her just to, don't let that happen.

MADELINE, TWELVE
BOSTON, MASSACHUSETTS

I live with just my mother and my brother. My mother is from Guatemala. She can't really talk English. So I have to speak Spanish to her a lot. I was born here but ever since I was little...my mom, she couldn't speak English. Even though she went to English school, she still couldn't speak English. She can't really understand anyone talking it. So I grew up speaking both languages.

I went to Guatemala last November with my mother. It's different! She told me that when she was little, when she was growing up, she was like poor. Guatemala's a poor country. She didn't have that many...like stuff. They couldn't buy new sneakers until they were really worn out and stuff. I think she's been living here for maybe twenty years. I don't know. She works, she's a nutrition assistant. She works every day and on the weekends she cleans houses.

I come to the Boys and Girls Club almost every day after school. I go home, I eat, I rest a while, then I come here. That's what I do every day. It's, like, to keep kids out of the streets. You can do your home-work here. They have different activities. Swim team, basketball teams. You can play in the gym and you can play on the computers. I'm always home alone and I'm bored 'cause my mother's never home and my brother's never home. So I come here.

My brother came here for a while, but then I guess he grew out of it, 'cause he doesn't wanna come here any more.

When I first joined, I couldn't double dutch at all. I couldn't. I could not jump in right. The rope would go down and I'd jump in, and it just messes up the whole thing. I would just step on the rope. Then I got into the ropes, but I would just mess up once I got in. It was frus-trating at first. You have to practice a lot. You have to get used to jumping into the ropes and staying in there. Just jumping with two ropes, you have to get used to it. The more used to it you get, the bet-ter you get. My coach, she worked hard. She made sure that we did everything right. Like when the rope goes up, we jump in, and we just go one–two–one–two–one–two. We just go with the rhythm of the ropes. I went to every practice. Later on I got good at it.

At the competition, first you do compulsory. That means she has thirty seconds to do certain tricks. She has to turn around twice, jump on one foot eight times, going around in circles. Then she has to crisscross her legs two times, and do high steps twenty times. We also do freestyle. We each have our own tricks to do. Stephanie turns around so she's hold-ing the ropes backward as they're swinging. Then I jump in and she turns around. Then I have to do a 360 and I have to clap under my legs and touch the floor. I have to jump out and the next person does their tricks.

At the competition, I was surprised 'cause the other team, they were like mad good. They were really good at it. They could do a lot, they could really do it good. But me and my team, we were like bad, we couldn't get it together. At the tournament we were really nervous, 'cause we thought we were gonna mess up a lot. But we just went out there and had fun. At the end, we won first place. All the girls got a little trophy. It's like an angel.

My mom went to the competition last year. She was real excited. She told everybody. I didn't mind. I don't really mind my mother being around me and my friends. It was my idea for her to come.

I would tell other girls, double dutch is real fun. You don't have to worry about messing up, 'cause the more you do it, the more you get used to it. Once you jump in the ropes, you don't want to get out. It's just the fact that I'm good at it... I'm kinda good at it. It's just like fun, jumping in the ropes, jumping in and out of them. And it's fun practicing doing tricks. Last year girls did back flips into the ropes. "Can we try, coach?" "Next year," she said, "OK."

I'm planning to go to college. I wanna go. I'm good at... I don't know. I don't know what I'm good at. Probably — science? I think, maybe? I don't know. We don't really take that many tests. So I can't really tell if I'm good at it or not. I like... I used to like gym and health, but we don't have that any more. I like theater arts. That's fun.

I don't think my brother wants to go to college. He doesn't talk about it. He doesn't even talk about school. He just... talks about everything else besides school.

My brother is older. He's sixteen. We get along pretty well, but he's kind of conceited. 'Cause he has like a moustache and a beard and everything. And every time somebody says, "You look good," he'll be like... I don't know, he's real conceited. And... he's bad, though. I don't want to say it, but he's bad. He likes to skip school. He got arrested once. He's on probation. All this stuff. I can't really consider him my role model. I wouldn't want to be like him, but in some ways I would, 'cause he's really nice. My brother, he's cute. Very popular and nice to people. I look up to him because if he's around adults he's like real nice. "How's everything, how's your family?" real polite. I think that's what people see in him. I see that in him, too, but damn, I don't know.

He has girlfriends. That's the only people who call him. Girls. That's it. Every time the phone rings, it's always for him. Jackie, Sara, Elizabeth, Yajida. His girlfriend right now is Sara. She's real nice. Sometimes I hang

out with her. But not a lot. He likes to go out, my brother. He has a job. He's at work right now. But he likes to be outside a lot.

He has bad influences. He hangs out with a lot of boys that are real bad. He hangs out with this boy Jafiz. That...um...he got ganged up. This boy...Jafiz, he was walking down the street. And this gang called the Crips, they all ganged up on him, and they were planning to kill him. They hit him with a hammer in the head. And they cut him. They cut his face and everything. He was like very badly hurt, and he had to be in the hospital for three days. He lives in my upstairs building. He's like my neighbor, upstairs. And my brother, he tries to be like him. He told me — my brother — he told me today that the Crips were...they were chasing him. But my brother got away.

My brother...my brother's in a gang. He's in the, um, Young Bloods. When he got arrested, my mother, she found out that. And he was wearing always red. So she went out and she bought him new clothes, she bought him all green. She bought him a green coat. They stole it. So. But...I don't know. He still hangs out with them.

My brother is not scared. He's not scared of anybody. I know that's kind of stupid. I don't really like his friends. I don't want my brother hanging out with them. But I can't do anything. My brother's not gonna listen to me. I tell him, "Don't do that." He's like, "OK, I won't do it." And then the next thing you know, he's in trouble again. My mother talks to him. My brother just gets tired of listening to my mother. She can't really do anything about it.

The girls...well, they're with the boys a lot. They're like always wearing red. The girls are just with the boys constantly. They skip school. They sell stuff...they're bad.

I don't think I'm gonna be like that. Well, my mom thinks I'm not, right? But I can't really tell if I'm gonna be like that. I hope that I won't be like that. But I don't know. I think it's pretty stupid first of all, 'cause the girls think they're so tough. 'Specially like fifteen, sixteen, they think they're like real hard, and they think that nothing's gonna happen to them.

A lot of boys bother me, they hit me and stuff, and I'm like, "Just leave me alone because I don't like you!" I just hit them and they get away from me. I just get real mad, and say, "Leave me alone, I don't feel like messing with you!" If a boy comes near me, I just hit him. I'll just be like, "Get away from me!"

If my brother would listen to me, I would be like, "Can you please wake up?" I'd say to him, "You know what you're doing is wrong." And he'd be like, "Yeah, I know." He tells me that he does stupid things. I'm like, "Then," I would tell him, "Then why do you do them?" He thinks he's a man. But to me, he's not a man. He's not a man until he knows what he's doing. But he thinks he's real big.

I think my brother wants to get out of the gang. But he doesn't want to, at the same time he does, for some reason. When he started being in the gang and they jumped him in — they beat him up, they jumped him. And then he is considered a member. And to get out they have to jump him again. He said . . . he told me once that he doesn't want to get out. But then again sometimes he does. I don't know.

If I had my way, well, my brother would be good. He could go wild and stuff, like he has his times. He would have his times that he could be bad, but not this bad, like he is now. And my mother . . . she would be like . . . she really can't control my brother. She would be able to tell him, "That's bad!" And my brother would be, like, "OK." She would work hard, she would like keep everything together, she would keep us three together. And I would be just as I am right now.

Sometimes I feel like I want to grow up. When my mother says no to me, in little things, I'm like, "I wish I was older 'cause then she might have said yes." Me and my mom, like we're real close, but sometimes she gets on my nerves. She's always worrying about me. She's says I'm smart and I make good decisions, but sometimes I feel that she doesn't let me do that. I think that she doesn't trust me. Well, she does but . . . if I wanna go out with my friends, like just to walk around, she'll say, *no!* I don't know why.

My mother thinks I'm real perfect. I try to tell her, "Just because I do good in school doesn't mean you have to treat me like an angel. 'Cause I'm not everything that you think I am." She's not with me twenty-four hours. I have my problems. She's always telling my cousins, my brother, why can't they be more like me? And that makes me feel bad, 'cause she thinks that I'm real perfect, and I'm like . . . I'm not. She makes me feel so uncomfortable when she says that. It just makes me feel too *good*. And I don't want to be like that. It's like . . . I'm not everything that you think I am.

JANICE AND REGINA, BOTH SIXTEEN
NEW YORK, NEW YORK

Janice: I was thirteen, playin' double dutch, having fun outside, at a party, dancing, weekends with my friends. It's a new life, I'm into junior high, it's a whole new world. It's bigger now and you got more privileges than when you was like eleven and ten. You want to explore this. I was out there being a tomboy, having fun, it was the life. I was thinking about my friends, all the freedom I had, trying to get all my fun in between curfew hours.

Regina: When I was thirteen, me and my friends were like, "What you gonna eat for lunch? Is my mother gonna let me hang out after school?" I was playin' volleyball every day. There was a girl at my school, she was in the seventh grade and had a baby. She was the talk of the school. Me, I was like, "Please, I don't want no kids." My mother, she strict. My mother would have broke my neck if I came home and told her I was pregnant.

Janice: I was fifteen when I first had sex. It hurt. I wanted to do it. I felt, I love this person. I felt like it was the right move. But I regretted it a whole lot. He took my virginity. We didn't stay together. I'm not gonna be a virgin no more, you know. I was personally feeling sad about it. You s'pose to hold that, that's a special moment in your life. You supposed to save it for somebody that you really care about. It was foolish for me to have sex at fifteen. If I would have waited a while, things would have been different. I'm not proud that I was fifteen having sex. Being a virgin is special. Having sex with someone you love is supposed to be special. Not just 'cause you found this person that's actually willing to have sex with you. That's not right.

They take your virginity, and this person say, "I love you, I love you," and do all that little pillow talk, whatever. Then once that's gone, he's gone, too. It's a divide and conquer thing. He got it, he conquered it, he left his flag, now he left. That's it. He's not coming back.

Some boys say they want virgins so they could break them in. That's not right, either. You're not supposed to take a girl's virginity and run. You supposed to take it slow and don't rush into it. My first time, it hurt. He rushed! I was like, I gave it up for this—a measly five minutes, come on. No, that's not right. Five minutes, instead of a whole lifetime I could have been waiting, sharing with somebody in the Bahamas somewhere. No, I'm stuck here in your one bedroom apartment, for five minutes, when I could've had it somewhere else? No, that's not right. Then you see the person, and you be like, "Just get out my face." When you see him, you be like, "Five minutes, um hmmm." You always look at your watch when you see him, "You that five-minute brother. No, don't talk to me no more."

Regina: You naïve. You naïve. I was fifteen when I lost my virginity, too. My best friend was having sex. She told me one day in gym class. My boyfriend was asking me, and I keep on making up excuses. Then one day I was like, all right.

When you lose your virginity, you think that person love you, you gonna be married, you think you gonna have kids, you want to spend your life with this person. I could picture all of the kids. But when he broke my virginity, he had a girl already that was pregnant. I didn't find this out 'til after he already done took it. I was so ashamed. I was embarrassed and I was hurt. I had nothing to show for it. I sure did learn my lesson.

Janice: The hard way, but we learned it.

Regina: If you a virgin and if your boyfriend tell you he loves you . . . if he loves you, he'll wait for you. Until you more certain.

Janice: It's not like you can go in they pocket and be like, give me that back! You can't! It's gone! Once it's gone, it's gone. You could kiss that bye-bye.

Regina: He consider you used goods, especially these boys around here, in Harlem.

Janice: Anywhere. They ask you, you a virgin? You say no — bye bye. You used goods.

Regina: I was fifteen when I found out I was pregnant. That was the prime of my life, me and my friends, get up, go out. I was neglecting school. We was just going out, hangin' out, being with our friends, just chillin', doing what teenagers do best, just hangin' out, front of buildings, just talk about everybody, making fun of people, that's how we was.

I got real sick, I got real sharp pains through my stomach. And

I was praying for chocolate, chocolate cake, chocolate doughnuts, everything chocolate.

My friend kept telling me, you pregnant. I was acting like a real bitch (if you don't mind me saying). I had a real bad attitude. I was, "No, I'm not pregnant! Me, of all people, no." I didn't like children. I can't stand bad kids. I couldn't be having a baby. When the lady called my name and I came in the office, she was like, "Your test came back positive." I got dizzy. I had to sit down. I almost fainted.

Janice: I didn't think I was pregnant. I thought my period cycle was changing, to be honest. I was like, "I can't be pregnant, it's just changing, it's just changing, that's it, Janice, calm down." The day after I turned sixteen, I got my first sonogram. That's when I realized I was four months pregnant. I was sorta like shocked. There is no way possible that this happened to me.

During my pregnancy I was like — oh gross, having somebody living inside you, actually taking over your body. They took you captive now, everything you want is no longer for you. Like, if you hungry, you not feeding for your stomach. You gonna eat and it goes straight to your baby. It feels like it just skips your stomach. You still feel hungry.

The first time she moved, I was like, "That felt nasty! Oh, gosh, somebody actually kickin' inside me!" My boyfriend saw her move and he's like, "Oh, gross." Then after a while we got used to it and it became fun being pregnant. She'd wake up in the morning and that's your alarm clock, right there, when a baby wants you up, you up. Even if you want that extra sleep, if a baby's hungry, it's gonna let you know. It's gonna kick and turn, kick on your ribs. You gotta get up, you gotta obey that baby's every wish, even though it's not here yet to demand it. But you gotta do it.

When I was pregnant, I stayed in the house, I did not go outside. I was on my bed watching my friends from the window outside playing spades on the car. I used to call my boyfriend out the window and tell him bring me some Oreos or something upstairs. I thought, it's not right for me to be out on the street with this big ol' belly. I even started crocheting. I was in the house making hats. I turned into a little old lady. I'm just sittin' there watching TV, eating cookies, making things in the house.

Regina: When I started showin', I stayed in the house. I did not come outside until my doctor's appointments. I look out the window. My mother look at me. She was like, "My poor baby." She never put me down. She never said, "Don't you wish you was like them girls out there?" She never said that.

Janice: The hardest part of my pregnancy was gainin' weight. I hated that. When I got pregnant, I was 96 pounds. When I gave birth, I was 180. I almost doubled my weight. Every time I went to the doctor, I was like oh, 115 now, oh you 125 now. Constantly going up, and I was like, "Oh, no! I'm getting fat! This is embarrassing! I'm not gonna be a size two no more! Oh, gosh, this is horrible!" All through the winter I looked like a little penguin, walkin' through the snow.

When you see your baby, you hold her for the first time, that is the happiest moment in your life. You just looking at this little person that depends on you, and they so quiet and so small and they just look at you like there's no worries in the world. Even though you know there's worries. I cried for like two days after I brought my daughter home. I was thinking maybe this was gonna 'cause problems between me and my boyfriend. I cried, I hope we not gonna break up over this. Once you get your feet on the ground and reality hit you — you got them five o'clock feedings, and you got to be up —

Regina: Five o'clock?!!!!

Janice: — your breasts is leaking every time your baby cry, you be like, this is really startin' to irritate me.

Regina: Five o'clock, what you talking about five o'clock, my son was getting up two ... four ... sometime he wake up on the hour. I did not get no sleep. You was lucky you got 'til five o'clock in the morning!

I think about before my son was born, how I used to go out. I wouldn't have to worry about, "Does my son have enough Pampers, enough milk?" Before him, I could go out and I don't have to worry about nothin'. You got a baby now. If you young, don't have no baby now, enjoy your teen years.

If a boy says he love you, well, he could wait. If y'all is sexually active, use protection, use any kinda method — use it. There's a lot of stuff I wanna do and I can't, 'cause my son comes first.

Janice: Yeah, it's no longer just you. It's you and your responsibility. If you want something, "Oh, that's nice, I want to buy that for myself," you gotta stop and think twice. "Well, my daughter needs Pampers, she needs new clothes." Babies grow, and that's gonna be money, all the time. And money for laundry, every time you turn around, you got laundry. No matter how many times you go the laundromat, you was at the laundromat yesterday, you will be there two more days doing laundry, dirty clothes, back to back. You can't sit outside with your friends, or go out to the movies, 'cause not everybody is gonna want to babysit for you. You gonna have to think, "I don't really want to go the movies with my baby, my baby gonna make noise through the movie." These are things you gotta think about, these are consequences that comes with being a parent.

Regina: You not as free as you used to be. It's real hard struggling with a baby. The only place I go is his father's house. I don't hang out like I used to. I go to work. My mother keeps my son. I go to school. I'm making sure I'm not one of the statistics out there. You hear a teenage mother is on welfare, do not go to school, just sit there, dependent on the system. I do not want that at all. I want to make a better life for me and my son. I want him to grow up in a better neighborhood than I did. We raising each other. I'm still growing myself, I'm still a teenager. I'm still learning things as I go. I'm learning new things about him every day.

Janice: Exactly. I regret, I don't totally regret, but if I could do it, I'd go back. I look at her and see her go, "Mama!" and that makes me feel good, just to have somebody greet you at the door, forever laughing. You know that person love you. This is somebody that actually love you. But it's still hard. I wanted to travel the world. I always said, "I'm going to Egypt, I'm going to Spain." The closest I get to Egypt is on a map. I'm not getting there no time soon.

Regina: Girls have babies 'cause some of them feel like they need love. That's not it.

Janice: A baby don't know what love is anyway. All a baby knows is that you're the mother, you're supposed to take care of them, you're the person that feeds them, you're the person that changes them, you're the person that they see. They don't know what love is exactly. So that's no way to get love, understand? If you want love, get a puppy! Don't have a baby. And giving birth and labor and all that, that's hard, that's painful, I won't wish that on my worst enemy. That's no way to find love. If you want to find love through pain, get a tattoo or somethin', don't have a baby!

Regina: I'm not saying having a baby is all bad, 'cause it's not. My son smile at me, I love to see him smile. But if you ain't no mother, and you just want to have a baby 'cause your boyfriend says he loves you, so he tells you to prove it back to him by getting pregnant? Some men sticks with you and some men don't, and some men tells you lies. It makes you feel real bad that at one time this man tells you he loves you, then as soon as you get pregnant, things start changin'. It hurts.

Janice: If you pregnant and you home thinking about your boyfriend out there with the next girl, that's only breakin' your heart. 'Cause you know he out there cheatin' on you. You didn't make this baby by yourself and this boy's gonna tell you, "This ain't my baby," or, "Prove it." That make you feel bad. That make you feel worthless. Like, "He tell me he love me couple of months back. Now that I'm pregnant, all of a sudden he go try and tell me this is not his baby. That's not right."

Girls tend to wait and depend on a boyfriend. But if you know your boyfriend, when you met him, he was hangin' outside with his friends. What make you think that gonna change? If he can't hold a stable job, why do you think he's gonna hold one because of a baby? Understand, if he's used to his everyday ways, outside with his friends, drinking, get high, a baby's not gonna make him change. It's only gonna make you, the woman, change, 'cause you're a mother.

Regina: I get frustrated. I love my son to death. But if there was a chance, if somebody was to come, and say we could bring you back to before you had your son, I would go back. 'Cause right now, until I get a job, I'm dependent on my mother. I'm living in her house, I'm eating her food, I'm sleeping in her bed. If she want to get angry and decide to kick me out, she could do that, 'cause that's her house. I wish I could have waited, 'cause there are so many things I still want to do. I want to go out on Fridays, Saturdays. I can't do

that. I gotta take my son with me. You should wait. If a girl out there thinking about havin' a baby, wait. Please don't do it, 'cause once you have that baby, you gonna wish you would have waited, and wish gonna be too late then, 'cause you is not goin' back in time. I'm tellin' you, girls, it's *hard*.

 PASSION

Passion is suffering, and Sanne and Stephanie break and bleed for what they love most dearly. They're synchronized swimmers, expert in a sport that is a perfect model for girls' adolescence. They present a smiling, graceful face above water. Their surface is smooth, serene, sparkling with rhinestones and beads of silver water. Beneath the blue, where no one can see, they are kicking like crazy. To support their perfect posture they struggle secretly, madly, and with all their might.

SANNE AND STEPHANIE, BOTH SIXTEEN
CLAYTON, CALIFORNIA

Sanne alone.

Synchronized swimming is definitely harder than it looks. The better you are, the more smooth you are, the more graceful you are. Your breathing doesn't get so hard and labored. That's stuff that you learn. It's part of the training. Your coaches tell you, "Don't breathe so loud, don't gasp like that," or "That arm movement's too jerky." That's something you learn. When you see the younger girls swim, it looks as hard above the water as it does under the water. That's something that you learn. It's still there, though, when you're older. You still struggle, trying to keep yourself looking graceful.

Compare it to something that people can understand, like gymnastics or ice skating. People realize that there's a lot of pressure in those sports. That's what synchro is like. I train twenty-five hours a week, I've been doing it since I was six years old, I travel all over the country. It's really hard to explain to someone who has never seen synchro — what it is. I mean, I don't know how to explain it. There's a lot of ridicule about it. I'm always careful not to criticize other sports, 'cause I've been on the other end.

Sanne and her former duet partner, Stephanie.
Sanne: We worked really well together, because we have a lot of the same work ethic. The way we worked, and the way we set goals, was so similar that we worked really well together. We wanted to work.

She would count and I would sing to the music. She would teach me how to count and I would teach her to listen to the notes in the music. She was really good right side up and I was better upside down. We just complimented each other really well. We had been friends for a long time before we swam together as a duet, so I guess we understood each other. I know what she looks like when she's nervous. She talks! Before a meet, we'd be ready to swim and she'll be talking about — I don't know, something totally unrelated to the meet — where I just sit and stare at the wall —

Stephanie: In her own world! I think we helped each other *and* we made each other worse. I think we helped each other more. We had worked with a sports psychologist to set up a program, because Sanne likes to be organized. She likes to have an agenda. So we would do breathing exercises together, and arm movements together, with our eyes shut — even swimming synchronized when we were warming up, just freestyle — to create the idea of being one and being a duet. If I talked to her before we swam, it would make her crazy. So I always talked to our coach instead. Sanne would be off in her own world. I knew when to leave her alone.

Sanne: Mostly I was just visualizing the routine over and over again. At a national meet, you swim each routine twice, in preliminaries and then in finals. I would always be going over the mistakes that I had made in the first swim, so I wouldn't make them again. That's usually what I was doing. But, then again, I tried not to think too much about it, 'cause then I'd make myself more nervous.

Stephanie: She's a perfectionist.

Sanne: Yeah. I'd always like to give last-minute corrections.

Stephanie: Oh my gosh, we'd be walking out on deck, ready to dive in for our routine, and she'd be saying corrections! I'd be like, "Sanne it's too late, we just gotta swim!"

Sanne: I was always afraid that people would forget something.

Stephanie: The trust issue is very important with duet. You have to trust your partner.

Sanne: With duet it was more like mutual corrections that we had. But with team, I was trying to remind people of things they had to do, 'cause I didn't want them to forget. I don't know if it helped them at all, but it made me feel better. I was never trying to control anyone, or be controlling. But a lot of times on my team, I felt like… I was the one who was trying to keep everything together. I was the one, when we were supposed to land drill, and everyone else was talking, I was the one who was trying to get everyone back on track. Get the music going, and get everyone land drilling. So I sometimes took on a motherly role. I was like a little mother hen, trying to get everyone together and focused.

Stephanie: Sanne was always very focused in her swimming. The perfectionist part of her always came out, whether at practice or a meet, even when she was coaching. She was very much like the mother hen trying to get everybody together. I think because Sanne demanded a lot from herself, she demanded at lot from others, too. Not demanded, but, like, expected people to demand that much of themselves. Sometimes other people are just not as motivated as you are. Because Sanne was motivated and she was a perfectionist, she expected others to be motivated and perfectionist, too. Critical of themselves like she was critical of herself.

Sanne: I was too critical of myself, too hard on myself when I made mistakes. I would get hung up...angry at myself when I made mistakes. Too angry, so much so that you can't really focus on what you're supposed to do any more, you're just so angry.

Stephanie: Even if you placed very high.

Sanne: I just didn't think it was acceptable...it wasn't acceptable for me to make mistakes, and I just got really angry when I did, so. That's destructive.

I was putting way too much emphasis on the sport. Now, today, sports aren't just sports any more. They're an avenue to college scholarships. They're avenues to success and money and everything. Plus in synchro, you're with eight girls who are pretty much your family and you don't want to let them down. There's just a lot of pressure. So I would make a mistake and I wouldn't just see that figure being wrong, or that routine being a bad swim. I'd see everything down the line falling apart. It became way too much for me.

I wouldn't listen to my scores. I'd go underwater, and I would just put it out of my mind. Then when I saw the results, I would get angry.

When I got angry with myself, I would scratch myself. I would scratch my legs and my arms, just to...inflict pain on my body.

'Cause it was easier for me to deal with that than with the emotional pain. That was just punishment for myself. I don't really even remember the first time I did it, and I don't really remember the last time I did it. People have told me of incidents where, I guess it was really bad, and I don't even remember that.

I don't really remember how bad it was. I don't think...it was that bad. I don't remember. Someone told me it...maybe...it was to the point where...maybe...I mean, I was just...it was just my fingernails, which were never really that long. But they say that... maybe...it was to the point where I was bleeding...which I don't remember. I don't even really remember to that extent. I don't know. I don't know how bad it was.

I guess it gets really bad, it gets bad enough that you mutilate your own body. That's saying a lot right there. There's no other way for you to express that anger. You just can't...the bottle...the bottle becomes too full with too many emotions. That's how bad it gets, that you would do that. I don't know how else to explain it. I don't know what it looks like from the outside. But from the inside, it's not pretty.

Stephanie: She says that she doesn't remember incidents, but I remember a lot of incidents. I can give you the pool, and the event we were on, and how old we were, and stuff like that. Sanne and I have a really close friendship. We were close before we swam. I was very aware of when she had had enough, or when she was really upset with herself. She gave off certain signs that said, "This is it, I've had it." As her duet partner and also as her friend, I was able to pick up on those signs and when the destruction set in, I knew she was upset with herself. At the beginning, I was scared. I didn't want to get near the situation at all. I overcame the fear because I think I understood the problem. I mean, I'm a perfectionist, too, and I'm her duet partner. It was scary, sometimes she'd be really shaken up afterwards. I always worried about her. People on the outside don't wanna get involved. They don't want to make things worse. If they want to make things better, they don't know how.

Sanne: I didn't really care if anyone saw. I probably wanted people to see, because I wanted help. Which many people were just running away from. They didn't really wanna help me. Coaches would come and say, "Cover yourself up." I would put my shorts on, and they said, "No, put your pants on. We don't want anyone seeing that." Presentation. That's what the whole sport is, presentation.

I had Stephanie, and I had one coach who really helped me. She set up this whole thing with a sports psychologist. My parents never even knew about it. The coach would pick me up from school and we would go. There were some tough times, in that room, with the psychologist. But my coach was always there for me. She was so supportive. When I think about it, there were really only a few people who helped me, but what they did was incredible. They gave so much of themselves. When I had finally come to terms with it, and I think I was coming out of it, I wrote the coach a letter and really thanked her. I know that she is the main reason I was able to do it. When it really came to a head, people at the swim club, they said, "You fix this or you get out." Which to me was kind of a little insulting. It didn't seem like they were being really supportive. That one coach was there for me. And I guess my mom finally had to find out. But the people who I thought should support me—I didn't feel like I was wanted, or that they wanted to help me. I felt like I wasn't wanted because I wasn't good enough. I wasn't a main talent on the team. I was just someone who had been around for a long time. I wasn't like a synchro prodigy like some people you see. I felt like they didn't care if I left, because I wasn't really good enough score-wise.

The sports psychologist helped me kind of put everything in perspective. I had to let go of the whole college thing, let go of all those expectations, and just focus on the sport. Focus on the little goals, the little tasks at hand, which has helped me. And learn that the performance was wrong, and not...that I'm wrong, and it's my fault. That helped me a lot. I haven't really been as angry with myself as I was during those years with synchro. But I definitely feel

sometimes, that you get that urge to be angry with yourself and to be destructive. It's always there. It's hard not to . . . get angry with yourself when . . . I struggle to not be so angry. 'Cause I don't want to go back to the way I was before.

I don't really . . . I actually . . . I haven't really learned another way to deal with that emotion. What I've learned is to try and not get there. Separating my self-worth from my performance really helped. If you identify yourself with what you do, if your whole self-worth is in that one routine, then you can't handle it when you make a mistake.

I knew it was time to leave. I couldn't do it any more. It stopped being fun. It really started to be more stressful. When I was at the pool, I was worried about everything I had to do. It lost what drew me there in the first place. It wasn't fun any more.

Up to that point I never really thought I would quit. If you asked me, I'd say I'm never gonna quit. I was surprised myself at how sure I was. It just . . . it lost its allure, I guess. I still . . . the family that you develop there is one of the things that draws you to it the most. But I was confident that if I left the sport, I would still be able to maintain those friendships, because they were so strong. So in that sense I felt like I could leave, and still be happy.

But when I left the sport, you do go through a period when you feel like you have no purpose. I felt lazy, and I didn't know who I was any more. For so long, when your parents introduce you to someone, "Oh, this is my daughter, the swimmer," y'know, that's what you identify yourself as. And so when I left, I didn't really know who I was. I had trouble identifying what I was, or what drove me, or what my goals were. So it's been —*(sigh)*— interesting, the past couple of months, trying to find what I want again.

Now I'm just trying to get involved in other stuff. I'm trying to figure out what other interests I have, which I haven't been able to pursue for the past . . . since I was six or seven years old. I'm finding that things that I thought I liked, when I was swimming, I don't really like. I've only been out of swimming for five or six months now, so I really haven't exactly figured out what I'm interested in. I don't know if anyone really figures out exactly who they are. I mean, I haven't figured it out yet. It's a journey, I guess.

Stephanie: Our last competition, I fell apart completely.

Sanne: For my Stanford application I wrote about my last swim with Stephanie. It was funny, 'cause I thought I would be the one totally breaking down, but it was Stephanie, in the end.

Stephanie: I think she needed to get out of the sport. She knew that it was time. I was fully warned about it, months in advance, that come July it would be over. She was my duet partner. You spend a lot of time with your duet partner. A lot of myself depended on her. I confided in her, not only as a duet partner but as a friend. We worked together every day at practice and we spent so much time together. When it came down to the end of that routine, and it was time for her to leave, I think she was looking forward to another life. But for those of us who were still left in the sport, just facing the sport without her, and not facing something new, it was, in a way, more difficult. I was crying during the routine. I was crying at the end. I lost it during the last part and I was gone.

Sanne: I still love being in the water. It's really therapeutic for me. I've been doing other kind of things to keep in shape, running and rowing. But being in the water is really therapeutic for me. I don't know, maybe it always has been and I didn't realize it. I like getting in and I love hearing the music underwater and I love laying on the bottom of the pool when it's raining. Just hearing water around your ears. I love hearing the bubbles. I love being surrounded and just kind of feeling like...you know how to use the water, it's not threatening at all, 'cause you know what to do and it's kind of like your friend. I mean, some people get in the water and they're thrashing around and they look like they're gonna sink. But me and the water are like this *(crossing fingers)*.

I'm thinking of studying environmental biology — environmental engineering, something like that, nothing really sports-related at all. Nope.

Stephanie alone.

I've learned a lot from Sanne's experience. A lot of stuff that I ended up having to deal with — not to the extreme, to the physical extreme. But to the mental extreme.

When I first started I was seven years old. I had tried soccer and I had tried ballet and I had tried piano. Nothing really appealed to me. I was too big to be a gymnast or a ballerina, or I wasn't flexible enough. I was a little girl who didn't know where she wanted to go, really, as far as a sport goes. All I knew was I loved the water. I loved to swim. But lap swimming just wasn't for me.

I came to synchronized swimming because I liked the glamour, I liked the makeup, the idea of wearing sequined suits. I wanted to be — you know, the Miss America idea. Little girls always want to be like Barbie. They always want to have the great hair, she always has makeup on her, she has beautiful clothes. Some of them are sequined or shiny, so when you think about being a model or a synchronized swimmer, it's the same effect.

I'm sixteen years old and I've been swimming for nine years. I hope to make it all the way to the Olympics. My age group would more than likely be 2004.

It's kind of funny, because you go into something thinking, "Wow, I'm gonna be glamorous, I'm gonna be gorgeous." And then you find this athletic world. And I love it. I love training, I love being part of the team, and I love being a synchronized swimmer. The athletics, the grace, I just fell in love with the sport.

I don't think the glamour matters as much now. Unfortunately, I think synchronized swimming is often thought of as "the glamour sport." It's the sequins, it's the makeup. We train to make it look easy, so people misinterpret what we do. They don't think it's hard. They think we're standing on the bottom of the pool. They say, "Oh, it's just glamour. It looks so easy." And they don't see the other side of the sport.

One of the hardest things about being a synchronized swimmer is how much time comes out of your regular life. I train twenty, twenty-three hours a week in the water. It's five or six days in the water and a day of land training. I run, plus we do medicine balls, stretching, land drilling. Our coach gave us a lecture. I got the extended version yesterday. It was: go to school, go to practice, do your homework. You can go to the prom, but that's it. No social life. It's time to swim.

Relationships and love and even friendships, you have your whole life to figure those things out. We talk about marriage, we joke about having kids, but it's never a serious topic. I don't think anyone on the team gives it a lot of thought. Because right now you want an education and you want a career and you want to go to the Olympics. Those are your goals, and everything else falls where it falls.

This is my life. It always has been my life. I know that I've declined from relationships because it was our highest competing season and I did not want to deal with anything else. Because for me, this is it. This comes first, right next to school, right next to my family.

It's a female sport. It's a new sport, compared to things like baseball, football, that have been around for ages. They are the male sports. You don't see women out there in the NFL throwing around a football. So it's not only being a women in a man's world. It's being a synchronized swimmer where there's maybe one or two men. Definitely the pressure's put on you to be an athlete and to be accepted into the world of sports.

I think that there are still different standards in what is expected of a male and what is expected of a female in a sport, whether it's basketball or baseball or softball or whatever. Maybe because men don't do synchro, they think, "It couldn't be that hard or else men would be doing it."

When it looks like we're standing on the bottom of the pool, we're really treading water, which is what water polo players do. "Support scull" is what we do to keep ourselves upright, with our legs out of the water. It's a lot of shoulder strength when you're upside down and a lot of leg strength when you're right side up. You have to learn how to work with the water—that's the whole point of sculling. Learning how to work with your muscles, with your body, with the water to keep yourself up. It's not just floating.

The worst feeling is the lack of oxygen under the water. You know that you're not coming up until a certain count and that count is sixteen or seventeen counts away. And your heart starts beating and your stomach starts throbbing and your cheeks just pphhhfffttt! It's an intense feeling. It's very scary, yet it creates a nice challenge, because when you come up, you know that you've won and you're there. A lot of us have blacked out underwater. I've passed out. It's scary, but you know that you have all of your teammates and coaches right there and they're not gonna let you drown.

When you talk about synchronized swimming, people either say, "Wow, that is so cool, I respect what you do," or, "Go find a real sport." That hurts a lot when you dedicate so much of your time. It hurts even more when it comes from your peers or other athletes. I consider myself an athlete. I train as hard as they do, or more hours than they do. But we can't get the respect that their sport already has. It's because it's a new sport and a female sport, and all the things that go along with that. I think there's a lot of misconceptions: no, we're not standing on the bottom of the pool; yes, we train like other athletes do; no, we don't float around the water. So I wish people wouldn't criticize what they don't do. I wish they would have a little bit more respect.

We swim in teams of eight girls. I'm a soloist, I have a duet and I'm also part of the team. A lot of times people say, "What is the point of *solo* in *synchronized* swimming?" But it's judged totally different than any other event. They're looking at how you interpret yourself, how you cover the pool, how you use your music, can you hold your own in the pool? For my solo this year, I'm a belly dancer, and it's definitely a part that's gonna take a lot of character. It's fun, it has a little attitude. If you're out there and you're swimming to boring music, who's gonna wanna watch? But if you're a belly dancer with an interesting suit and a fun little spark in your eye, then they will wanna watch.

Something that I had to learn last year was that it's half physical but it's half mental. The mental part is not only how you portray yourself or your character in your routine but also how you see yourself as a swimmer. Do you have self-esteem and confidence in yourself to succeed? Last year I had a battle with my self-esteem and my confidence in my swimming, which I feel I've overcome.

We have what we call Junior National Team. That's the top ten girls in the country. We go to a Junior National meet. You have to qualify to get there. The top three hundred or so girls are invited. Then they make cuts. We have what we call "figures," compulsory figures. Everybody does the same thing, we all look the same, and we all get judged. All three hundred girls do those, and then they come up with the standings. They take the top fifty and we do a different set of figures. After that, the top thirty do another set. Then the top eighteen do a routine with music.

Last year, I was in eighth place, but, all of a sudden, I absolutely had the biggest lack of confidence in myself that I'd never had to deal with before. And so if you look at my standings, it goes eighth, eighth, thirtieth, average nineteenth. So I didn't make the team. And by far that was the greatest loss I've had to deal with in this sport.

I absolutely let my mental side get to me. I was definitely having a struggle with myself. Sometimes it's really easy to get a negative attitude about the way you swim. I'm a very critical person. I'm definitely a perfectionist when it comes to my swimming. I'm not gonna quit until it looks the way I want it to look. Which is why I don't mind all the practice. When you do one spin twelve times and it's not right — I refuse to stop until I get it right.

I don't know what I was doing. This negative attitude had totally taken over in me, this, "I'm not good enough. It doesn't look the way I want it to. How can I fix it? I just don't have it in me to fix it." That was totally the wrong attitude. The right attitude is, "I've been doing this for nine years. I know exactly what I'm doing. I've been practicing for eight months. If there was a problem my coach would have told me." I needed to feel it from within. I needed to say, "I know what I'm doing. This isn't new to me. This is what I love to do." I think for a second I lost what I loved about the sport.

It's understandable when people crack. Everybody cracks sometime. But I've worked on it a lot. So I don't think we'll be seeing any more of that.

Stephanie at the National Meet.

It's kinda funny, you can say that you love to swim, and I do love to swim. But to feel that love while you're swimming—I haven't felt that way in a long time. I love going to practice, but I haven't been really happy about swimming in a long time. I don't know what it was that changed. I just know that ever since I had my little problem last year, it just hasn't been the same.

Here, it's not practice, it's competition. It's a totally different field. It's kind of like you're facing all your competitors, and you're not... It's the nerves that get involved. Last year, I think I was concentrating more on the nerves. I wanted to swim well, but I wasn't focused on having fun. That's a problem sometimes with sports, you lose sight of having fun. When something's not fun any more, even though you love to do it, there's just something that's missing in your swimming. I think that's kinda what happened.

Last year at Nationals, I just swam horribly. As much as I love to practice and love to swim and I wanted to go to the meet, when I got to the meet, I was totally a different person. It went horrible.

You have to feel very confident when you walk out there. This year I've had a lot of fun swimming. If I don't accomplish anything else this meet, I'm glad that I got that back.

The one thing that I definitely came to do was to make the national team. Because that's something that I have to prove to myself and I didn't do that last year. As I start crying. You have to give me a minute. Nerves and everything. Mom, can I have some Kleenex?

Anyway, that's something that I need to accomplish. For myself. Hopefully I have a good shot at that. I was there last year until my mental breakdown, so. I should be there this year, a little more mentally solid. I hope.

I'm really glad that I found the love in my swimming again. That's what it's all about. It has to be fun. You have to love what you do. I felt really good today after my swim. As far as my placing, it's totally out of my control. I think I did well. I did better than I did last year.

Last year... It's kinda like this thing where I can shut my eyes and see myself doing it. I can see myself doing it perfectly. I know that I can do it, because I've done it. But when I go out there and I get in front of a bunch of people, I feel like they don't think I'm good enough to do it. So I kinda sink back into this little hole. And I don't swim the best that I can. Afterwards I'm like, "That felt horrible." Not my best. And so at the national meet when I did badly on one figure, I was like, "Oh my God, I don't belong here." Everyone was like, "Yeah, you do," but I said, "No, I don't." And I let it get the best of me. So, it won. So, I didn't belong there. Not then, because I wasn't mentally ready.

The nerves build up as the week goes on because you get more and more tired. Since it's competition you always become sore, you work your hardest. So by the time Sunday rolls around, and it's finals, your arms are sore, like my arms are sore right now. And it's day one.

Stephanie's mom.

Last year I wasn't here. It was very hard for me to be at home, and to have her here without the support of the family. This year being here, I'm probably as nervous if not more nervous than she is. But I see a lot of growth in Stephanie and I see the love. And that love will give her strength. I think she's mentally ready. Everything is the luck of the draw sometimes. It's a subjective sport just like it is in ice skating. It's out of her hands. As long as she does her personal best.

We have a really strong relationship as mother–daughter, and a friendship between the two of us. She has always felt a strength, an inner strength from me. I think it's easier for her if I'm here because she can voice her own inner feelings and get rid of them—any upset-ness or things she needs to talk about. It's hard to do that over the phone. It's hard to convey it. I couldn't convey it last year. When I hung up the phone, I knew she wasn't listening.

Stephanie is solemn and silent through the figures competition.

I would never want what happened to me to happen to anybody else. I think that in a lot of ways I recognize the signs. I can tell when other people are stressing or when they're having difficulties. I think I'm

pretty relaxed considering the circumstances. Whereas before I was like, "Oh my God, visualize! Do this! Do that!" I just needed to relax and do what I did every day in practice. So, I think that's helped me a lot. I've been placing well and with a lot less stress.

Synchronized swimming is half routine and half figures. It's kinda like the ice skaters used to do. They would do maybe the figure eight on the ice and everybody does that and everybody gets judged. There are 370 girls here, the top 370 in the country that qualified to get here. We all wear black suits, white caps. So you can't tell us apart. In front of the panel of judges, you do your figures. Eventually you get a list and it should tell you who's at the top and work its way down.

So they're testing you. Are your arms strong? Do you have core strength? Are your legs strong? Can you hold your breath? Are you going slow? Are you traveling? It's a way of testing everybody on the same skills. You do want that look of smoothness, that still look. That's what they're after. Calm and high and extended and very . . . and it's not supposed to look difficult. That's what we do.

Stephanie makes it to the finals. There are eighteen competitors left, young, strong, and fiercely biting their nails. They will perform a grueling swim-dance to music, over and over and over again. Judges sit high in lifeguard chairs, stern, severe, unsmiling. They rate each girl down to hundredths of a point. As she swims, Stephanie smiles winningly, adorably, convincingly at the judges. She moves like a glamorous sprite, sleek, sparkling with droplets. The music ends. Her smile crashes. Her face turns as gray as the face of a girl long drowned. She shivers and sobs at the side of the pool.

Stephanie on the swim-off.

What happens now is they need ten girls. But if the scores are a hundredth or a tenth of a point apart, there has to be a swim-off to decide which is the one. None of us know whether we're in or whether we're out. Just because I'm not in the swim-off doesn't mean that I'm on the team. It means that I could be *not* on the team at all. No one knows until it's fully announced.

But what these girls will have to do is swim this routine over and over again until one beats the other. Last time there were girls who swam this routine six or seven times until they got enough margin so that they could justify the top group. So, this is evil. This is cruel and evil punishment. I'm glad that I'm not doing it. This is bad, those girls are exhausted.

I can honestly say that my body feels like Jell-O right now. I'm lucky I'm walking after a week of competition. It's just unbearable. Everything pretty much rides on this one for them. This right here is nerves. This is it. I'm glad I'm not in there right now.

Stephanie watches the swim-off. The girls are gladiators, smiling pretty. As the music ends, one warrior girl slips underwater like a seal. Her competitor moves painfully toward her. She lifts her from behind in a fireman's carry. They struggle for the poolside, both girls gasping. The fallen girl is crying. Her head nods off, her face falls down in the water. Her neck snaps up when her face hits, only to collapse again. She's like a baby fighting to stay up way past bedtime.

That's straight endurance right there. And they don't know if they're done yet. They have to re-figure the scores. In another twenty minutes or so, they'll come back and maybe do it again. So these girls are going to have to wait in agony, not knowing. Last year it was bad. Last year it was never-ending. It just went on forever. I think they had to swim seven or eight times.

There is no second swim-off.

Stephanie waits with her mother for the announcement of who has made the team, and who has not. Stephanie twists her mother's fingers like the worried handkerchiefs of waiting women everywhere. They gaze into opposite walls. No one speaks. The air is thick with chlorine, fog, and fear.

At the first syllable of her name, Stephanie rockets from her seat. Her

*mother barely grabs a brush kiss. Stephanie stands with her new
team. She is proud, and shy, and smiling.*

I just found out that I made the National Training Squad for Junior
National Team. I ended up ninth overall out of originally 370. This puts
me right now where I want to be. So, it's good. It's the quiet after the
storm. I spent a week in that pool. I'm ready to go home and I really
can't wait to go home. It's the mental pressure. I'm surprised I'm not
crying with the release of stress. It's intense. Now, you've come, you've
done what you needed to do and that's it. You're free.

 REFLECTION

F̲ew girls can stand the scrutiny of their own gaze in the mirror. We're refracted like Picasso portraits. We grade our features separately, like chicken parts. The body we trusted in childhood betrays us now, with changes as wrenching and thrilling as those of a movie werewolf, come full moon.

If we're not pretty, smiling, and slim, ridicule slaps us in the face like a bucket of suds. Effortless perfection is the dream, and a girl can be cast out for trying *too* hard.

Katie, Jen, and Morgan reflect on the mirror's tyranny.

KATIE, SIXTEEN
HARTSVILLE, SOUTH CAROLINA

I was free, when I was a little girl, I was rambunctious. No, really I don't know. I think I was pretty much shy when I was little. I was a Daddy's girl and I was a tomboy. I played baseball. I loved to get out in the yard with the boys. I just...when I was little, I don't really know what I was. I just don't think back that far. I don't know.

My mom works at a hospital and my dad works at...it's like a factory with like, ah, let's see...I don't know what they do. I guess it's with cloth or something. I'm not sure. My mom's a pediatric nurse. My brother went into the Air Force, so it's me, my mom and my dad. We eat dinner together, breakfast together. Just basic family life, I guess.

Me and my boyfriend broke up. We dated for a long time, and we were in love. It's just...we had problems. We still talk. But he's in a lot of trouble. He just turned out...bein' kinda rough. He left home. And, um, he just kinda got on the rough side. I had to get outta that 'cause it got bad on me. I am a Christian, and I want to stay that way. I didn't want no guy to bring me off like that. Take me away from my family. I still love him.

I was in a few pageants when I was a baby. I was in my first grown-up pageant just a few weeks ago. I did pretty good. I was surprised. My self-confidence has been really low, 'cause I don't like my smile. I don't think very highly of myself. That's how I figure I gotta get over this, I gotta be in pageants. When I was in that pageant, my self-confidence just went up to a high. I feel a lot better about myself. I can get up on stage and smile.

I don't think my smile is very beautiful. My jaw, my bottom jaw is like growing out faster than my top. It just juts out. It's like my lips poke out. It's got my smile all bulky and I don't like it. It's just...my smile... that's what brings me down. My face is like real long and my lips are like...And, um, it's gotten worse. Everything gets worse before it gets better, but, um, it's been like six months maybe, and it started getting worse and worse. I don't wanna smile. I just don't like the way it looks. I don't like it because it's not normal. I mean, that is a low part of my self-esteem. I think it's really ugly, I really do. I mean, I know inside beauty is what counts, but I just think...I think I'd be a whole lot prettier if this was fixed. I think that's what throws me off now. Not

with girl friends, but like with guy friends. Being able to get a boyfriend. I just think guys don't like me, I just think they...y'know, my jaw makes me ugly. But that's just my jaw. I guess it's just me. I'm me and I can't help that. Which I love myself, so.

I get picked on about it. They always call me "Chin" or "Big Lips," or like "Bubba Gump," offa Forrest Gump. Guys are just like that. Just immature. They don't really care about nobody but themselves. They just always like pickin' on girls. It's basically...a guy's a guy, so. (*Laughs.*) But I kind of got over that, 'cause I respect myself more than that, y'know, to let something like that get me down.

I'm gonna have it fixed one day and I'm gonna like it a lot better. I'm gonna have surgery on my jaw to take my jaw back. They're gonna come in and cut the bones, I believe, and take it back, so it will be even and normal like it's supposed to be. 'Cause it's really not normal right now. It's really like, off, and out, so. I'm gonna have surgery. It's gonna all be better one day. Won't have to worry about my smile.

The operation will change my face and I'll feel so much better about the way I look. See, when I look in the mirror every morning, this is all I see, is my chin, just two miles out, y'know. I'm supposed to get this fixed and, um, hopefully it'll...I just think I'll look prettier. I know people see this, and it kinda shakes me up. I'm ready to get it fixed. I think I'll be so much more beautiful. And normal, I guess.

My hair, well, um, my hair color's like fake right now. I always try new experiments with my hair. I left for the summer, I lived with my aunt to babysit for her while she worked. When I came back, my hair was a different color and cut off short. That was a real change for my mom. It's like I was a totally different person. I like doing experiments with my hair. I just don't want it too short. I've had it short before 'cause my...it got burned off one time.

My brother kinda threw a firecracker at me and it burned all my hair off. It doesn't really bother me 'cause it was like an accident. They... I mean, he didn't get in trouble and that was good, because he didn't really mean it. But the coincidence was, he hollered, "Merry Christmas, Katie," y'know, and it just landed in my hair. And it just burned all my hair off. And this was like Christmas Eve.

My dad was on the porch and me and my brother were out in the yard, poppin' fireworks. I wasn't payin' no attention to my brother. I had my back turned to him. When he said, "Merry Christmas," I wasn't thinkin' nothin' of it, y'know? All of a sudden that thing landed in my hair and my hair caught fire and I just went crazy. I was just runnin' around in circles in the yard. My dad said I looked like a lightening bolt going past him, and I wouldn't stop, and my dad was chasing me.

My mom runs in the house and calls the hairdresser. "Katie got all her hair burned off!" And the hairdresser's like, "Why are you callin' me? You should be callin' the hospital!" My mom was just pullin' out handfuls of hair. My hair had been down to my hips. It was awful. That's why I respect my hair. *(Laughs.)*

I love my hair, though. Love it. Actually, I love everything about me now. I got more confidence in myself. I just love myself and I respect myself more than I used to when I was younger. I guess I got older and matured and just learned more. By following God, I've learned to watch my actions. I've learned to respect myself through him. I realize how much easier it is in life, if you respect yourself first.

Before, I didn't care about myself. I always put myself down. I had a bad eating disorder. That's what I'm struggling with now that I cannot get over. I've had it for two or three years now. I'm trying to get over it and I'm like depressed, y'know? But I mean I just...I feel a difference...I feel like a different person.

I had anemia and anorexia. I did not have bulimia, 'cause everybody thinks I had bulimia, but I could never make myself throw up! I was anorexic and anemic and this time last year I was in the hospital.

I thought for sure I was gonna be back in there this year 'cause of the way I was goin'. I was really downhill last week. But I've worked my way back up.

I'm still struggling with my eating disorder. As I get older I guess I come out of it more. But then sometimes I do slip back down. I don't know what 'causes me to slip back down, but sometimes I get depressed. But hopefully I will get over it soon. And I won't go back downhill again.

I don't know...it's like, um, I don't know...it's like, maybe when I was younger, it's just, um, maybe when I was younger, it started as me...I felt like I didn't get enough attention maybe when I was younger. Yeah, maybe that's what it was—because I didn't get attention when I was younger. And that's when it started. I was just so depressed from,

um, just, um, I didn't feel like I had any friends, and I don't know what really — I guess I just thought I was fat when I was younger, but I've never been really big. I've always been really small. I guess I felt like I didn't have any friends, and I felt like there was nothing for me to, y'know...I hated school. I didn't like to come to church either. God wasn't in my life then. As I get older, I get out of it, and feel better 'cause I got God in my life now. That makes me feel so much better. I just feel like I have so much more here for me, y'know?

When I was younger I was such a tomboy and I started changing. I was like, what is goin' on? I was just totally clueless. I was, like, I don't like this. All the changes I was goin' through, I really didn't like it. That might have been another reason I became anorexic. Oh, I hated it! I didn't know what happened, I really didn't. I was like, "What is this? What is happening to me?!" I didn't know. Like, I hate getting my period! I hate shaving my legs. That's the worse thing, I hate shaving my legs! I mean it's just things I hate. I feel like if I was a man it would be a whole lot easier, you know?

God's my first priority, then family, but family goes in with God. I go to church on Sundays. God is like, He's like...the light of my life. He's like there with me though thick and thin. Everybody says they're gonna be there for you, but it's not like God is, y'know. 'Cause God is there and you know He's there. It's like...I was in a car wreck, um, a year ago. It almost took my life. But I know I had an angel sittin' in my lap. 'Cause if I didn't, I wouldn't have made it through. I think about Him every day, just every second I think about God. I ask Him...I mean, I talk to God. I'll be driving in my car, and I'll be talkin' to God. Like, "What's gonna happen next?" you know? He's just got a lot of power in me. I sing for God. I go to church and I sing for Him. I sing in church, I love to sing. And if it wasn't for Him, I wouldn't be able to. I sing for Him 'cause He gave me the voice to sing with. That's how I feel about it. See, God's a lot to me.

All my confidence and self-respect, it comes from God. To be able to get up on that pageant stage, it's like God is walkin' right in front of me, and I'm followin'. He's like right there. He's walkin' beside me, in front of me, behind me. God's there, because if He wasn't, I wouldn't be able to walk out there. I couldn't do it. I wouldn't have the strength to walk out there, 'cause I just get so nervous. But then I pray, and it's all better. All the girls stand around and pray, before our pageant, and it just makes it so much better. We pray to Him. We thank Him for allowing all of us to be there, and allowing all of us to have the strength to be doin' it. We glorify his name, 'cause He's the one that's there. He's the one who's helping us though this. He's the one that's making this happen. We just thank Him and ask Him for help and stuff. It makes us get through the day.

Somebody told me once that wearin' makeup was like a sin. I didn't wanna believe it. I was like, "Why?" y'know? But then I realized you have to be natural, because He was natural. And so I quit wearin' makeup. But then, when it comes to bein' up on stage in front of everybody, you gotta show yourself. I mean, all you're really doin' is adding color to yourself, where people can see you. 'Cause if you're just up there plain and natural then nobody's gonna look at you. They can't see you. I mean, you're just adding color and brightening yourself up. With all the cameras and lights and stuff, you have to have makeup on or they won't see you. I wear makeup for stuff like that, being with cameras and lights. But I usually go natural.

I love white. White's my color. My pageant gown is white and it's got beautiful pearls. It's not showy. It does cover me good, and I like stuff like that. I ask God, "Help me pick out a good dress." I pray about mostly everything, all of my choices and stuff, 'cause I can't make up my mind. I have to have someone there to help me out. I pray and ask for the Lord's advice. I do that on most stuff I do. It's hard to make choices on my own. I can mess up. It's not that He can tell me, "Wear this one," y'know. I just...I think white is pure and He is pure and that's why I love white. That's why I picked white, I guess. I don't know if it's necessarily signs that He gives me. It's just...I just fall in love with it, and when I see it it's like I gotta have it. I don't know what he does to help me do it, it's just there. It's like a...I just have a feeling, I just have a cleansed feeling, y'know. It's like, when you have chills, it's something like that. I don't know how to explain it. It's something like a... it's a feeling something like when you have chills, that certain feeling.

Oh, I love competition, it's like one of my favorite things. The day's gonna come when I have to compete with a really close friend, and I'm not gonna like that. But it's all in fun for me. It's not like, "I gotta win this or I'm gonna die." I just do pageants for fun. When me and my friends compete, I'm gonna want them to win more than me, because I guess it's just the way I feel. I don't know how they feel about it. I'll put all my effort, and I'll do the best I can. But my mind is basically gonna be on my friends. Because I'm like...I don't want them to be mad at me. I like the competition, but then, I don't, 'cause it's like you're picking out who's the prettiest and I mean, there's nobody better than anybody in this world. There's nobody prettier than anybody, anything like that. Competition is good in a way, and I don't like it in a way. But that's the whole thing about beauty pageants.

You gotta get your eyebrows waxed and stuff like that. It's a pretty stressful time, it's pretty...out there. It's like you got a lot of stuff to get ready for. I mean, you really gotta eat right 'cause if you don't you're gonna get nervous and get sick. It's just so much to have to worry about. Your hair and your makeup, just everything. Your fingernails, your hands, your arms, your legs, everything. And, um, just things you wouldn't even think of. Everything has to be perfect. When you're in pageants, it's a stressful time. There's so much you gotta do and there's so little time to do it.

Now that I'm in pageants, I have more confidence. I mean, you just don't know how bad I was, with my low self-esteem. I was just a poor little kid, y'know? I didn't think highly of myself and I pushed everything away. Now, I feel so much better, but I still have health problems, and I can't help that. But, um, hopefully it will get better one day, with God's hands. I'll really feel so much better when I get my jaw fixed. I'm just in small pageants now, but when I get this fixed, I'm gonna be in big pageants. And I won't worry about smilin'. Right now it's harder for me to smile than it is for anybody else. Because of the way I am. But I try my best, I get out there and try. When I get my jaw fixed, I'm gonna be in bigger pageants and I'll be a whole lot prettier person on the outside.

I mean, everybody's pretty to me. Everybody has got their own beautiful ways. Everybody's beautiful on the inside, I think. Somewhere inside, everybody's beautiful. I know people these days...criminals and stuff. But there's somewhere beautiful down in there—everybody's beautiful. Outside beauty...I think it counts in a way because...God made everybody and everybody's gonna be beautiful inside and outside, because they came from God and I think they're gonna be beautiful inside and outside. That's what I think. I don't know.

JEN, SIXTEEN
CAMERON PARK, CALIFORNIA

People expect girls to be happy all the time and act like life's wonderful and great and blah blah blah. I don't know why people expect teenage girls to be like that 'cause *sooo* many of us aren't. It's one of those insane expectations that people have of girls. We're supposed to sit there and smile and not talk and be stupid. If you feel bad, just cover it up with a smile and keep going.

Everybody goes through down times. People act like it doesn't happen. But everybody gets sad sometimes. People pretend it isn't normal for girls to act like that, but it's totally normal. I don't spiral down like I used to. After a day or two I come out of it like most people do. Just keep going.

I was one of the prissy little girls, like, *(whining)* "Oooooh, that hurt!" and I cried all the time. My Grammy used to tell me I had a bladder behind my eyes. If anybody called me names I would cry. I was very round, like I am now. Bugs grossed me out, and the thought of playing in mud was just sickening to me. I was very girly and I wore dresses and little clips in my hair. Pink was my favorite color for quite a few years!

I was wearing a bra in like fourth grade. I developed way before most girls. Kids at school thought it was strange. They didn't know how to react. I'm like a double D right now. But it wouldn't look right if I had really small ones, because of my size. I'm proportioned correctly.

I had two Barbies. I liked to do their hair, and I chewed on their feet. I just kind of nibbled on them. They had little teeth marks. Just 'cause they're that rubbery consistency that you can kind of put your teeth through. When I was like eleven, I would cut their hair off. And then I was like, "Oooh, burn Barbie!" That's when I went through my little pyromaniac phase. I went through, "Cut off Barbie's hair. Burn Barbie's feet." Burning stuff just for fun.

It was two days before my twelfth birthday. I was at summer basketball camp. My cousin's a basketball coach and we were in Idaho then. And oh, my God! I got my period for the first time. I didn't know what to do. It was something my mom had been preparing me for for a while, 'cause she saw how early I started wearing a bra. She said, "OK, we have to talk." I kind of freaked out, 'cause I didn't know what to do, and I was all, um, um, um, um. So I went to my cousin's wife. She was

all excited for me. I was like, "What, is it something good?" I just thought it was strange. I was like, "Why are you so excited?" I guess I can see why she was excited. I don't get excited any more!

Junior high was horrid, junior high was horrible, I hated junior high. It's the most difficult time. Everyone's in little cliques and groups and if you're out of the norm, you are ostracized by *everyone*. I wasn't one of the norm. I was kind of strange. I thought, "Oh my God, there's gotta be something totally wrong with me!"

I was like I am now. I was "big boned." And it really is big bones, 'cause my wrists are huge. I'm not meant to be a skinny person. That's the fashion model type these days. All those really bony chicks. You know — stick-like bones sticking out everywhere. That's when you eat ice for lunch. I think that's kind of gross, but I wasn't one of those people. I was a size C bra in eighth grade, so I was just bizarre. I was the weirdest thing. I assumed I was fat, and that that was a horrible thing. Everybody else said, "She's fat! She's fat!" Actually I wasn't fat, I just developed before everybody else did. But I didn't see it that way and neither did they.

Growing up, I saw in all my little *Seventeen* magazines all these little skinny girls. I thought, I have to be like that or no one will like me. I have to be like that, or no boys will like me. I tried to be like that, but it didn't work.

See, junior high was really a horrible time. I ended up becoming bulimic and I was hospitalized and everything. I ended up in the hospital for trying to overdose on Tylenol and aspirin. I ended up being put in one of those...hospitals. I was there for like a week as an in-patient, and I was an out-patient for two weeks. I ended up trying to overdose one more time.

Then I realized, wait a minute — this isn't what I want to do. I don't want to die. This isn't right, this isn't what I want to do. I didn't want to die. I did not want to die. But I got to the point — feeling jaded, like there was nothing left for me. This is lame, all life is gonna be is just painful, so I don't want to live. I didn't want to die, but I didn't want to live either.

I ended up surviving it. I just barely survived it. I guess I have like clinical depression. They put me on medication for it. And, y'know, I'm pretty happy. I don't know if it's the medication, or the fact that I'm maturing to the point where I realize I don't have to be what everybody thinks I'm supposed to be. There was nothing wrong with me. I was just not really like most everybody else. I consider that a good thing now. You're not a freak because you're outside the norm.

But I've always got those images in the back of my head. It's kind of like society is pressuring you. "This is what's right, this is what's right, this is what's right." After growing up for sixteen years, seeing that that's what I'm supposed to be, it's kind of difficult to pull away from that. It's always in the back of my mind, "Oh, I should be doing that." It gets smaller and smaller, less and less.

It's a lot my parents' doing. Telling me that I can be anything I want to be. I'm really lucky to have my parents, 'cause most other parents would have given up on me. My parents haven't. I love my parents. I don't understand how some kids say, "I hate my parents, I hate 'em, I hate 'em." I mean, yeah, I get angry with them sometimes, but I could never hate my parents.

So I got to high school and went, "I guess I have to grow up. What am I gonna do, to prove I'm not a baby any more? I could play a sport, but what sport would want me?" I'm not exactly the athletic-looking type. I'm naturally big boned. I'm a pretty good size. I played basketball when I was eleven. I kind of liked the contact there. But I would always foul out of games! I'd get like, too *into* it. I thought rugby sounded kinda interesting, so I went out for rugby.

The mud's fun. I like to play in the mud. Last year, it was this girl's birthday and we all took her down, and we just got into this huge slinging mud fight. I'm a little boy trapped in a girl's body. Well, that's not true. Not totally true. I don't know.

The bulimia — OK. It's kind of a way . . . you don't have to feel anything. You eat all this stuff, throw it all down, throw it back up, and — there — it's gone. Everything that you felt is just kind of gone. And with rugby, it's a way to get out your aggressions and your feelings in a positive way. 'Cause you're not really hurting people and you're not really hurting yourself. You get kinda bruised up, but you're not really hurting yourself that badly.

My sophomore year I still believed I was, y'know, just a cow. I've sort of gotten over it. You grow out of it. You learn, "Well, hey, if I'm a little bit bigger than everybody else, big deal." My size is a great advan-

tage in rugby. It's harder for girls to take me down, and it's easier for me to take other girls down. I can take the hits.

It makes me angry when people condescend to me because I'm a girl. Guys will do that in the computer store. I'll walk in there, and they'll think I'm not intelligent. I've done so much work on my own computer, I'm probably just as knowledgeable as they are. That drives me up the wall. I realize it could be a lot worse. It's amazing to me how women dealt with it before, 'cause I can barely deal with it now. I'm just ready to stand up and go, "OK, I *will* punch you in the face if you do it again." The boys' rugby team, they tend to do this a lot: We're practicing and the guys' practice is over and they walk straight through our scrimmage. And our coach is like, "Can you guys go around?" and they walk straight through our field.

I got to make up posters and put them all over school about our next game. Nobody ever comes. It's very difficult, we're so looked down upon. It makes me mad. The other sports are like a big thing because they bring in money. But we don't get a chance to bring in money. Our games are normally short notice. We don't charge because not a lot of people know what rugby is. I have a feeling that if people found out about it, we would have crowds like we do at our football games. The average Friday night football game, there are tons of people, snack bar is open, all the cheerleaders going rah, rah. The stands are full, they're packed. Everyone wants to go and see how the teams does, blah blah. It becomes this huge social thing. We'd love to get crowds like that.

My whole family comes to see me play. It's nice to have them there. I live with both my parents. I have a five-year-old brother — oh my God. Being sixteen, that is very frustrating. My brother was born when I was eleven. I was the baby of the family. Everybody's little baby. Then this little brat came along and took my place, and I was pissed! I have a thirty-one-year-old sister. My cousin, she's eleven, she lives with us. My sister is from my dad's first marriage. Pretty normal family situation.

Jen with her mom.
Mom: I hated high school with a passion. I really did. I was fat and not popular and — smart, but didn't want to be a nerd.
Jen: I like being a nerd.
Mom: Yeah, well, nerds are a lot better off these days than they used

to be. It wasn't 'til I got into my early twenties that I started really being comfortable with myself. Growing up is very tough for girls and it's really difficult when you don't look like that standard that they show on TV or whatever.

I think it has been very difficult the last couple of years for Jen. I think the most important thing was just making sure she knew how much we loved her, no matter what. I've always wanted just for her to be happy, to be herself and to be comfortable with herself. I was like Jen. I wasn't this svelte, skinny little girl. I've always tried to make sure she knew that she was special even if she wasn't the cheerleader, little skinny girl type.

Jen: God forbid that I would be.

Mom: *(laughs)* Because she is the person that she is — smart and funny. Sometimes I didn't think she loved me. She didn't show it, but I still loved her. You tell them when they're little, "You can talk to me about anything." But you have to make sure you're here whenever they want to talk. We tried to tell her that there was nothing that we couldn't talk about, or help with. She could always come home.

Jen: Don't get all sappy now, please. In junior high it was worse, not being skinny and not being popular and not being like everybody else. In high school you have a lot more people to choose from, different groups and a lot wider range.

Mom: I think it's different than it was years ago. In junior high we were still pretty much kids. High school was more like junior high now.

I always was overweight when I was younger. My mom and my grandma had me on every diet. Then you start hearing about anorexia and bulimia. With Jennifer, I always wanted to make sure that I never made weight an issue at all. But society makes it an issue. Even if they don't feel it in the home, they feel it everywhere else. They're bombarded with that. She had a real, real, real difficult time. A lot of it I just assumed was just normal teenage angst, just going through what she had to go through. Hormones. It still breaks my heart that I didn't realize it was much deeper than that. When she was little, when she skinned her knee, I could pick her up and say, "I will make this better." I couldn't make this better. And I'll always deeply regret not identifying earlier how really bad it was.

Jen alone in her room, dressing for a blind date.

I'm getting ready to go to a basketball game to meet my Winter Ball date, a blind date that my friends have set me up with. I've never met the guy before. They say he's pretty cute and he's really funny. My friends say he's tall and kinda skinny, and he plays baseball. He's got red sideburns but brown hair. Hmmmm. That's all I know. I don't know what to expect.

I'm hoping he likes me. At least enough to stand me for one night. I hope we don't completely hate each other. My friend says, "Be charming." And I do that by . . . ? Doing what?

I've never had a boyfriend before. I mean, there have been guys that I've like, liked, and then they've never liked me back. They're always like, *(whining)* "Let's be friends," and I'm like, "OK, kiss my butt." That's what's happened so many times that I'm trying not to get my hopes up. I know I should be optimistic. But I want to protect myself so I don't get really hurt. But I don't want to . . . not be open if someone really likes me or . . . shows an interest or whatever.

He would have to be intelligent, because I can't stand people that are slow to catch on. He doesn't have to be a jock, but it'd be cool if he played rugby. Skinny guys, I feel really awkward around skinny guys, 'cause I outweigh them by like twenty pounds, so I could like break 'em in half if I wanted to. He has to be funny. Someone I could get along with. That's why I always end up liking my guy friends. We'll get along and we'll like totally click and then it'll be like phttt . . . and nothing will happen.

I don't know what to wear. Normally when I go out with my friends I don't really care 'cause I'm just with my friends. I'll probably only have one dress change. But tonight I'm meeting this guy and I want him to like me or whatever. I'll probably be changing three or four times.

Jen's finally ready. She gets behind the wheel.

I've had my driver's license for a little more than six weeks. I put a lovely dent in the car the other day driving to school. CD falls on the floor. I'm trying to go straight and trying to pick up the CD. Hit a big bush, knocked out a light and nice little dentage. Cracked part of the windshield up top. Everybody has their first little accident. That was mine. Didn't injure anyone. The only accident so far, I'm hoping, knock on wood, oh, God, no wood in the car.

Of course, I'm exceedingly nervous. I try not to care what people think of me, but in this case, I do care what he thinks of me. I'm nervous 'cause there's already this kinda obligation to go to Winter Ball together.

I just don't know if he'll think I'm very cute. I don't think I'm very attractive to guys. I don't know why. I've never had a guy actually like me as more than a friend. So if a guy ever did, I'd probably go, "What are you, on crack or something?"

I have some good qualities. To guys it's probably not that attractive, but I'm affectionate. I'm funny. I've got a strange, sick, and twisted sense of humor. I'm outgoing. I'm loyal. I'm kinda protective, 'cause I don't like it when people hurt people that I care about. I try to make people realize that they've hurt others. Normally not in a violent way.

I can't believe that next year I'm gonna be a senior. It is the weirdest feeling in the world. 'Cause it feels like it'll never end and then it's like, what do we do when it's over? Did I actually learn anything?

I want to be an actress or a writer. I liked my drama class. It's one giant sexual innuendo. We're all obsessed with sex and it's all we talk about, all we joke about backstage, it's horrible! During *Little Women,* we were so bad. Backstage slapping each other's butts — everybody grabbing everybody else. The running joke throughout the play was that I was a pole dancer. I made up a little pole dance 'cause we had these poles holding up the second story of the stage. I would never be an actual pole dancer or anything. Not even to pay my way through college. Mostly because you're just selling your body, with yucky drunk men leering at you. Not my idea of something that educated people do. I've always wanted to be educated. Everybody says curiosity killed the cat. Well, I'm gonna die at a young age, 'cause I'm really curious. I want to know about everything.

Now we're in suburbia. We were in suburbia before, but this is real suburbia. This is more upper middle class than my neighborhood. I'm just plain ol' middle class. The kids at my school, their parents buy them new Beamers and Mercedes. My family, we have no excess money. But I'm happy being where I am. I know the value of a dollar whereas a lot of kids here don't. I know you've gotta work for it. We're definitely not poor, but they're not gonna buy me a car, because they can't. We're building a house down the street because we're renting our house. Kids at school live in mansions. It's really odd to be around those peo-

ple. I almost get embarrassed. I don't invite a lot of people over, and people wonder why that is. I'm not necessarily embarrassed. It's just like what if . . . I'm not normally friends with the kind of people that would go, "You're not as rich as I am. I'm not gonna be friends with you." But there's still always that thing in the back of your mind.

After the blind date, before the Winter Ball.

He was nice and cute and funny. He's got a cute personality which makes him cuter. He's kinda skinny. Guys that are skinny, I don't like being bigger than a guy 'cause it's just kind of awkward. "Oh yeah, I could beat you up." But some guys are just skin and bone. He's got some muscle.

He's got a girlfriend. But he doesn't really like her a whole lot any more. He wants to dump her, but he's not really sure. He's asking me for advice. I'm like, "I don't know, what do you want to do?" He confronted her last week and she acted like she didn't care. That's a hint right there. I don't understand that. People don't want to be mean, so they act like they really like you. You end up thinking that they like you, and they don't. It ends up hurting more.

I think he knows that I'm kinda fond of him. But we both know that nothing is gonna happen. I'm not gonna make big moves on him, considering he's got a girlfriend. That kinda kills it right there, so. He's telling her the truth about the Winter Ball: he's going out with some guys on the baseball team. Not the whole truth — but it's partially the truth. His girlfriend would freak out.

I just kind of understood this as a friendship thing. That's the way I perceive it from him, I don't know how he sees it.

Something might happen. But, any big thing that might happen soon, I don't think so. We'll probably go out, do stuff a little bit more, that would be cool.

Jen shows us the formal dress she bought for the Winter Ball. It's long, simple, lavender, sweet, like a 1965 bridesmaid or a Jackie Kennedy A-line, to the floor.

This is my dress. I just bought it. I got it on clearance for sixty dollars. I'm really glad, 'cause it's a Jessica McClintock.

I always feel like I'm gonna get it dirty or something when I'm trying on nice clothes. I'm just a big tomboy. Well, I'm not *that* big of a tomboy. Well, I'm kind of a tomboy. It makes me feel like…I like to try it on, but I'm always afraid I'm gonna rip it or break it or get it dirty or something. I don't normally like pink, but it's a long gown, and it makes me feel pretty. I know that's so stupid. Oh, well. It does, it makes me feel really girly. And I'm not used to that.

I kind of like that it has a high neck. Low necks bother me, I don't know why. It doesn't look really slutty or anything, not too much skin. Not that that's a bad thing. But I'm not really comfortable walking around like half-naked. I had to get a dress that I could wear a normal or semi-normal bra with. It's very difficult to find all those neat-o bras with the cool little strappies, or strapless in my size, which is like a 36DD.

When I was younger, I wore shirts that made my breasts look even bigger. I used to have this pin on my backpack that said "Don't talk to my breasts, they're deaf." It's true, guys will look directly at your breasts and just kinda nod with what you're saying. You could say just about anything, and they'd still nod. And you're like, "Hey, I'm up here!" And they don't notice that. Especially with ones like my size. I feel bad saying that, but it's true. The size mine are, no matter what I wear, they're always gonna go, "Uuhhhh…" and look directly at them and talk to them. Boobs, tits, hooters, we know guys say that to each other. But to us, they just call 'em boobs.

I'm OK with it. But there are so many problems with them. I probably have a higher risk of breast cancer. I've got these grooves dug in my shoulders from bra straps. I have upper back problems because of 'em. But if they weren't so big, I'd look strange because I'm proportioned correctly. If they were any smaller, I'd look like a cow. They draw attention. If they are the first thing that grabs a guy's attention, but then he gets to know me, and realizes that there is more to me than just my breasts, then it's OK, and I like them. But if they draw a guy's attention and that's the only thing that keeps a guy's attention, then, it wasn't worth it.

Everybody else knows about hair and nails and makeup. I'm really retarded at stuff like that. My hair, I can pull it back in a ponytail. I can braid it in really bad little…it looks like a boy braided it. For the dance, I'll probably have the hairdresser put it half up or something. Get it curled or whatever. I don't know. Believe me, I've had bad experiences in the past with my hair at formal dances. Freshmen year it was all big and ratted and it looked like I had a poodle on my head. At homecoming it just looked poopy. I've never had a really great hair experience. Makeup, don't even ask me. I don't know what I'm trying to enhance. Then my nails. My nails are pretty short 'cause of rugby, but I paint them anyway. I paint them really bizarre colors and it always chips, so I'm not really an expert at nails. Like, if anything, the epitome of me is chipping purple nail polish.

After Winter Ball.

Winter Ball was a lot of fun. We went to dinner at the Pasta House. The guys had little balloon-animal hats made. We had fun at the dance. I got to know Nick a lot better. I think he got to know me a little bit better. I thought I looked really good. I liked my hair, I thought that was cool. We went over Christian's house after the dance. I ended up falling asleep. Like, Nick was sitting on the couch and I was like laying on him, like falling asleep.

I think I asked him to Sadie Hawkins, that's a dance where the girls invite guys. I did ask him to Sadie's. I was like laying there on the couch and he was standing there telling me he was leaving and I was thinking to myself, I've got to take him to Sadie's. I didn't know if I had said it out loud. It turned out that I did say it out loud, so.

He's supposed to be dumping his girlfriend, but we've been saying this for a while now. Now he says he like actually is gonna dump her. Chris says that he kinda likes me but he's really confused because of the whole girlfriend thing. Chris says he kinda likes me so... I'm getting kinda excited. I really like him. He's really funny.

I don't know if he likes me as more than a friend. I'd like him to, but I really don't think he's gonna want any kind of relationship once he breaks up with his girlfriend. I'm not figuring on anything happening, but if it did it would be really cool. You know how you learn not to care? Then if nothing happens or we go out and we break up, it's OK.

We didn't kiss. Nobody kissed anybody. That's cool with me. I've kissed a couple guys. I've never had like a serious relationship. I like guys though. Everybody talks about their boyfriends. It's like, "Shut up! I've never had one." They're like, "Oh, it's not that great." Can I figure that out for myself? They say, "It's better being alone." Well, let me draw my own conclusions, OK? 'Cause no matter how many people tell me, I have to experience it myself.

A week or so later.

I talked to Nick last night. He called me just to say hi. I thought that was kinda cool, he called me just to say hi! I'm trying not to get too excited because of it.

As for the girlfriend, he said it's really really close to being over. OK, Nick, sure, whatever.

I don't know if anything serious will happen. I figure if he dumps her this weekend, which he says he's going to, which he probably won't, 'cause he said he's going to so many times, maybe something will happen. But I know he's not gonna want a relationship like right after he breaks up with her. If anything serious happens, I don't expect it to be for a while. But it's cool being friends with him, 'cause he's really a sweet guy.

I want a boyfriend. I don't know if I want one *that* badly — I don't want one bad enough to wear dresses every day and wear a whole lot of makeup. Every girl pretty much wants one.

One of my friends, he likes to tell me that I should be more girly. "Jenny, you should do something with your hair. Jenny, don't paint your nails that color, it makes you look like you're dead. Jenny, don't dress like that, put on a dress once in a while." "Shaun, when are you gonna figure out I'm not the average girl?" He thinks...he believes that's what a girl should be. I realize I don't have to be that. I can be what I want to be.

MORGAN, SIXTEEN
LEXINGTON, SOUTH CAROLINA

It's just a peer pressure thing, I guess, to change from what you are to — a girl. I've always been a girl, but to act and dress and talk like a girl. Everybody starts changing through middle school. The girls start growing up and the guys start noticing the girls. Eventually you want to say, "Hey, I'm not one of the guys any more! I'm a girl! Look at me!"

When I was a little girl, I played a lot with my brothers. I didn't have Barbie dolls. I had Tonka trucks. We'd sit out in the driveway, and scoop

up sand in the buckets of the trucks. Our favorite thing to do was jump off the trampoline into the pool. I don't know what changed me.

It was awkward, because your bodies are changing. You want to look good, but you look in the mirror and think, "Ugh!" I was short and I was kinda chunky. My hair was very short. In middle school every girl feels like, you don't know what's going on. You just feel kinda out of place. Not with the older people and not with the younger people. You're just kinda stuck in the middle.

You just have to suck it up and say, "Hey, Mama, is there anything you can do to help me?" When I was going through that transitional period from little girl to teenager, my mom was real supportive. She's a girlie-girl, so she set me down and she said, "Hair, makeup, and clothes!" She said if you want to look like a girl, you got to act like a girl, and you need to walk and talk like a girl, instead of, "Hey, I'm one of the guys."

You have to work at it. It's the way you carry yourself and the way you present yourself. I think it has a lot to do with self-confidence and the time that you spend putting into yourself. You start trying new things, letting your hair grow out, cutting it. You start playing in Mom's makeup. Mom starts putting it on you. I guess that's when you really decide, "Hey, I'm finding…myself."

I've changed, but that underlying person never changes. You try and keep that and say, "This is who I am." That little girl is still in me. If you lose that part, you're nobody. I'm still that little girl.

I was scared about competing because of the stereotypes that are presented with beauty pageants. The blonde, the airhead, no brains. I didn't want to present myself as that type of a person. I've always wanted people to look at me and say "smart" instead of "pretty." A beauty pageant just didn't seem to fit that. That scared me a lot, what my friends thought.

I met a girl and she was in them. She seemed really nice and she said, "You meet so many people. It's a great experience." I had the dress, and I had everything, so I said, "OK, I'll do it."

After I got into it, it was hard. It's like a softball player training to play softball. There's a certain way to stand, a certain way to look. It's hard. I have a coach. She is Super Woman to me. She can do it all. I thought, "It's a pageant. All I have to do is walk across the stage." And she told me how to get in stance. It's the hardest thing! My stomach hurt, my rear end hurt, my shoulders were tight, and it was uncomfortable. But she helped me. You put yourself forward and you try to be your best.

I was so nervous my first one. And I was skeptical about doing it. It turned out totally different than anything I ever thought of. I walked up, did what I was supposed to do, or so I thought, and I won! It was like, I don't know what I just did, but whatever I did, it worked.

You have to stand out and you have to look good to yourself and to the judges. You have to say, "I need you to look at *me*, instead of looking at these other eight girls up here."

If I get nervous my whole chest and my shoulders and my neck just break out in these horrible red splotches. And my hands are shaking. You just have to breathe and say, "I can handle this." Everybody has their nervous quirks. And you say, "Everybody's going through this. I have to breathe and I have to chill out." I haven't really figured out what makes me nervous yet. I guess it's the competition. You put yourself forward. You have to say, "I'm going to be my best and if my best isn't good enough, then it's not." That makes me nervous. Thinking that this other girl, her best might be better than my best. I'm wondering about this chick over here. But you can't let anybody else know that they're scaring you.

It's a competition with yourself. You have to block out these other girls and say, "This is me against myself." I have to be the best that I can be. If I'm being that best and this other girl is being her best over here and that is better than my best, she should win. You just ham it up, eat it up and say, "Hey, I'm here." And the nervousness goes with it.

If you're doing a swimsuit competition, you want to get everything pushed and poked and ready. Then you want to walk in front of the other girls, and just —*whoosh!* It's just a mind game, I guess. "I'm not really better than you, but I'm gonna act it." But you're friendly. When it comes down to dirty competition, that's what you do. It's what I do.

The preparation for swimsuit is especially mind-boggling. I work out about an hour a day, five days a week. I run two miles a day. You want your body in top form. You want muscles to pop. And you just want to say, "Hey, I'm in shape. I am an American teenage girl — I'm athletic," but yet it's a beauty pageant. You just try to get your body in the best form that it can be.

Firm Grip is a lifesaver for the bathing suit competition. It's a spray, a sticky spray that wrestlers use when they wrap their hands. It's wonderful for spraying your rear end and pulling that bathing suit so nothing — so you can't see. It keeps your bathing suit from riding up. That's one of the best tricks. Tape, tape's always a good one. Usually it's masking tape or duct tape. You tape the part of your body that you want pushed in or you want pushed up. Usually you're taping either your stomach, because you don't want a pudge, or you're taping your breasts. If you tape your breasts, you want to push them all the way up. Then you start under your arm and tape around, and put your breasts over the tape so they're pushed up. You want 'em to fill out. Or, if you want your stomach flat, you just start at your side and tape it down, so you don't have any wrinkles. You want it smooth.

This was mean: I walked in the bathroom and I brushed my hair, like every other girl in high school does. A very derogatory comment was made. Like, "Morgan's always got to look perfect." And it upset me. Because I don't want to be pictured as someone perfect. I want to be pictured as a regular teenager who has a hobby and who enjoys it. You just want to really blend in. At school you try to blend in, but at competition you want to say, "Hey, I'm different. You need to look at me." But at school you just want to say, "I'm one of you, blend in with me, go along with me," instead of, "Why does she look like that?" I have a zit right here that I'm trying to hide but everybody faces that. This is me. I have to deal with that. And I can't change it, so I'm stuck with being myself and kinda happy with it.

Morgan and her mom.

Mom: You don't know what the judges are looking for. They might want long dark hair, they might want a blonde, they might want little makeup, they might want a true beauty queen: lots of makeup, big, pretty hair, that kinda thing. It's you against the judges, and either they like you or they don't. You just have to do the best you can. If they like that, then good. If not, they're gonna choose someone else. If not, Mama sits and cries. And Mama sits and cries if she wins.

Morgan: The very first pageant I was in, I won. And Mom jumped out of the seat, yelling, "That's my baby!"

Mom: I did jump pretty high, but it was uncontrollable. It was her first pageant and her first win. So I was very excited. I did just shoot straight up! When she placed for the semi-finals for the state, I just slid right out of my chair to the floor. My husband was going, "Mama, sit up, Mama, you got to sit up!" And the tears were just streaming down my face. The tears flow when she wins, when she loses, it puts things in perspective.

Morgan: It's good for you every now and then.

Mom: Maybe you did everything right and it goes back to the judges again.

Morgan: You still want to be yourself.

Mom: 'Cause it is a competition, if against no one but yourself. She has a competitive spirit that I don't have. I've done everything but walk across that stage with her. I take every step she takes, I'm taking it right along with her. If she falls, I fall. If she wins, I win. If she loses, I lose. But I'm there to pick her up — always, every time.

HOPE

Bianca and Michelle say they're traditional girls who long to marry and raise children of their own. But they suffer the scorn of boys and men, and they hate that disrespect. They want to rebuild gender roles and explode the narrow icon of the good American girl. They don't realize how radical their vision really is. Like girls everywhere, they want to raise their daughters in a fair, free world. They say, "Maybe by that time…"

Like girls everywhere, they *hope*.

BIANCA, SIXTEEN
SHAW AIR FORCE BASE, SOUTH CAROLINA

Me and my mom, our relationship is on again, off again. When I was younger she was just my mom — she was great. Now that I'm older, I want to break away. She's still trying to... "Let's wear matching shirts," or, "Let's go to the mall." I wanna go with my friends, not my mom. I wanna break away, and she's still, "No, come back!" It's nice to know that she still...even though I try to push her away, she's still wanting to bring me back. We're not...I wanna be more...she's...she wants to be on a mother-daughter *and* friends basis. That's a hard thing to bring together. 'Cause she's an authority figure and you can't be equals. She swears we can, but I don't know. There've been a lot of struggles between me and her. I'm a big Daddy's girl, and she has always tried to pull me away from that. I get along more with my dad than I do with my mom sometimes. But I can always come back to her and I can always relate to her because she's female, just as I am. There are things I would tell my mom that I would never tell my dad in a million years. So, we're very close on certain things, and we're way far apart on others. But she's still a great person.

Both my parents are great, they really are. They make me very mad sometimes, but I know that they do it because they love me. It's a hectic family sometimes. Everything's OK. We move around a lot. I was born in Wyoming, then we moved to North Carolina, and we moved from there when I was three or four to Germany. We lived there for six years. Now we've been in South Carolina for six years. It's constantly changing, but it's a great opportunity to live different places and meet all kinds of people.

My dad, he's from Detroit, it's a big city. He had like a rough childhood. He lived with his mom. He never really talks about it. He went into the military when he was real young so he could have somewhere to go, so he could have a job, and he could get his life on track. My mom, she had an amazing childhood. She's been all over the world. Her dad was with an embassy, and she lived in Brazil, Florida, and Wyoming. She rode wild horses, she lived in the Amazon jungle, she danced in parades in Brazil. She's done adventurous things, like dirt-bike races.

I have an older brother, he's eighteen. He gets to do whatever he wants. It's hard to see him do things that I can't do. He's a boy, and parents tend to let the boys go before they let the girls go.

I really like school. Everybody's like, "You big nerd!" But I make As. I love learning. I like life science, human anatomy, animals. Not plants, plants are boring to me. But I really like living things, humans. The human body just amazes me. I find it fascinating.

My teachers, they always tend to gear more toward the guys when it comes to the more scientific heavy-duty stuff. Everybody's like, "Well, you probably don't find this interesting." I don't know why, because girls are just as interested in science as boys are. I only have two guys in my biology class and they sleep most of the time. They're not even thinking about science. They don't find it amazing like some of the girls in my class. Every science class I've had, the guys always do worse than the girls. The girls always succeed and the guys are always falling behind.

I have classes that are taught by coaches. Big buff male coaches who think that girls can't do anything. I had a football coach last year, he was my world-geography teacher. Everything was football. We'd be talking about Saudi Arabia, and he'd link it to football. I'd be like, I'm not here to learn about football. He would talk to the guys more than the girls. All the girls were sitting in a little corner. And the guys were all sprawled out. Me and my two friends, we were really opinionated in his class, 'cause he was always talking about women. He called us the "estrogen corner." We always had an opinion about what he said, 'cause he was very, "Well, girls are not as good as men." That's not something I want to listen to.

This year I have a football coach for my U.S. history teacher and he does the exact same thing. He says, "Women are just...they play sports, but they'll never be as good as men." Maybe men are a little more aggressive in certain sports. But women can be just as aggressive. And that doesn't have anything to do with learning capability. They think just 'cause they're good at football they can excel in their class. That definitely isn't true at all, 'cause we have some football players in my class that just aren't cutting it.

Everybody thinks cheerleaders are just big ditzes. But that's not how it is at all. Nobody sees cheerleaders as athletes. We have athlete passes, just like the football players and the volleyball team. Everybody's like, "Why do y'all have them? You don't do anything." But if they tried to get on the floor, and lift a 120-pound girl by themselves, they'd see that it's a hard thing to do. It takes a lot of concentration, and it's very time-consuming. Just 'cause we wear a short skirt, they think we're not as important as anybody else. This year we had a football team that didn't win a single game. We still had to get out there and cheer for them. We're trying to encourage them to do their best and meanwhile these people are scowling at us.

Some people look at cheerleaders as the tramps of the school because they're wearing a short skirt. But we have done something to earn this skirt. This uniform is a symbol of what we have done this year to work toward this.

I don't think looks are that important. Some of the girls on the squad disagree. We had a girl try out and one cheerleader said, "What does she wear when she comes to school?" I was amazed. It doesn't matter to me. I'm definitely no fashion model when I go to school. I go to school to learn, not to impress anybody else.

But I think it really . . . it does matter how you look. We have a girl on the squad who's not as attractive as everybody else in some people's eyes. And they push her aside. She's as important as everybody else, but people push her away. They're like, "Why is she a cheerleader?" And they down her, but she tried out, and she's here. I think a lot of people are angry that she's here. The way she looks, the way she dresses. It's a big deal. People have like a cheerleader type. When girls try out, they're like, "She doesn't look like she could be a cheerleader. Look how she's dressed." And I'm like, "How can you tell, until you see her cheer?"

Cheerleaders pile in pyramids and throw their stars into the air in elaborate gymnastic stunts. Within the squad hierarchy, in terms of their stunt positions, some girls "base," others "fly."

Weight is a huge issue. I wanted to be a flyer. I really wanted to go up in the air. I couldn't 'cause there were other people who were lighter than me. The chunkier girls always have to be at the bottom. I always have to base. I never get to fly. I could do the same stunts that everybody else could do, but I couldn't fly because I wasn't light enough. It's unfair to treat somebody like that. You put your uniform on, and people are like, "That uniform's a little tight, isn't it?" It's a big issue. People are like, if you're not thin, you can't be a cheerleader. And that's not true. There are girls who are heavier than me, that can do a lot more than I can. There are people out there doin' flips that are a lot heavier than me. And I can't do flips. People who are heavier set, they can do just as much as the skinnier people can do. But they never get the chance. People automatically assume they can't because they're heavy. Weight really is a big issue on the squad. People whisper, "Oh my god, look at that chunky cheerleader."

All my friends are a lot skinnier than I am. I say, "Oh, I wanna wear your jeans," and I go to put them on, and they barely make it to my thighs. Definitely, weight is an issue. It's an issue with every girl. It's part of your self-image. I feel like I'm on the heavy side, but I'm OK with my…I'm not, "God, I have to be thin." You can be OK with your weight, but you'll still feel that you're not perfect.

Everyone says, "Oh, you're so pretty, you're a really nice looking girl," but I don't look at myself as everybody else looks at me. My hair, ugh, I hate my hair. Everybody I know has straight hair. I want to have long, straight hair and be able to run my fingers through my hair. I've always hated my hair. I've always wanted to have straight hair like everybody else, 'cause I've always stuck out. Everybody's like, "There's the curly-haired girl." I hate my hair. And my eyes, I hate brown eyes. I don't hate them on other people. I just don't like them on me. I'm just…I'm plain. I have brown hair and brown eyes. Brown skin. I just want something that stands out. The eyes are the one thing that everybody looks at. My eyes are plain. I would like to change them, maybe make them green or blue, something that would shock people, something that would make me stand out. Definitely.

I look in magazines and I'll try to do my hair like that girl, 'cause she looks really pretty in that magazine. I look on TV and I see models and I'm like, "Oh my gosh! Wow!" You tell girls, "If you look like this, then you're gonna go somewhere." That's a big thing to put on somebody. And then you hear people say looks aren't everything. You see beautiful women and you see how much money they're making because they're beautiful, but then you look at other people and they're not as pretty, but they have a lot more talent. People see the beauty first, before they see the skills.

We have a lot of pretty girls at our school. They've got the perfect figure, they've got the most beautiful eyes, the prettiest hair, the prettiest clothes. People look at them and they're like, "Wow, they're so beautiful." They have everything, they have…they may…y'know.

You don't even know the person, you don't know if they're dying inside. All you see is that outer shell and you look at them and you want that. There are girls at my school and I just look at them and I'm like, "Why can't I be like that?" But then again, I don't know what their life is like. I've never taken the time to ask them. I just always assume it's good 'cause they look good on the outside.

I always dream that I'm gonna be the girl that everyone wants to be. I've always had that dream, that I'm gonna be the girl that everybody looks at, and they say, "Wow!" There are girls at my school, they walk into the room and everybody's mesmerized. They're just, "Wow, man, I wanna be her!" And I've always had a dream that I'm gonna be that girl. Y'know, it hasn't come true yet. But I've always had that fantasy dream, that I'm gonna be that girl that everybody wants to be. And when I walk into a room, everybody's gonna turn, and everybody's gonna look at me. That's pretty much my main dream. I just want everybody to be, "Wow!" Wowed by me.

I'm happy now, but if I looked like that I'd be flattered. You can never have too much flattery, never, no matter what anybody says. It probably wouldn't drastically change my life. I know it wouldn't. I don't know. Just knowing that people are looking at me and saying, "Wow!" I think that would make me feel amazing. Looks are important. They are. Looks can get you a lot of places. They can. I don't think it would change my life drastically. It would be an immense feeling, though.

I was told that if you eat a lot of cheese that makes you smile. I eat a lot of cheese, I love to smile. My competition smile, I have a fierce, uptight smile. My face is just frozen in that position the whole time I'm out on the floor. When I get on that floor I turn it on. I'm just ecstatic. Even if I'm feeling crappy that day, I get out there and I turn it on. My face is just a whole new face. I'm really excited, my eyes are open wide, I show teeth, millions of teeth. I want to prove to the judges that I have spirit and I'm excited to be there. By the time I get off the floor, I'm praising God that I can release my face, 'cause my cheeks are so tense from smiling so hard.

I have a boyfriend. We've been together for two years and three months. When I first met him I was like, "Oh, man, he's adorable." But I always thought he was way out of my league. I'd never have enough nerve to go up to him and say, "I like you."

I met him in marching band. He played an instrument and I drilled flag. I looked at him from far away. I'd write letters to him when I came home from band practice, and tear them up as soon as I was done, and throw them away. 'Cause I thought, "He'd laugh at this."

One day I told one of my new friends from the band, and she told him. Luckily he said, "She's cute, I like her, too." We got to know each other and things just went from there. It has been an up and down relationship, but I've enjoyed every minute of it. He doesn't live here any more, he lives far away. It's kind of hard not having him here. But I know I can deal with it. It's OK.

One cheerleader on our squad, she has a baby. It's the hardest thing in the world for her. But she loves that child. It forced her to grow up and to take on a huge responsibility. But everybody is susceptible to that. Everybody is susceptible to everything. We had another cheerleader get pregnant. She's no longer on the squad, but it happens, and that goes to show, it can happen to anybody. It's an issue in my life. But I don't worry about it. I just try not to think about it. But, yeah, it's an issue. And it's an issue with a lot of my friends. It's an issue actually with every single friend I have.

Up through fifth grade, when I was in elementary school, everybody looked the same. Everybody was wearing dorky clothes. We didn't care what our shoes looked like. We didn't care what our hair looked like. I got to middle school, sixth grade, and I saw people wearing bows in their hair and some of them started wearing makeup and cool clothes. I was just like — ugh! I was still wearing teddy bear shirts and those people were wearing teenager clothes. Sixth grade was the worst time of my life. My mom cut my hair short. It was really curly, and I couldn't take care of it. I didn't . . . I don't know, I didn't progress like other people when I went to middle school. When I got there everybody . . . clothes were a big thing, makeup was a big thing. I'm looking around, and I'm still wearing my hair real funky, I'm missing a tooth. I'm like, "Oh, man!" I was like, "I gotta do something about this!" In seventh grade, I started to change a little bit more. I decided to grow my hair out, 'cause I wanted to have long hair like everybody else. I noticed a lot of changes in myself. I wanted to be more feminine. I wanted to be like the other girls. I wanted to wear my hair in bows, I wanted to wear earrings. I went from looking at teeny bop magazines to looking at *Vogue* magazine.

I got my period at the worst time, in my sleep. I was in seventh grade, and all my friends had had theirs. My friend got hers at a sleepover in sixth grade, and I was like, "God, when am I gonna get mine?" And—oh, now I wish—ugh! Oh my gosh! Take it back! Then, I was excited, I ran to school. "Guess what girls! I'm not the only one left out, I'm with y'all now!" But now as the years go by, I'm like, "Oh, man, no! Not that time again!"

I miss being a little girl. There's so many pressures now. Especially in high school. Everything you do now is gonna affect your whole life. When you were younger, you made mud pies. "I'm gonna eat some mud, I'm gonna play with my friends, I'm gonna go climb on the jungle gym." Sometimes when I get into bad situations, I'm like, "God, I wish I was two again." Somebody was there to take care of me. Somebody told me what to do, to make sure I didn't do the wrong thing, to make sure that I always did the right thing, to be there to guide me. It's...it's different now. It really is. *(Big sigh.)* I definitely wish I was little again sometimes. But then other times, I wish I was older and I was bigger and I could do other things that older people get to do. So it changes from day to day. My parents still won't let me pluck my eyebrows! And I'm like, "God, I wish I was eighteen so I could do what I want!"

I would tell younger girls to take things slow, to enjoy everything you do each day when you're young. Because when you get to high school, there's no going back. I wanted to wear makeup so bad when I was in seventh grade. I'd sneak out of the house with my mom's lipstick, and I'd get to school and I'd put it on. If you try really hard to grow up when you're younger, you're gonna miss all the things that are going on around you. It's really sad if you miss everything. I work in a store and middle-school girls come in, and they look older than me. They're gonna miss their childhood when they get older. They won't have a chance to go back and make it up.

I'm not on the cheerleading squad any more. It got very hectic. It was very frustrating. Everybody had to be number one. The girls are at each others' throats. We were unified one minute and hating each other the next. It gets really hard when you have a group of girls and you just bunch 'em together and you expect them to be perfect. People have emotions and you have to put those out the door. It put a strain on

everybody. Our friendships were just really shaky. When I was on the squad I was like, "Ugh! I can't stand you right now, don't look at me!" And now, I mean we talk and everything's OK. I'm a weakling when it comes to that. It means more to me to keep friendships than to be the best at something. I'd rather be down here with my friends than be up there with no one. I felt bad because I quit. You almost feel like you failed at something that you really wanted to try hard and do.

I don't want anybody fighting, I don't want anybody ripping each other's hair out. I just want everyone to get along. That would be the perfect world, if we didn't have anybody angry at each other, if everybody loved each other. Everybody's holding hands, singing songs or something. Just very peaceful and a very happy environment to be in.

I wanna have a big happy family, when I'm through with college. I want to go to work and have a husband. I wanna have two kids, a boy and a girl, but I'll take what I get, definitely. I've always dreamed of having a nice house. There are things I wanted when I was younger that I didn't wanna ask for, because I knew it was too much for my parents to give me at that time. But I want my children to have everything. I want to spoil them rotten. I wanna have a dog and I wanna have a cat and I wanna have fish, and I wanna have all kinds of animals running around. I want to have a big yard. I always dream about that. I see commercials on TV, and there's like a family, and they're doing family things or eating dinner. And I'm like, "That's gonna be me." I'm gonna have a big dining room table and we're gonna sit down and we're gonna eat dinner together. I'm gonna take my kids to school, and I'm gonna pick them up from school, and we can talk about what they did that day.

MICHELLE, EIGHTEEN
EL DORADO HILLS, CALIFORNIA

I'm so not a nineties girl. I want the house, the car, the kids, the husband. I wouldn't even mind being a housewife. Isn't that terrible? I don't think women say that any more. But I wouldn't mind that at all. I don't want a big house, I don't want a nice car, I mean, one nice car. I'm not after the boats and the cars and the money and going out to dinner at nice restaurants every night. I just want a normal life. I sound like I'm seven, but I'm a girl at heart, I can't help it. That's what I want. The typical American life.

I don't know if I could handle actually being a housewife and sitting around the house all day. But when you have kids, they need you home with them when they're little.

When I was a little girl, gosh, I used to be really sweet and shy. I used to be painfully shy. I was afraid to talk to people, afraid to order in restaurants. I had other people order for me.

During my sophomore year, I decided that I wanted to join something. I joined rugby because you didn't have to try out, like all the other sports. I was too afraid to try out.

Since I've played rugby, I've become really outgoing, especially when I'm out on the field. I love to be out there yelling and stuff with the other girls. I kinda felt left out until now. Playing rugby, I feel like I'm really involved in my school and just in *something*. I play pretty well. I never thought that I could play a sport, or that I would be good enough to play with other girls and be athletic. It's made me feel a lot better about myself.

I don't think I look like one of the big burly girls that you'd expect to play rugby. None of the girls out there are stereotypical jock girls. It's just fun to go out and be a part of something and play and tackle. It's fun to play in the mud, you don't get that chance too often.

Tackling is the greatest part of the game. I play for the tackling. It's kind of a way to get your aggression out. It's really fun when you tackle the bigger girls. People are like, "Wow, she's a lot bigger than you."

There's a lot of techniques we practice. You have to get down low and wrap your arms around the girl. But when you get out in a game, you're not really thinking about it. You just do it. You're running and your adrenaline's up so high. You just tackle. You're trying to take that girl down. She's got the ball. We tackle the girls with the ball so that they stop running up the field. It's basically, stop the ball from going any farther.

You've got your adrenaline going and it's so exciting to know that you can take these girls down. I mean, it sounds crazy, but you do feel powerful. It's fun to know that you can do it, and that you don't have to be big to do it. That you don't have to be strong. You have to have the techniques and just do it.

I'm really energetic about the tackling part. Even when we scrimmage with the girls on our team. You feel bad sometimes. I remember a

scrimmage where I tackled one of our girls and made her cry. I felt kind of bad, but it was kind of exciting at the same time.

There's a lot of bruising, a lot of cuts, cleat marks. After a game all the girls get together and compare bruises. It sounds really weird and kinda tomboyish, "Oh, look at this one." It's like a contest, who has the best bruises. We don't mind 'em. Nobody's really scared of 'em. 'Cause it happens. You've got those cleats on, you're gonna get kicked. But injuries are overplayed. We've only had two major injuries since I started playing. One of the girls screwed up her leg really bad. She had pins put in her leg, and now she can't play, ever, or anything. And Erin did something to her elbow, she had like a half cast.

I was dating this guy and he said, "You can't play rugby, you'll get hurt! You'll get beat up!" It's really not that bad. You come up with bruises and stuff, but not broken bones. I've never had a black eye out of the game.

People think girls can't play rugby. We get derogatory comments from men. The other day I had my rugby shirt on and this guy starts going on about, "Oh, I'm sure it's really soft," and, "You don't tackle, do you?" Girls can do it. Physically, we may not be as big and strong as boys, but we can play as well as they can. It's a rough sport and when girls play rugby, people are shocked. Especially men. It drives me insane but it's kinda fun to shock people.

I really hate stereotypes. I hate sexism, I hate homophobics. People are so prejudiced. We go out and we play rugby because it's fun. It has nothing to do with being girls. We can be just as rough as anybody else. It's unfair for people to think less of us because of our gender.

We have a hard time dealing with our rugby boys. They make jokes about us and they laugh at us. They don't think well of us being girls, playing rugby. We're not as fast or as strong as they are, but we try really hard. It's disappointing that they don't respect us as their female counterparts. But we get over it. We just keep going out and playing.

Girls are typically — or stereotypically — thought of as being these little weak things that play volleyball or tennis. Every year I guess sexism decreases a little bit, but there's still a lot of things that you have to deal with, being a girl. You get used to it. You stop noticing it. I mean, you can't even really point out the stereotypes, they're like everywhere. Like, there's a stereotype that girls aren't as good in math and science.

Gosh, I could beat out a lot of the boys I know in math and science. We can do whatever we want to do. That's the thing—we can. I've never thought I couldn't do something because I was a girl. I do what I want to do.

You just fight back, and you do what they say you can't do. You do the jobs they say you can't do, you play the sports that they say you can't. I mean, I'm not exactly a feminist or anything. I still like guys to open my door and pay for dinner—but I'm not gonna let anybody put me down and tell me I can't. It doesn't matter, being a girl. You can do whatever you want. I mean, boys are not better than me. I can run faster than quite a few of them. I've beat them out in sprints and things.

I don't know if girls are brought up less aggressive on purpose, or if it just happens. Girls aren't taught to be aggressive, and boys are. Since they're little they go out and play football with their brothers. A lot of girls around here, their parents have a lot of money. So they turn out to be the really foofie kind, buying clothes and makeup. Not that it's a bad thing to be feminine and wear makeup, but they're not as aggressive. I think I fall somewhere in the middle. I'm not really the jock type. I just like to play rugby. I'm not very manly. I'm not exactly girly-girly either. You should be a little bit of both. You can't run around in pink dresses all your life.

I change every year. I become more outgoing. When I'm out with the girls on the rugby field, the first year players are not as aggressive as they should be, and so I like to get them riled up, get them ready to play. Teach them how to tackle, how to be aggressive, how to get an attitude. You can't let people run over you.

The whole "women rugby players are dykes" thing. I think it has to do with girls doing things that aren't exactly girlish, or what's accepted to be girlish. I know our girls are homophobic, they'll say things about college women we know, oh, she's gay, she's a lesbian. We do know some gay women rugby players, I mean, it happens. I don't know what everybody's so scared of. I like what I like, and everyone else is entitled to like what they like. I'm not afraid of people thinking I'm gay. I may not be, but I'm not gonna deprive anyone of their rights, of what they choose and what they think is right for themselves.

I'm not traditionally moral. I'm pretty immoral, as bad as that sounds. But what I do believe in, I believe in all the way. One of my major things is gay rights. There's a lot of homophobia. But, I'm so for gay rights. You hear a lot of, "I don't care what they do, as long as I don't see it." It's not fair to be like that. Gay people might as well have the same marriage rights as straight people. It's just wrong the way people think. I'm not always right, but I do believe in things.

The community I live in, it's a very white, homophobic kind of community. If you were to get into a discussion about gay rights, people go crazy around here. "That's wrong, it's against the Bible," that kind of thing. My parents are so anti-gay, it's crazy. My mom knows... to some extent she knows that I'm for gay rights. She's brought it up when she's mad at me. She'll yell very obscene things out. I can't even repeat what she says. That I think such and such an act is OK. Usually it pertains to guys. My parents are old-fashioned, they were raised up to be hard-working. I'd like to take these qualities, but there's other things I don't want to take with me. My parents don't always agree with me. I can't help that. I am who I am and I believe what I do. I'm not my parents and they're not me.

My mother has a lot of problems with the things I think, so we don't talk about it. She has a lot of problems with my religious views, that I don't believe in God. I was brought up in a private Christian school, where we had Bible study every week and went to church every Sunday. I'm glad that I was raised up on a religious background. I have something to found my arguments on.

I say what I think. Premarital sex is such a big thing in high school. I'm not the type to say you can't have sex until you're married. As wrong as that sounds. I really believe high school kids, we're not getting enough sex education. I'm not talking about the kind where it's abstinence or nothing—I'm talking about teaching kids, if you're gonna do it, how to protect yourself. I tell my friends where they can go to get on birth control, I tell them I'll go and buy them things if they need them. I try to protect my friends. I'd say 75 percent of the kids in my high school have already had sex by our senior year.

My parents were just like, "Don't have sex." That was it, that was the end of the story. That's all I've ever been told here at home. I know it's the same for a lot of kids. "Just don't do it." I don't even know where I learned about sex. You learn from other kids, a lot of weird stuff. Starting in junior high, sex becomes a big topic that we all talk about. The big taboo subject.

My parents tried really hard, but I plan to learn from their mistakes. I'm not afraid to tell my kids about gay people. I'm not afraid to tell them about sex. I want my kids to be smart. I want them to come and tell me what they're doing. I don't want them to hide things from me. 'Cause they're liable to get in more trouble and get hurt more. I want my kids to be able to call me and say, "Mom, I'm at a party, everyone's drunk, I need a ride home." I know I've been in that situation. Drunk driving is such a big problem around here. There's so much money and so little to do, a lot of it ends up in alcohol and drugs. Parties are the big thing and everyone gets drunk, and people drive around. Everybody's like, "It won't happen to me." I know I've been like that.

I didn't go to school today. I stayed home and slept on the couch. I got home from work at 1:30 A.M. There was stuff I had to do, so I couldn't go to bed 'til 4:30 A.M. I thought, there's no way I'm going to school.

My mom works, so I'm by myself. I get tired getting home at 12:30, 1:30 in the morning. Everybody's asleep. The only time I'm home, I'm sleeping. Weekends come around, I don't even go out. I stay home and sleep. I'm not home a lot 'cause I have school, rugby, and I work full-time.

I turned eighteen last month. Things aren't exactly ideal here at home. I got kicked out once. It could happen again. I have to have some money. I don't even make very much working full time. Sometimes it doesn't seem like it's worth it. But I try.

Most kids, they kind of start acting up around sixteen, but I never. It didn't happen to me until about seventeen, eighteen, when I started getting a little bit of an attitude with my parents. I don't know, it just kind of happened.

It was the week of my birthday. Friday night. We got in a fight about trivial stuff. I told her I was going out. She didn't want me to. I told her I was going anyway. I never talked back to my mother like that before. I was being a little brat. I went out. When I got home, she had packed up everything in my room, taken it all into her room. She told me I could leave with nothing. I moved in with a friend for a few weeks. That's why I got a job in the first place. I wasn't working before that.

After a while, my sister took me to her house, and my mom was there. I so didn't want to talk to her! I tried to completely ignore her. She started yelling at me. My sister left, and it was me and my mom

alone! We got in this huge fight. Somehow it got resolved. She said she wanted me to come home. So I came. It's easier. I was gonna have to pay rent where I was staying. It's hard enough trying to make enough money to support myself and then to have to pay rent, too? It just didn't work.

I've always been an obedient kind of girl. I never talked back to my mom. I still don't talk back to my mom the way my friends do. We did have a little bit of a tiff over my clothes. First couple of years of high school, I used to wear flannels and boy clothes. I might have been a tomboy. I liked the boy-looking clothes. They decided I needed dresses to wear. So my dad and mom took me shopping and picked out my clothes for me. All dresses. I was allowed to wear jeans once a week. 'Cause they were tired of the way I dressed. I didn't dress like a girl at all, they said. And my dad's kind of old-fashioned so I had to wear dresses. People were shocked when I first started wearing them. I wore nylons and dresses and little shoes and it was a big change for me. I liked the way I was dressing before.

I turned eighteen and I just got this attitude where...you can't tell me what to do! I mean, it was just the week of my birthday, I was really excited, so I went overboard and she got really upset with me. I got myself in trouble.

It's just the big birthday of your high school life, where you legally become an adult. I know I'm not very mature at this point, I mean, I'm only eighteen. It's just one of those birthdays. It's kind of like sixteen, only more important. I don't know, my sixteenth birthday wasn't very important. It's not like you feel different.

Things have settled back down now. I'm just trying to finish high school and move on with my life. I know I don't have the money to move out of my home or not depend on my parents. I'm trying to work a full-time job and it's just killing me. I couldn't handle it if I had to pay rent and all sorts of things right now. Things are OK. My parents are all right. For a while I did want to move out. But just foolheaded kind of stuff. You know, "Oh, I'm eighteen, let me move out." Where? Basically, I'm just gonna graduate high school and go to college.

I'm definitely planning to play rugby in college. Definitely, as long as I can. I'm hoping to come back here and help coach. I'd like to go start a rugby team up at a school that doesn't have one. Teach some girls how to play. You almost never see rugby on TV. I can't imagine seeing a girls' game on TV. 'Cause girls' rugby...those damn stereotypes about girls. I don't think that will ever happen. I watch guys' games on TV or whatever, and oh, they're so good! I wish I had that talent. They can jump higher, they can throw harder. They run up the field, they're more aggressive. That's what we need, aggression. You've got to get out there and be rude, not rude, but you've gotta be tough. It's something you learn as you go, to be aggressive. I wish I could play like that, but I try.

Boyfriends, they're the curse of high school. I've been through my share of little relationships. Everybody wants to have a boyfriend. I put a lot more stock in having somebody you can trust, communication, finding someone you enjoy being with, no matter what you're doing. I'm looking for someone...a guy who cares about me and is my best friend. I'm trying not to rush into anything. I'm only eighteen. My sister got married at eighteen, my mom got married at eighteen. I'm not ready to get married. Sometimes I feel like I'm still twelve. But I've always got my eyes open for someone. I figure it will just happen. You can't go out looking for it. You get yourself in trouble that way.

This has been an agony of mine for years. "What do you want to do when you get out of high school?" I've bounced through several ideas. I'm thinking about going into computer science. I have a computer at home — it's kind of my passion. I spend so much time on the Internet. It's kind of my hobby. It's basically just crap — it's entertainment. You go in the chat rooms. They're known for their perverts! But it's fun to go on and talk to people. I've actually met some people that live around here. I know you shouldn't do that, it's kind of dangerous. But I do it from time to time. It's just something to do. Not that I have a lot of time. I might be on it at 1:30 in the morning. Sometimes that's why I stay up.

Really what I'd like, long term — I don't know if I'll ever do it, it's one of those dreams. I'd like to have a horse ranch in Montana, but I don't know if I could do that. The ranch would be my ideal life because it's easy going and laid back. It's not so much making money and having things. It's about just living and doing what you like. Having a job I like is very important to me. I see a lot of people, they get stuck in jobs they hate and I don't want that.

I hate my job now, but I feel good working because it's something I can do. It makes me feel like I'm supporting myself and not depending on my parents. The job itself is not exactly my ideal dream job. Gosh. I hate telling people what my job is. I work at McDonald's, serving food and cleaning and all that stuff you see fast food people do. I can't stand it, it irritates me. It's a terrible job, but you gotta get paid. You have to have money in high school. Especially at this school, you have to have money. It's a necessary element.

There's a couple of levels of money at school. There's the stereotype that there's the rich area and the poor area. Not that we're all poor. We have pretty nice houses. But some of them have really expensive houses. My parents worked hard to get where we are now. I have a total work ethic. I get it from them. I feel better when I'm making money and trying to support myself. Money's not important, but you have to have it. You can't live in the streets. Well, you could, but ideally, I mean, there's things people want. Money does drive the world. As much as people say it doesn't, it does. It drives what people do. There are things I want. There are things I want for my kids. You have to work for them. Just thinking about working for the rest of my life is driving me nuts. I get worn out. I get frustrated with the other girls on my team, 'cause they're like, "Where are you going?" I tell them I have to work full time.

I spent a lot of money last year on rugby. It was the biggest money I put out — buying my cleats. I was so proud of those cleats. They're expensive, and so's your jersey and all the little things you want that go along with it. But it was important to me to have the cleats and the jersey and the practice clothes.

I'll spend a lot on a formal dance, too, buying a dress, getting my hair done. I like floor-length gowns. They were my one splurge. One of the last ones I bought cost $160. People love my dresses, they borrow them, like some girls are borrowing my dresses to go to the Winter Ball formal dance on Saturday night.

I have great taste. I'm sorry, I have the best taste in formal dresses. I'll spend a week, hours and hours looking for the dress I want. They're not dresses other girls would look at. But when I pick them out and put them on, they're like, "Man, that's the best dress!" That's what happened at the prom. I found this floor-length white kind of princess dress that was great, and it had rhinestone straps. I wore white gloves and silver shoes. It was just the greatest. That was a good night.

In high school there's not a lot of opportunities to get dressed up and go out. I get really picky and I like to look just right. Everyone's gonna be there. It's the one time I do care what other people think of me. I want them to look at me and go like, "Wow!"

This is the first year I won't be going to the dance. I have to work Saturday night. I've never missed a formal dance before. I feel terrible! I want to go so bad. But it just didn't work out. Sometimes you can't do the things you want to. And you gotta accept that.

There's not a lot of time to have fun. I feel so old sometimes. I know I'm not, but I don't mess around a lot like others girls do at this age. But I like who I am. I've got my share of problems and there's things to deal with and I get upset. I get tired and I get worn out. But I like the way I think, I like what I believe in. I know I'm not gonna spend the next ten years searching for who I am. Because I know who I am. I know the things I value, and what I think is important. I think that's a good thing to know, and be able to say.

It's really weird, but sometimes I feel like somewhere along the line I lost eighteen years of my life, y'know? I don't feel like I lived them. So right now my goal is to live the rest of my life, and try to be a part of it. I don't want to look back fifty, sixty years from now and be like, "What did I do?" I want to live out my dream. I don't want to be so sad years later 'cause I didn't get to. I don't want to have any regrets. I don't want to regret the way I lived and the choices I made. I want to make good choices ahead of time, and not look back and say, "I should have done this." I want to end my life on a happy note. It sounds really morbid, God. Most kids wouldn't contemplate the end of their life. But to me it feels like it's rushing so fast, years go by, a year is a long time, but it's not, they seem long, but before you know it, it's over. It's not important to me to make some sort of statement and leave my mark on the world, nothing like that. It's important that I do the things I want to, the long-term goals I want. Have my house and my car and my kids and my husband, just not be unhappy in general. Just be generally happy. I think that's something a lot of people just don't get.

CONCLUSION

☙

My mother makes wedding gowns, and her hand sewing is exquisite. She says the underside of embroidered satin or lace should be as neat, precise, and lovely as the side that people see. She says this is the mark of good work.

She ties her silk in tiny, tidy knots and bites them clean with her teeth, or snips them with a satisfying click from her "good scissors," gold-handled surgical steel.

I measure my own work against her standard of craft and I find my work wanting. The undersides of my films and of this book are tangled with dangling threads. There is no neat conclusion, no clean cut, no satisfying click. I've done more than three hundred interviews, but I still have many questions for girls, maybe even more questions now than when I began.

Girls will be fine, I guess. We are famously resilient.

I do hope people who care for girls will be inspired to listen to them more keenly. I think of what Teresa said. She was sixteen, with a two-year-old daughter.

My sister is the age right now that I was when I got pregnant, fourteen years old. I see her going through all of the things that I went through and I just want to protect her.

When she was younger, she'd say, "I'll never end up like you. I'm not going to let some guy get me like that. I want to be able to go out with my friends."

Now, she's getting really tight with her boyfriend and she's doing whatever he says to do. I tell her, "Please don't follow in my footsteps. Be your own person," and she's having a hard time with that.

It just takes one person to believe in a girl, to help her turn out right. I just hope that other girls find that one person.

The never-ending challenge for people who care about girls is to *be* that person. It may be demanding and difficult, chaotic and complicated. You may become tangled in a web of loose threads. But the call is clear: be the one.

ABOUT THE AUTHOR

*

CAROL CASSIDY is one of five sisters from a working-class Philadel-phia home. She is the producer and director of the PBS documentaries *Run Like a Girl* and *Smile Pretty* and the ITVS film *Baby Love*. She co-produced and co-directed *Wildwood, New Jersey,* and directed *She-Crab Soup* at the American Film Institute's Directing Workshop for Women. Carol has worked as a journalist, a playwright, and a filmmaker. This is her first book. (Unless you count *Huntsman, Huntsman,* but that was in kindergarten.)